PENGUIN BOOKS

TORNADO DOWN

Pilot John Peters and navigator John Nichol were shot down over Iraq at the start of the Gulf war in January 1991. The two RAF flight lieutenants were held prisoner for 47 days and their battered faces flashed across the world's television screens. John Peters, 32, joined the RAF in 1980 as a university cadet. Married with two children, he currently flies Tornadoes in Bruggen, Germany. John Nichol, 30, joined the RAF in 1981. He has served in the South Atlantic, Norway, Denmark and Kenya. He is now based at RAF Leeming.

**RAF Flight Lieutenants
John Peters and John Nichol
with William Pearson**

TORNADO DOWN

PENGUIN BOOKS

PENGUIN BOOKS

UK | USA | Canada | Ireland | Australia
India | New Zealand | South Africa

Penguin Books is part of the Penguin Random House group of companies
whose addresses can be found at global.penguinrandomhouse.com.

First published in Great Britain by Michael Joseph 1992
Published in Signet 1993
Published in Penguin Books 1998
Reissued in this edition 2018
001

Photographic acknowledgements

The authors and publishers are grateful to the following for permission to
reproduce copyright photographs: BBC photographs, 20; *The Daily Star*, 3; Stanley
Dolphin Photo Ltd, 1; *The Journal*, 19; Fit Lt C. Lunt, 14, 16; Sqn Ldr P. Mason, 4;
John Molyneux, 7, 8; Harry Page, *Daily Mirror*, 17, 23; Pilot Press Ltd/Aerospace
Publishing Ltd, reprinted from the partwork *Warplane*, published by Orbis, 9;
Press Association, 21; RAF Germany Photographic Section, 15; Rex Features,
11, 12, 18; Times Newspapers, 22; Wg Cdr D. Wilson, 10; Flt Lt R. Woods, 5, 13.
Every effort has been made to trace the copyright owners, but if there have been
any omissions in this respect, we apologise and will be pleased to make
appropriate acknowledgement in any further editions.

Set in 10/12 pt Plantin
Typeset by Datix International Limited, Bugany, Suffolk
Printed in Great Britain by Clays Ltd, St Ives plc

A CIP catalogue record for this book is available from the British Library

ISBN: 978-1-405-93757-3

www.greenpenguin.co.uk

This book is dedicated to
the members of XV Squadron,
all of whom served
with such distinction during
Operation Desert Storm

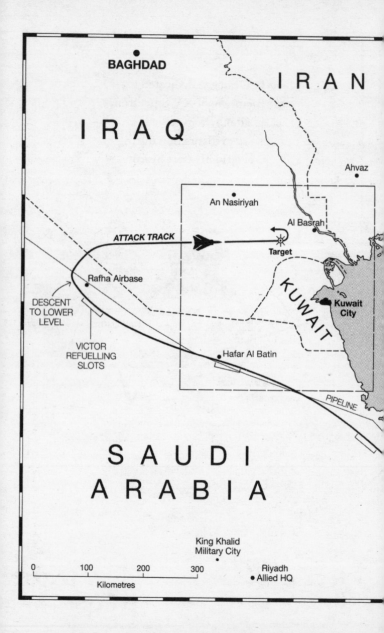

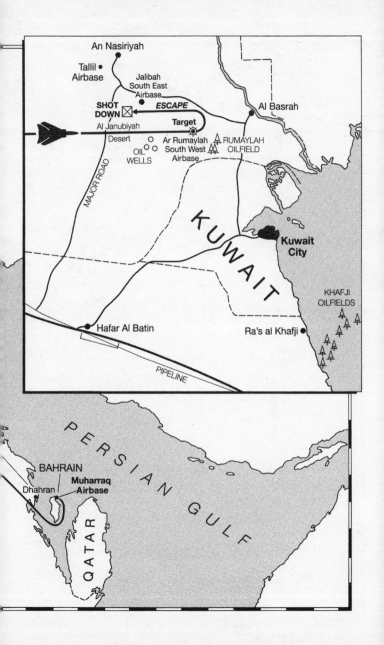

An Nasiriyah

Tallil • Airbase

Jalibah South East Airbase

SHOT DOWN ⊠ *ESCAPE*

Al Basrah

Al Janubiyah

Target ⊙

Desert

OIL WELLS ○○○

Ar Rumaylah South West Airbase

RUMAYLAH OILFIELD

Kuwait City

K U W A I T

KHAFJI OILFIELDS

Hafar Al Batin •

Ra's al Khafji •

PIPELINE

P E R S I A N   G U L F

BAHRAIN

Dhahran

Muharraq Airbase

Q A T A R

Contents

CONTENTS

Acknowledgements

Writing a book, especially one of this nature, is not a simple project. We are indebted to a number of people for their help, encouragement and support.

First and foremost we must thank Will Pearson who actually put our words onto paper in a manner that we could never have achieved; without his time and dedication there would be no *Tornado Down*.

A number of other people guided us through the literary minefield and we are very grateful to them. Our agent Mark Lucas at Peters Fraser & Dunlop deserves special mention for being our mentor over the last year.

We are forever in the debt of the teams of medics and psychiatrists, led by Wing Commander Gordon Turnbull, who were there to meet us when the Red Cross flew us out of Baghdad. They ensured our return to normality was as smooth as could be expected. Others who showed great understanding and support were our Station Commander, Group Captain Neil Buckland, and the Squadron Commander who led us to war and was there on our return, Wing Commander John Broadbent DSO.

Wing Commander Andy White took over XV Squadron a few months before it was disbanded in 1991. His support, and that of the RAF Public Relations Department, was especially appreciated at what was a very difficult time for the whole squadron.

A vote of thanks also goes to our solicitors, Richard Taylor and Charles Artley from Simkins, for their legal expertise and advice during some very trying times.

Finally, we must thank the many thousands of well-wishers who sent messages of hope and support to our families during our imprisonment and to ourselves on our release; we are indebted to you all for your concern.

Many of our experiences have been shared, but we would also like to add our personal thanks.

John Peters: I would like to thank all my friends at Laarbruch who supported Helen and the children during my captivity; in particular, I would like to thank the two Maggies, Mrs Buckland and Mrs Broadbent.

Finally, but most importantly, I thank my mother and father, brother and sister, and Helen's family simply for being there. They didn't ask for the worry and stress, the speculative horror stories or the constant media barrage. On my return they asked for nothing more from me.

John Nichol: My family had an extremely trying seven weeks whilst I was missing in action. In some ways, thanks to the intense media harassment and mindless speculation, they were subject to worse treatment than myself. There were a number of individuals and organisations who supported and protected them over those distressing weeks.

Inspector Tom Hilton and the Northumbria Police had their work cut out shielding my family from the forces of the media. They did this with the help and co-operation of the personnel from RAF Boulmer who also ensured that help and advice was never more than a telephone call away. Flight Lieutenant Ian McNeill was particularly supportive in his role as their liaison officer. The staff at British Telecom were invaluable in ensuring that unwanted telephone calls never bothered my family. The Rt Hon. Neville Trotter MP was a constant source of encouragement, as was Father Dominic McGivern and the parishioners of St Joseph's Church. Finally, the Post Office staff ensured that the many thousands of well-wishers' letters arrived despite the fact that few were correctly addressed!

On a personal note, I must thank Steve Barnfield for helping to take care of my affairs during my enforced absence. Thanks also go to Bernie Middleton, John Wain and Yvonne Andreou for allowing me to use their flat as an office and also for providing a memorable homecoming party along with the rest of the Avenue Road Mafia!

Finally, and most importantly, I send my love and gratitude to my family for being there and supporting me on my return from Iraq; to Paul, Angela and Christopher, to Brendan and Margaret, to Teresa, Stephen, Kate and Clare, to my parents: thank you.

William Pearson: My thanks go to Arianne Burnette of Michael Joseph for her sound editorial advice; Flight Lieutenant Simon Pearson, RAF, for his technical expertise and encyclopaedic knowledge of modern combat operations; and special thanks also to Gaynor Williams.

January 17, 1991. UK: BRITAIN SAID TO
LOSE ONE FIGHTER-BOMBER

LONDON, Jan 17, Reuter: A British
Tornado fighter-bomber has been lost
during raids on Iraqi targets, according
to military sources in the Gulf quoted
by the Press Association national news
agency.
The agency said it was understood to be
the first loss among seventy-five
British warplanes in the region in
Thursday's fighting.
The precise location of the incident and
the fate of the two crew were unknown.
The aircraft was engaged in a second
wave of daylight raids after the initial
attacks under cover of darkness.

REUTER NEWS SERVICE

Prologue

John Peters: The Tornado was doing 540 knots fifty feet above the desert when the missile hit. A hand-held SAM-16, its infra-red warhead locked onto the furnace heat of the aircraft's engines. Some lone Iraqi's lucky day. Travelling at twice the speed of sound, the SAM streaked into the bomber's tailpipe, piercing the heart of its right turbine. Five kilograms of titanium-laced high-explosive vaporised on impact, smashing the thirty-ton aircraft sideways. It shuddered, a bright flame spurting from its skin; fifteen million pounds-worth of high technology crippled in a moment by the modern equivalent of the catapult. The computerised fly-by-wire system went down, transforming the air-craft instantly from thoroughbred to cart-horse.

We had just completed our attack run on the huge Ar Rumaylah airfield complex, in southwestern Iraq; I was pulling the Tornado through a hard 4g turn, with sixty degrees of bank, to get onto the escape heading. The aircraft was standing on one wing, at the limits of controllable flight. The fly-by-wire loss sent it tumbling, the stick falling dead in my hands – a terrifying feeling for a pilot. I was pushing the controls frantic-ally, the Tornado falling out of the sky, the ground ballooning up sickeningly in my windshield. The huge juddering force of the blast had knocked the wind out of me. Gasping, hanging off the seat straps, I yelled: 'What the hell was that?'

'We've been hit! We've been hit!' John Nichol, my navigator, shouted from the back seat. Urgently, he transmitted to the formation leader: 'We've been hit! We're on fire! Stand by.'

'Prepare to eject, prepare to eject!' I yelled. 'I can't hold it!'

'Don't you bloody well eject! Get hold of it!' he shouted. It steadied me.

Fast jet aircrew do not survive collision with the ground at 540 knots. There is a one hundred per cent certainty of death. The Tornado's wings were still swept back at forty-five degrees for the high-speed dash home. I threw the lever forward, desperate to prevent the looming crash. Incredibly, it worked: despite the fire and the enormous loss of power, the aircraft responded, lurching back under something like control as the wing surface, swept forward now at twenty-five degrees, bit harder at the airflow. Still wallowing horribly, the aircraft began to climb, but with agonising slowness. I nursed the stick back to gain precious altitude. Having avoided immediate collision with the ground, I had an awful awareness that the best thing would be to climb to a safe height. But we were still in a high threat area, not far from the target. We had to remain low until we were clear of the road, crawling with Iraqi troops, that we had crossed on the way in, before zooming to height for the return home.

It was then that our problems really started.

The deafening warble of the right engine fire warning blasted out, a Christmas-tree panel of red failure lights flashing on.

At that moment a quadruple-barrelled 23-millimetre gun opened up, from one of the dozens of Anti-Aircraft Artillery (Triple-A) sites surrounding the target airfield that had been tracking and firing at us. Four of its shells peppered the AIM-9L Sidewinder missile nestling on our right inboard wing pylon, igniting the Sidewinder's rocket propellant. White hot, the fuel began burning up through the top of the slender white missile, the airflow fanning it back in a die-straight, incandescent line. The Sidewinder had become a giant oxy-acetylene torch, slowly but surely severing the Tornado's wing.

During the few seconds since being hit, I had been utterly absorbed in the struggle to remain aloft. Now, as a crew, we had to get through the emergency action drills the pilot and navigator must carry out if they are to have any chance of survival.

'We have a right-hand engine fire. Give me the bold face checks!' I shouted.

John began reading off his check list. 'Left throttle ... HP [High Pressure fuel] shut!' he commanded.

'It's the right engine!' I screamed, closing the right throttle. This should starve the burning engine of fuel.

'Left LP cock, shut!' he persisted. Left LP cock? He was trying to get me to shut down the left engine, our only and dwindling chance of getting home in one piece.

'It's the fucking *right* engine!' I screamed at him. I glanced at the warning panel. The fire had not only not gone out, it was worsening.

'Sorry! Right LP cock, shut!'

'Right Low Pressure fuel cock is shut!'

'Right fire extinguisher, press!'

'Right fire extinguisher pressed.'

Then I heard John shout, 'We're on fire! We're on fire!'

'I know we're on fire,' I said.

'No! We've got to get out of here! Look out the side of the aircraft!'

I glanced up. A bright orange glow in the rearview

mirrors made me twist backwards sharply in the narrow seat. It wasn't just the wing: the back of the aircraft had disappeared. There was no sign of the Tornado's massive tailplane. In its place a huge fireball was devouring the fuselage whole. Already it was halfway along the aircraft's spine, just behind the UHF aerials – about three feet from where John sits. But it was the wing he was worried about. I could see him staring horrified at it. I, too, stared, transfixed for a second by the swiftness of the fire's progress. Its back end ablaze, the aircraft was like some comet, trailing orange fire and long grey plumes of leaking jet fuel.

John called up the formation leader again. 'Ejecting, ejecting,' he transmitted.

No one ever received the message.

1

Whispers of War

LAARBRUCH, GERMANY. *John Peters:* The first whispers of war fell on deaf ears. I was part of a four-aircraft formation operating out of RAF Laarbruch, hoovering around Germany on a low-level flying exercise. John Nichol was off posing at some airshow, which is what he's good at. It was in early August, the eighth, a few days after the Iraqi invasion of Kuwait.

We landed at RAF Brüggen, to refuel. While the jets were being serviced, we breezed into 17 Fighter (F) Squadron, to say hello, grab a coffee, and brief for the next sortie. Some of the guys from 14 Squadron, which is based at Brüggen, were in there as well. Looking slightly flushed and excited, which should have been a clue that something was up, they said, 'We're going. We're going out to the Gulf.'

It's a favourite air force pastime to see how far you can get someone to believe a totally fictitious story: the bigger the spoof, the better. It's called 'rumour control': start a rumour and see how far it goes before it comes winging back to your ears as 'the truth'. What these guys were telling us looked like the biggest spoof of all time. Squadron Leader Gordon Buckley, our formation leader, turned to us and said quietly, 'Look, guys, they're just winding us up – they've obviously planned this.'

'No,' they said, 'listen, we're off to an air-to-air refuelling brief, we're getting a quick intro and a couple of training missions to get us into it, then we're going out – in a week's time.' This was a mite disconcerting; it did have a certain ring of truth about it. Tornado crews in Germany do not normally train for in-flight refuelling, there is no need: the aircraft has sufficient range for the job. In the Gulf it would be a different story, since the distances involved in reaching some of the targets and returning would be enormous. But we still refused to believe them. It seemed incredible. Next thing, the station Tannoy piped up: 'Telephone call, Squadron Leader Buckley'.

Gordon came back. He cleared his throat. 'We've got to get back to Laarbruch. Now.'

We stared at him in disbelief.

'No,' he said, 'this is serious. This afternoon's sortie has been cancelled. We've got to get back immediately. So it's back to the jets, gentlemen. Now.'

We jumped back into the Tornados, by now fully fuelled up for that afternoon's planned mission. The only instructions we got were: 'Climb to height, dump your fuel, and land.' This set the blood running. What were we returning to? If this was a spoof, they were certainly taking it a long way. Brüggen is only about fifty miles from Laarbruch by road – no time at all in a fast jet, especially if you are in a hurry. We were in a hurry. As we circled at 12,000 feet, dumping our excess fuel in the designated area, we had a god's eye view of Laarbruch. I wanted to be down there, in amongst it, to find out what was happening. The fuel seemed to trickle out with agonising slowness. I got even more excited when we heard over our radio channel, 'Guard', which is the distress frequency, so everybody over northern Germany could hear it: 'This is "Northern Fixer" on Guard: leader of "Kayak" formation return to base immediately.' That was us. He went on: 'Leaders of "Bobcat", "Mallet". . .' Northern Fixer was trying to recall all RAF Germany formations that were airborne that afternoon!

To say this was unusual would be understating things just a little. The message was repeated continuously, until all the units flying that day had acknowledged it. Even over the radio, there was an edge to that voice. When we reached Laarbruch, we were out of those jets in record time. Everyone was rushing around the station, not quite like the proverbial headless chickens, but there was a huge amount of extra activity. We shot into the Pilots' Briefing Facility, or PBF to the acronym addicts that inhabit the military. By now we were fairly keen to find out what was going on. Squadron Leader Gary Stapleton greeted us, his eyes button-bright. We followed him straight through into the briefing room.

'Right,' he said, 'there is a good chance we'll be going out tomorrow – to the Gulf. Make sure you pack an overnight bag, and make sure you've got all your bits together. We're on standby.' We stared at him in silence. Then everyone started talking at once.

All the 'war cupboards' that lined the briefing room were hanging open. These lockers, which contain special war equipment, were never opened under any circumstances – except the circumstance of war, or the very real threat of war. People were hauling kit-bags out and stuffing all sorts of operational gear into them.

We had had no inkling whatsoever that the Squadron was even being considered for deployment to the Gulf, but there we were, packing for it, at the double. Far from expecting we might go, the prevailing attitude was: 'Tornados only go to war at Armageddon. Tornados only go to war on the Central European Front. They do not go to war over some poxy little square inch of desert somewhere.' So much for the prevailing attitude.

St Mawgan, Cornwall. *John Nichol:* I was at the St Mawgan airshow that particular day. It was the Wednesday after the Iraqi invasion. John Peters was back in Germany.

It was a typical airshow: all your aircrew mates get together the night before, you go to the bar and have a few drinks, then you round off the evening by having a few more drinks. Occasions like this are all part of military aircrew culture, and have not changed since the first guy in a string-bag with a gun strapped to it got his wheels unstuck from the Flanders mud. The form is fairly easy to pick up; all you need is a hard head and a good line in bantering conversation.

Next day, the routine was: don the coolest available pair of aviator shades, strike *Top Gun* attitude, have photograph taken with members of the public, answer questions about the jet, be friendly. The public pays our wages, the public pays for the jet; so it is not unreasonable that people might want to find out how their money is spent now and again. One of the most common questions, from the smaller manifestation of boy, is: 'What's it like flying in a Tornado?'

This is quite a difficult question to answer. The reason for that is simple: it is like nothing else. In the grey pre-dawn drizzle you clamber up into your big ugly mechanical monster, snuggle down into your seat and snap shut the canopy. Now you are in a different world, enclosed, autonomous, completely shut off from the outside, with a beautiful cosy electronic whine in the background: a comfortable, well-appointed office for two, everything within arm's reach, a bargain at £15 million. You press a few buttons and glance around the cockpit to ensure that all the systems are 'up'. In seconds the turbine temperatures leap from ambient to 400 degrees Celsius.

After a call to Air Traffic Control (ATC), you taxi the Tornado out of its hardened concrete kennel to the take-off point. On the way, there is a continuous dialogue between the front and back seats, between pilot and navigator – essential challenge and response checks to ensure no stupid errors are made. Then you are cleared for take-off; you line up and do the final engines' check. Holding the aircraft on the brakes, the pilot advances the throttles through maximum dry power, to mid reheat, then to full reheat. In the dawn light you can see the glow from the flames shooting out thirty feet behind, feel the brakes straining to contain 30,000 pounds of raw thrust. Brakes off, and you are kicked back into your seat. The 0–60 mph acceleration time is slower than that of a Ferrari Testarossa, but the 0–200 mph time and the acceleration beyond that is certainly better. At 160 knots the airframe shakes itself clear of the runway, gear and flaps up, and at 200 feet you slip into the lowering grey undercast. With the throttles back out of combat power, where the fuel usage is an awesome 600 kilograms a minute, the pilot eases the nose up, you say goodbye to ATC and you are free, climbing steadily skywards through the thick northern European clag. The altimeter winds up and then suddenly at 12,000 feet you break out into that part of the world where the weather is always nice, the sun always shines and the sky is a beautiful deep blue.

The best part is looking down on 'civilisation' below, visible occasionally through the gaps in the cloud: it is only 0730 hours, but already you can see the rest of the world coming to life, waking up and going to work. Lines of cars in traffic jams stretch out below you, their lights on, wipers too probably, the drivers smoking, getting frustrated, checking their watches, listening to the bad news on the radio and a miserable weather report. And you have escaped their drudgery and trudgery and cannot help but feel sorry for the poor bastards, while you are high in the blue, in heaven with an electronic whine. It is hard, sometimes, not to feel superior. This is why some fast jet jocks, especially single-seater pilots, develop unmatchable egos and feelings of godlike supremacy. You have to do it to feel it.

Try explaining this, or even some of it, at an airshow without sounding like you are just trying to impress! But it's a different kind of challenge, at least, to flying the thing.

We were standing by the aircraft, soaking up endless questions, juvenile admiration, and the Cornish sun, when the station Tannoy system barked into life: 'The Captain of the Victor is to report to Station Operations immediately. The Captain of the Victor is to report to Station Operations immediately.' Within minutes of this announcement the whole Victor crew scrambled out of Station Ops, sprinting across the airfield to reach their aircraft.

On the way past, one of them shouted, 'We're on thirty minutes' notice to go! We're going out to the Gulf!'

And we were laughing at them! We called back, 'Tough shit, mate.'

Shortly after this little flurry of excitement, the 17(F) Squadron crew standing by the Tornado next door to us got the call. We had a laugh at them, too, but not for long. Twenty minutes later, the Tannoy system crackled out: 'The XV Squadron Tornado crew is to report to Station Operations immediately.'

'Oh oh,' I thought. 'Surely some mistake?' I looked at Cliffy, my pilot; he ran across to Ops. A very few minutes later, he came back, a changed man.

'We're also on thirty minutes' notice to move,' he said. 'To the Gulf!'

To which I replied, 'Naah – never. Don't be daft!' It was beyond belief.

'Yes,' he said, 'the Squadron is on notice to move to the Gulf. We've got to get this aircraft ready to go, now . . .'

That wasn't quite so funny.

This went on for the rest of the day. There was a Jaguar there, two Tornados and a Victor, and everybody was told to ready their aircraft for a return to base, immediately on signal. I kept thinking, 'We're going to go to war here, we're going to do what we trained to do, but never thought we'd have to do. They could've given us a bit more notice!' The atmosphere was amazing. I was scared, but it was electrifying.

By now most of the public had cottoned on to what was happening; they kept coming up to us and wishing us good luck when we got out there, wishing us all the best. It was like suddenly being plunged into a Hollywood blockbuster about war, but without having rehearsed the roles. It felt like all this was happening to someone else, but surely not to me? The news hit us with a real bang: the Victor crews were told they were flying straight out from the airshow at 0700 the next morning, and meeting fourteen Tornados over the North Sea for an immediate training exercise. They were going to practise their first ever air-to-air refuelling. These were the RAF Brüggen squadrons, 17(F) and 14, which were among the first to go to the Gulf a few days later.

Order and counter-order fizzled and flew. As evening came on, we were told, 'It's OK, stand down.' So all the remaining crews rendezvoused in the bar and stood themselves down. The storm had blown over – for the moment. We would fly the aircraft back to their squadrons the next morning. Meanwhile, the 'standing down' was going so well that a Scud missile explosion in the left ear would not have woken some people at the end of their standing-down sessions. There was a brilliant atmosphere; a feeling of slight madness in the air, of 'live it while you can' euphoria. Of course, nobody got 'drunk' – after all, we were flying the next day. But two people 'built a shed', one 'was off his trolley', another 'fell out of his tree', and the rest were 'completely off the plot'. 'Drunk' is not a word the RAF uses much.

Simon Burgess, a 17(F) Squadron pilot, was in the bar. We were laughing and joking. Towards the end of the evening, I was running around the bar with a tea-towel on my head, pretending to be an Iraqi.

'Nichol,' he called, 'you might regret doing that one day!'

He was right.

2
Early Days

John Peters: It was a coincidence that John and I had wound up together on XV Squadron. He doesn't much like me remembering this, but I was the pilot on John Nichol's first flight. It was in August 1987. As a Staff Instructor at the RAF's Navigation School at RAF Finningley, in Yorkshire, I was piloting a new batch of trainees on a 'get-acquainted' flight. We were chugging around over Lincolnshire in a Dominie, the military version of the HS125 business jet, used by the RAF for training its navigators. John was one of the new boys. They had to deal with the radio, do a few basic navigation exercises, look out the window to see where they were – that kind of thing. For some it was the first time they had ever been airborne. They didn't have to enthuse on landing, but they nearly all did. Fresh out of Cranwell, the RAF's Initial Officer Training College, Adrian John Nichol (John to all his friends) was the most enthusiastic.

'God,' he said, 'that was fantastic!'

'Yes,' I replied, glancing at him to see if he was joking. The circuit we had just completed was the shortest and most straightforward I regularly flew. I had flown it dozens of times before. But John's enthusiasm was infectious. Later, we got chatting in the bar. It turned out he had joined the RAF at seventeen, training as a communications technician. After four years at RAF Brize Norton, he had reached the dizzy heights of Corporal. Then he had put in for a commission, and here he was, a few months down the road, Flying Officer Nichol, trainee navigator.

Within two years of our meeting, our roles were reversed. Having been chopped from the Buccaneer Operational Conversion Unit in 1986, I had spent all my time at Finningley fighting to get a second chance at flying fast jets. So I was ecstatic when my posting to the Tornado GR1 came through. Somebody up there believed in me. After learning to fly this aircraft, I was posted to XV Tornado Strike/Attack Squadron based at RAF Laarbruch. Here it was my turn to be the new boy, under John Nichol's wing – one of life's little ironies. He had been posted there a few months before I had, and was consequently much more up to speed on Tornado operations. On a Tornado squadron, a pilot and navigator are paired up as a crew and will normally fly together. But people come and go for all sorts of reasons, and circumstances often dictate that either your pilot or navigator (your 'man') is not available. John and I were paired up occasionally, so for a while he was kept busy showing me the ropes. There were a lot of ropes.

John Nichol: Over the next couple of years after our first meeting, JP and I were not specifically crewed together, but we flew together often. My job, as a navigator, was to operate the Tornado, its systems and its weapons, as well as to navigate, all the while keeping in mind the big air picture. JP's job was to fly it.

Laarbruch being a front-line operational RAF base, we were invariably training for war against the Warsaw Pact countries. The sign over the door in one of the ground-defence training sections exhorted us that our 'Job in Time of Peace is to Prepare for War' – and they meant it. It applied to everybody from the cook in the airmen's mess to the front-line fighter-bomber pilot. Day-to-day, we flew ground-attack missions over the North German plain, simulating attacks on air-fields, bridges, power-stations, factories . . .

Flying a fast jet like the Tornado is not just about being airborne. A normal sortie would start at 0715 with a meteorological or 'met' – weather – brief, then we would plan a mission. Tornados most often attack in units of four, known as 'four-ships', or sometimes in units of eight. The targets we flew against in training were chosen for their similarity to the targets we might fly against in a war with the Warsaw Pact. Planning and briefing a mission like this usually ate up about two-and-a-half hours. Then it took about half an hour more to don the remainder of our flying kit, truck out to the aircraft, start it up and get airborne. Frequently, a mission would involve our own fighters making practice attacks on us, just to make the sortie a bit more difficult, and would culminate in our dropping practice bombs on a weapons range somewhere. We would then make our way back to base, perhaps simulating an emergency of some sort on the return trip. Having 'put the aircraft back to bed', we would have a chat with the engineers about how that particular Tornado had be-haved, and report any significant snags or defects. (The demands of maintenance mean that crews do not norm-ally fly in their 'own' Tornado, but take the first one that is available.) Then it was back to the crewroom for the obligatory cup of coffee, before a thorough debrief-ing to get the most out of the experience. This would include a step-by-step critical examination of the trip, going into every conceivable aspect of the sortie, from the 0715 met brief to the moment we clambered out of the cockpit again to the brand of coffee we drank. For our ninety-minute sortie, we had spent a total of four hours on the ground, preparing and debriefing it.

In the afternoon, we might fly again. If not, there were always plenty of jobs to do in the smooth running of a 6,000-strong, front-line RAF base, quite enough to occupy the time of the fledgling officer. Most of us had secondary duties, which could range from being in charge of the airmen's accommodation to organising the base Motor Club. Or you might find yourself doing something really menial like running the aircrew coffee-bar. This is widely regarded as the worst job in the world, as it is well known that you can never do it right. If you do not have somebody moaning that you have run out of sugar, you have some health-nut complaining about the lack of skimmed milk. Many a promising career has come to grief over whether to order good old sliced white, or brown bread with birdseed in it! I had to do the job for a year, which I hope was a compliment to my management skills, not a punishment.

3
Work Up to War

John Peters: Although XV was already a front-line squadron, and as such in a high state of operational readiness for war, it was less well prepared for a war with Iraq. For the first few days, the Squadron did not even have a map of the area. The Ground Liaison Officer photocopied one from his *Times Atlas*, enlarged it and used that as the 'intelligence board'! The initial briefs, giving us background information about the conflict, were mostly abstracted from editions of the *Daily Telegraph*.

Despite these little hiccups, everything moved up a couple of gears once we knew we might be going to the Gulf. For a start, we got some decent maps. Because we were unaware of the overall command strategy, the next four months were frustrating: follow-up order and amendment, rumour of war and rumour of rumour of war ... 'Yes, you're going. No, you're not.' The whole thing seemed absurd to us. People were annoyed at first, and then amused. At one point, we were told we were taking a brand-new weapon out to the Gulf, the ALARM anti-radiation missile. We spent a week sorting out how to use it in combat; we were to be the first squadron armed with it. It was so new, we dealt directly with British Aerospace, its manufacturers. Then that order was cancelled, and another squadron was earmarked to take over the role.

The Laarbruch engineers began working furiously to prepare the jets, beavering to make the necessary modifications for combat and for desert operations in the few weeks that remained. The most evident of these changes, and the most spectacular, was the salmon-pink paint-job the Tornados were treated to as desert camouflage. They were painted one at a time. When I saw the first one, it gave me a weird feeling in the pit of my stomach: war was dogging our footsteps now, all right. Death in a pink jet! At the same time, everybody wanted to fly the pink jet, because it was different, and therefore somehow 'special'.

As a Squadron, we began a special Gulf training syllabus. For a kick-off, this meant operational low-flying; in plain English, flying as low as possible. There are very few places this is allowed in peacetime, as the noise and the shock of a Tornado rocketing over their heads at 100 feet upset the local populace no end – not to mention the local livestock. In Germany, with the recent easing of tension between NATO and the Warsaw Pact, we had been told to stay above 1,000 feet when flying, at all times, which is about ten times as high as the aircraft would usually operate in war – plus a bit.

The Tornado GR1 is a ground-attack aircraft, so the sortie we practised most often was the 'Hi-Lo-Hi', as it is sometimes called. After the serene cruise from Germany at high level, you pop out over the North Sea to find England laid out before you like a map. Descending through the murk as we draw nearer to the target, we swoop out clear of the cloud base to the adrenalin rush of low-level flying. Rocketing along at 500 miles per hour at 100 feet, the airframe vibrating and shuddering, we are hedge-hopping, close enough to touch the tapestry of farmland flashing by outside. Greens, browns, the straw colour of ripe wheat, the bright yellow shock of rape fields succeed one another as we skim over lakes, flash down valleys. You apply power as the mountain ridge comes rushing up; the Tornado soars, in its element. Time and distance shrink. It's the ultimate white-knuckle ride. The trick is to try to stay relaxed.

Most people who paid any attention to the news were drinking it down in gulps during those anxious days. Intelligence called us to a briefing right at the beginning of this harum-scarum period. The briefing officer, Major Peter Moody, told us that Saddam Hussein controlled the fourth largest standing army in the world, with over a million men permanently under arms.

He then went on to analyse some of the underlying causes of the Iraq–Kuwait conflict. Saddam Hussein, he said, claimed the British had carved up the region with complete abandon, inventing little kingdoms in a way that was bound to result in trouble. (God bless the British Empire.) Iraq's aggression, if you accepted this thesis, was thus excused by its leader as historically inevitable – not his fault, in other words. But who accepted this thesis? Just to stir the pot a bit more, the Iraqi government was claiming that Kuwait had 'stolen' £1.3 billion of crude from the Rumaylah oilfield, which bestrides the border of the two countries. Kuwait had rejected Iraqi demands for compensation. Iraq then cancelled the £5.5 billion Kuwait had loaned it during the Iran–Iraq war. The Iraqis also accused Kuwait of selling Kuwaiti-produced oil at a cheaper rate than the official price agreed by the Organisation of Petroleum Exporting Countries which 'deliberately' cut Iraq's own oil revenue. At least that gave us a bit more background.

Watching the news over the next few days, I was surprised at how quickly everything escalated. The

United Nations Security Council adopted Resolution 660, condemning the invasion of Kuwait and demanding Iraq's immediate and unconditional withdrawal. Saddam Hussein ignored 660, goading the West still further by massing another 100,000 regular troops on Iraq's border with Saudi Arabia. Then, on 6 August, the UN adopted Resolution 661, calling for the immediate restoration of the legitimate government of Kuwait, and imposing mandatory economic sanctions on Iraq.

Next thing we knew, the United States had dispatched the first military forces to the area, on 7 August. On 8 August, the United Kingdom launched its own military contribution, which it called, with minimal charisma, 'Operation Granby'. That was the day I was called back from Brüggen.

The Squadron now began flying in constituted four-aircraft formations, the classic Tornado attack fourship. In other words, the same four crews always flew together in the same four-ship. Squadron Leaders Pablo Mason and Gary Stapleton were the crew of our lead aircraft. Gary was an organised workaholic, who used up whole rainforests of paper in his role as Flight Commander. Mark Paisey, tall, cool and self-confident, quiet but with a dry sense of humour, was paired with his navigator Mike Toft, a bloke you would always want around in a tight corner. Tofty was noted for his party piece, a 'Clog Dance'. Then there was Chris Lunt, 'Lunty', red-haired, always with a ready reply or a joke, and his Scottish navigator, Colin 'Stroppy Jock' Ayton. And then there was us.

These same pairs would eventually go to war together. Quite soon, flying as a unit every day, the eight guys in our four-ship had grown so closely-knit, we practically knew one another's bowel movements. We had immense trust and understanding going. Each of us could predict what the other guy was going to do in the air, without having to ask – useful when the chips are down.

We were flying a lot of 'parallel track', a favourite night or all-weather technique. 'Parallel track' is where the four Tornados fly in parallel pairs of aircraft, with two nautical miles' lateral split, and about forty seconds' longitudinal time separation between the lead and rear pairs. The tricky bit is getting each aircraft to stay in position and on time, at the planned speed, throughout the entire sortie, including the attack itself. This sounds as though it ought to be straightforward. The problem is that in the dark or rain you cannot see any of the other aircraft. You have to pray that their crews are 'following the green writing' – the information in the Head-Up Display (HUD) – to stay on their time-line and on track. Each crew makes sure that they know exactly where their Tornado is in four dimensions. Maintaining a constant four-mile separation from the man ahead and two-mile separation from the man abeam is no mean feat over a round trip of 900 miles. Remaining in position and on time is essential, since the risk of collision increases exponentially as a function of time/speed inaccuracies. There is also the very real risk of flying through the fragments of the bomb that has just been dropped by your buddy in the aircraft just ahead of you, should you happen to arrive over the target a few seconds early.

We also began practising air-to-air refuelling: first the day check sorties, because it was the first time we had ever done it, then the night sorties. This was thrill-a-minute stuff. At first, it was really difficult getting four Tornados onto the tanker, in daytime, with the expert help of air traffic control, not to mention dangerous. Then, suddenly, someone said, 'Right, now you are going to do the air-to-air refuelling at night.'

This was a bit hard to swallow. How could you possibly get four aircraft, and an enormous tanker, into one small piece of sky, at night, when they could not see one another? 'Don't worry,' they said, 'you'll do it.' And we did it.

Then they said, 'And now, you are going to do it silently. You are not going to have any help from air traffic control; you are not going to talk to one another; you are going to go and find a tiny tanker [all of a sudden, it seemed tiny] in thousands of square miles of airspace [all of a sudden, the sky seemed huge]; you are going to put four jets on it, in pairs, and when refuelled you are going to descend into the darkness of the North Sea as a coherent four; and you *will* refrain from hitting one another, or the tanker. You will be travelling at 400 miles per hour, and you will be separated from each other by twenty seconds.'

We gazed at one another in disbelief. We all said, 'It can't be done.' Then we went off and did it.

At night, the closure rate between your own and the other aircraft is very, very difficult to judge. In this situation, one thing the pilot and navigator must have is mutual trust: great hunking dollops of it, blind and unquestioning. John had to trust my flying skills when we were approaching the lead Tornado and the tanker, ten yards from another aircraft, flying off nothing more than two small red cigartips, the glow from the engines of the Tornado up ahead of us in the darkness. But before we even reached that stage, I had to trust his skill with the radar. As a pilot, I could not see the aircraft in front of me until we were right on it. So John 'talked down' ranges and heights to me as these decreased on the approach run. Basically, his job was to monitor the position of the tanker and the other jets at the tanker, then fly me into the Victor, literally on a course to hit it, until I picked it up visually. This only happened when it was very, very close indeed. Until I actually saw that black shape against the black sky, the only guide was John's voice in my ears.

The whole exercise certainly concentrated my mind. For John, sitting in the back, it was even more hair-raising. On our first bite at this particular cherry, he was muttering: 'I am not paid enough to do this. I am definitely not paid enough to do this.'

This was some of the most exciting flying that we had ever done; it was very, very challenging. When, aged fourteen, I joined the Combined Cadet Force at school so I could learn to fly, this was the kind of thing I dimly had in mind. The reality was hugely better. Every single day now, as we continued training for a new type of war in the desert, we were flying our socks off, flying ultra low-level, attacking Royal Navy ships out in the North Sea. We were improving our air-to-air refuelling skills, and dropping bombs regularly on the weapons ranges. Our dogfighting skills also improved radically that autumn. The UK Air Defence squadrons were organised to attack us, unexpectedly, usually at the most vulnerable moment of a given sortie. One minute we were sitting pretty, sucking juice from a nice Victor, then just as we had got back down to low-level and were en route to the target, a Phantom would come screaming out of nowhere, on our tail, with one of its Sidewinder missiles growling at us, straining to be let loose. Suddenly we were in the business of 'death' avoidance, jinking like crazy to break the Phantom's radar lock, the formation splitting to the four winds to escape the predators.

The fighters would claim kills on the radio, yelling triumphantly in our ears: 'Fox 2! [Sidewinder kill.] Fox 3! [Guns kill.]' When you were on the end of it, the 'death', if it came, did not feel simulated: it felt only too real. But it honed up our dogfighting tactics, all right.

John Nichol: All the exercises we had done abroad and at home were paying out dividends now. A lot of our training took us to far-flung places across the globe, like Goose Bay, Canada, where we practised operational low-flying (OLF); Decimomannu, Sardinia, weapons skills and air-to-air combat; or the high-point of every Tornado squadron's three-year tour, the Red Flag exercise in the Nevada desert, at the Nellis Air Force Base near Las Vegas.

Red Flag was particularly useful, as it was the nearest we could ever get to a major war, short of actually being in one. And it was Red Flag that I found myself remembering now, with the Gulf crisis in the news.

Although it is an American show, we flew as part of large multi-national packages, just as we would if we did get sent to the Gulf. At Red Flag the Squadron flew against real targets with real weapons, with all the associated fighter cover and electronic warfare support. And just to make it more interesting, the 'enemy' was similarly well-equipped. We were taking on surface-to-air missile and gun systems, Triple-A guns and associated fire-control radars, simulating the Warsaw Pact threat. On top of this, we were confronted by the 'Aggressor' squadron of *Top Gun* fame. This squadron is to all intents and purposes Soviet. The pilots drink vodka, their aircraft are painted in the latest Soviet camouflage patterns complete with red stars, and they go so far as to have the red stars of the Soviet Air Force emblazoned on their flying helmets. Some of them even spoke Russian. All this meant we were able to assess the effectiveness of our wartime tactics more realistically.

The only thing that is different at Red Flag is that the defensive SAMs do not actually come off the launcher rails at you. Which is just as well, sometimes. The other good thing about this exercise is that visiting aircrew live in a hotel on the Las Vegas strip, with all the lights, sounds, scents, sights and temptations that the gambling capital of the world has to offer. The good life aside, the main point of Red Flag is for all of us to practise the art of air warfare, alongside very large numbers of our NATO allies.

On the first day at my first Red Flag, something uncanny happened. It was in March 1990. Before we had even got airborne, we were sitting in the briefing room, listening to the standard flying safety briefing being given by a Red Flag staff officer, a USAF Colonel. He fixed us with a glittering eye.

'Gentlemen,' he began, 'you should make the most of the facilities we can offer you here at Red Flag. Train today as if you were going to be at war tomorrow. I am telling you now, although you may not believe me, there is every chance that in the next eighteen months, you will be fighting a war together. I am not saying this will be on the European Front. In fact I am convinced that it will not be. What I can tell you is that you will all be in the desert together somewhere, just as you are now; but you will be ranged against an Arab nation . . .'

We had had a million pep talks. This just sounded like one more: the usual stuff, designed simply to make us work harder. But he had foretold the future, as we were now discovering. We never found out where he got his intelligence from, but whoever it was must have had a crystal ball. Nearly one year later, in January 1991, we were at war in the desert. So were most of the other aircrew who had been sitting in that room with us.

John Peters: The training had never been put together in quite this way before, at such an intense, complex and unremitting pitch. With all this activity, we were pushing the Tornado right to the limits of its capability, its engines, its airframe, its weapons delivery and navigational systems. And we were being pushed ourselves.

In the middle of all this intensive training, on 27 August, I was on a Hi-Lo-Hi sortie, being 'bounced' – attacked – en route to the target by USAF F-15s and F-16s. The following morning, Helen, my wife, went into labour with our second child. Thankfully, in all the chaos, our next-door neighbours at Laarbruch, Rob and Lyn Woods, said they would look after our two-year-old, Guy. With the car fully fuelled up, we shot down to the RAF Hospital at Wegberg, about forty miles south of Laarbruch, with Helen doing her breathing exercises en route. Toni, our daughter, was born at 2050 that evening, weighing in at a tiny but perfect five pounds twelve ounces. I cut the umbilical cord myself, but there just wasn't enough time to be a dad *and* train for war at the same time. Wegberg hospital, with Helen and the new baby, was a magnet, which drew me to it every evening, but then so was the Squadron. We could be sent to the Gulf at any time. Excitement overload.

Helen bore the brunt of it. No sooner had she come

home with baby Toni than I was off, on 6 September, to RAF Wattisham in the UK for more training in operational low-flying.

A rollercoaster ride in the dark: 'Terrain-Following Operations', or TF Ops for short. Three other aircraft are very close. It's night. There's cloud. Left hand on the throttle reacting to the aircraft as it twists and surges over the unseen ground just below, the other hand rests on the right knee, twitching near the stick as the electronic systems point you straight down the black hole of a valley, its floor rushing up to meet you at 500 miles per hour plus.

Next turning point: the Tornado flips itself up onto one wing, hauls itself round the massive shoulder of an invisible hill . . . A violent pull-up into cloud: up over another obstacle, the blink of the anti-collision lights on our wingtips reflects off the grey mass of cloud, intensifying the feeling of blindness. Then we're slammed back down again, the Tornado aggressively in control, rolling itself sharply onto the next heading. Helter-skelter. Thrown around in the back, the navigator has only a 'commentary' from his pilot to prepare him for the next violent lurch: 'Check fuel. I've got a ridge at two miles, cut off at three . . . aircraft pulling up . . . painting beyond. Next heading . . . R and T dot, E dot, good ground returns out to six . . .'

I am concentrating very hard on the little screen at front left of the cockpit, the 'E-scope', a three-inch by four-inch display that shows me an electronic image of the ground ahead relative to our height and position. The Terrain-Following radar in the aircraft's nose projects a pulse ahead of us. This reads the folds and furrows of the earthscape rushing towards the plane. In automatic mode the aircraft flies itself, following the computer-generated climb or descend commands. The crew sits 'hands off', their lives entrusted to a smart piece of silicon. The Terrain-Following system means the Tornado can still press home its attack even in pitch-darkness and in bad weather. Really, it's a very sophisticated kind of automatic pilot. You have to have absolute faith in the technology. It comes – with practice!

Along with all the flying, we were delving ever more deeply into the arcane mysteries of our own and the opposition's weaponry. There was lots of extra book-work to get through, learning more about the enemy's capabilities and aircraft types, his radars and missile systems, in great and exhaustive detail. There was a disturbing amount to learn about the Iraqi Air Force. The 'worst case' intelligence assessments were that the Iraqis had over 700 combat aircraft, excluding heli-copters. Their massive inventory included some very modern and very effective types: more than fifty Mig-29 (NATO codename 'Fulcrum') air superiority fighters; seventy Mirage F1 fighter-bombers; thirty Mig-25 'Foxbat' interceptors; and whole swarms of Mig-23 'Floggers', Su-22 'Fitters' and Su-25 'Frog-foots'. This little lot was dispersed over sixty-odd air-fields throughout the country, many of which had plenty of spare tarmac to take off from, or 'substantial in-built runway redundancy', as the intelligence hand-out put it. Some of these places were gigantic: two or three times the size of Heathrow. To defend these well-equipped airfields, Iraq had a choice of missile and Triple-A systems bought off-the-shelf from both Soviet and Western sources. The country also had an almost inexhaustible supply of conscripted manpower, much of it battle-hardened from the recent eight-year war with Iran. Since it takes very little wit to fire a gun into the air, Saddam Hussein's threat of creating 'lead walls' – curtains of ground fire for us happy chappies to fly into – had to be taken seriously.

Aircrew always read the technical manuals anyway, in peacetime, but the work was much more emphatic now, preparing for the specific environment in which we would be fighting. We spent days on end attacking Iraqi airfields in the flight simulator. Everyone had this immense thirst for knowledge. Even the most junior people on the Squadron would question something, refusing to be fobbed off unless they were entirely happy: 'I don't agree. Why do it that way? Why not do it this way?' This attitude extended right down to even the smallest details of operational practice. With the prospect of death in front of them, people became much readier to question the wisdom of their superiors; and their superiors, on the whole, accepted this questioning as a healthy sign. The attitude of the Boss, Wing Commander John Broadbent, was: 'The Squadron is going to war, and I'd like the best out of it.' All the brainstorming was designed to achieve that objective. When everyone had chipped in their three-pennyworth about how this, that or the other should be done, the senior people – the Boss, the Flight Commanders, the Weapons Instructors and the Electronic Warfare Officers – all went into a room one day to make smoke. They emerged with our 'War Doctrine', that is, the operational flying bible for the Squadron. Broadly speaking, all RAF squadrons would be operating the same tactics – it was more a question of an emphasis here, a small procedural change there – but all these little things mattered hugely to us. Although they are much smaller, Royal Air Force squadrons are like regiments, in one respect: they are something of a family affair. The XV

Squadron family, about 200-strong, was spending a lot of time together, and finding out a lot about itself in the process.

4

The Last Supper

John Nichol: It wasn't all work. Our Christmas parties were brought forward, because we'd be out in the Gulf before then. JP and I found ourselves Entertainment Officers for the Squadron. The annual Lunch of the Year was coming up at Laarbruch, but, this being early December 1990, it was also a Lunch of the Decade, so something special was in order.

We called it 'The Last Supper'. Instead of balloons and party streamers, we had the whole crewroom blacked out, in swathes of velvet and dark cotton. There was a votive, church-like atmosphere: solemn fugues playing mournfully in the background, and people reading resonant extracts from the Bible. As they came into the crewroom, everyone paraded up to the tables carrying candles, putting them all down the middle. We had what we imagined to be Last Supper food: feta cheese, olives, 'Galilee Fish', 'Passover Lamb', fruit. Everyone was dressed in their flying-suits, but they had to wear something purple, and sandals on their feet. We had three seats set up at the end of the room. In front of each chair was a bowl, brimming with soapy water. The Boss and the two Flight Commanders took up position in these seats, washing the feet of all the sandal-clad fliers coming in to join the fun. To help them in this important task, they had huge, horrible great scrubbing-brushes . . . most people got quite wet, somehow. Between courses, there were further readings from the Bible.

It sounds sacrilegious, even blasphemous, but it

wasn't like that. As it was, we couldn't say, 'Let's go and have a church service, let's all pray together', although the chaplain did his best to encourage us. It just wasn't done. But done this way, it was somehow acceptable. People were letting off steam, and most of them got a little the worse for wear; but there was a breath of something in the air, of people coming to terms with events. It was as if the religious ritual, diluted and disparaged though it might be, provided some sort of answer to a question we had not yet even asked ourselves. As a lunch it was certainly memorable.

Everybody gave each other their Christmas presents early. We were told categorically that we would be out in the Gulf by 25 December. But even then, with the war looming daily in the headlines, I was still convinced it was not going to involve me. It just wasn't going to happen. I had been on standby to go to Lebanon, to Ethiopia; we had always got blown up ready to go, and then we didn't go. It looked very unlikely, what with all the shilly-shallying, that we would be going this time. I was quite happy with that. There were, after all, a lot of nasty men out there with guns, who would be trying very hard to kill us.

Talking about guns, in the bar one night we had all been joking about what might happen if the shooting really did start. The worst fear – and despite all the ribaldry it was a fear – was fear of capture. Everyone said the same thing: 'We don't mind being shot down and killed, but we don't want to be shot down and caught.'

By this time, horror stories had begun to emerge in the Western media about the things Iraq's ruling Ba'ath Party torturers were doing to the Kuwaiti people – like cutting off their ears and nailing them to the wall, or drilling through their eyes with a power drill. We knew from some of the excellent coverage in the more 'serious' newspapers that the Ba'ath Party, with about one million members, was the political instrument with which Saddam Hussein held onto power in Iraq. We also knew that the Ba'ath Party was to Iraq what the Gestapo had been to Nazi Germany: it held its own citizens in the grip of abject fear through the systematic exercise of terror. And these were the nice gentlemen who would interrogate us if we were captured. So the consensus, although it was hard to say whether people meant it seriously or not, was that if it looked like you were going to be captured, the thing to do was to put your service-issue pistol to your head, and blow your brains out. Looking at the smiling faces all around, joking about the whole thing, it struck me as being very unlikely, in the event, that any of us would actually do it. But we all had images, absorbed from films and books about the POWs in Vietnam, of rat-infested pits, of prisoners standing tied to a post in a freezing river for a week, with rodents chewing at their vital parts. Also, the British press was busily hyping away, printing stories saying that captured Allied pilots would be torn limb from limb by the Iraqi people, and so on. We didn't necessarily believe this sort of stuff, but these were the things we were reading about, that we were inevitably thinking about. I suppose all the bantering about self-destruction was a way of getting the subject out into the open, where we could discuss it. I said I'd play it by ear (pun intended) if the time came, but JP said, 'What if they cut your balls off and sewed them into your mouth? That's what they used to do to captured RAF pilots in the Yemen back in the Twenties. You'd kill yourself if you thought that was going to happen . . .!'

'As long as it was my own balls,' I rejoined, 'but I'm not having your balls sewn into my mouth! My own, yes. Yours, no.'

We carried on this semi-serious conversation later, at JP's place, with Helen. One problem, we decided, was that the new regulation issue 7.65-mm Walther pistols were so weedy, the bullets would only sting us if we fired them at our heads ('Gosh, that hurt!'), unlike the massive old Browning 9-mm, standard issue until recently, which would, as the man said, 'Blow your head clean off'. Appropriately enough, given our lengthy conversation about testicles, we had been practising with the Walthers that very day, using air-filled condoms, tied to posts, as the targets. Helen said that the prospect of having JP's balls anywhere near you, without having asked for them, was enough to make anyone shoot themselves. So that decided it: suicide.

There was quite a lot of discussion in the bar about the ethics of war, about how we felt about going to war. Non-RAF friends in particular would ask, 'How do you feel about killing – or about getting killed yourselves?'

The answer was very simple: we had taken the Queen's shilling. We had been trained, at enormous expense to the British taxpayer, about £3 million per head, or some such mind-bending figure, to do a job. We had led a pretty nice life in the Air Force, varied as to experience, with good prospects, good mates, an adequate income, and plenty of travel. But in the end we were professionals. Going to war was part of the job. It came with the turf, as the Americans say. The taxpayers had to have some return for all that money they had pumped into us – something more than our shining presence at airshows. Yes, it was a shock, and, no, we had never expected to fight, but that fact, the simple fact of being a professional, with a job there to be done, that was for us the overriding factor in the whole business. This attitude, which may seem cynical or even callous, was hard for some of our friends to grasp. It is the difference between random feelings about war – the sort of feelings people outside military life might have – and the attitude of aircrew like ourselves, to whom war is something they have to train for day after day. It was our duty. Having said that, many people wanted to use their training for real. They were extremely pissed off when they were unable to deploy to the Gulf with the rest of us. There just weren't that many aircrews needed. But guys were trying to delay postings, or get out of courses, so they could come with us.

Some people questioned the rights and wrongs of our involvement in the Kuwaiti cause, though. As one guy put it, 'What if Kuwait exported bananas, instead of oil?' These days in the RAF it was no longer a matter of 'Theirs not to reason why, theirs but to do and die ...' People asked if the West was right to intervene. Would it not be better left to the Arab nations to sort out? There were almost as many different opinions on this subject as there were voices to express them. For one or two guys, it was wrong in principle that we should be taking part in a war when we weren't defending Queen and Country. To others, Saddam Hussein was a kind of second Hitler, with the mass gassing of Kurdish villagers and a long list of other well-documented crimes against humanity on his conscience. He had to go.

On 2 December, we finally got our marching orders – the big move to Bahrain. The twelve aircraft of XV Squadron had been divided into two flights: the eight that had already gone out to the Gulf with 14, 17(F) and 31 Squadrons and our own remaining formation of four Tornados. We would be the last to go out. Just before leaving, we had the Squadron Children's Christmas Party. This was always fun. But we suddenly realised that this year there was one very bad fairy at the feast: the Walthers. There we were, walking around on a Sunday afternoon, about to attend a kiddies' Christmas bash, with our guns and holsters strapped to our shoulders. Not really in keeping with the spirit of the occasion, pistols – just a touch out of place among the chocolate rice cakes, the Twiglets, the jelly and the balloons. We popped into the mess for lunch, just before the party was due to start. Helen was there with the children, Toni and Guy. She had Toni's pram with her, so we whipped off the shoulder-holsters with the pistols in them and hid everything in the pram, under the blankets with the baby.

That afternoon, straight after the party, we shipped out. This was the hardest thing we had done so far – much harder than the night tanking in pairs! We had verified the life-insurance policies, made the wills, telephoned our relatives, written the letters. JP had given Helen one of her Christmas presents, some exotic lingerie. All of this made for an extended goodbye. But saying those farewells, sitting there in the Sherpa van that would speed us down to RAF Wildenrath and our flight to the Gulf – that was a bit of a choker. Some of us, even if it were only one or two of us, would not be coming back. The odds were not in our favour. It was hard to swallow, looking at Helen and the other wives, and at the kiddies all excited in their pretty party clothes, clutching their precious new toys, and thinking that we might be looking our last. People veered between tears and jokes, but the predominant reaction, from the male side at least, was a sort of hollow bravado. Some people cracked a few beers to help them through the pain of parting. It was four o'clock in the afternoon when the transport set off.

John Peters: The Tornados had already been flown out to the Gulf, because there were far more aircrew going out than there were aircraft. We were travelling there in slower, more stately style – by Hercules transport. This great, lumbering, bone-shaking beast of an aircraft didn't really take a lifetime to reach Bahrain, it just felt like it. It took about eighteen hours, in fact, including a refuelling stop at Akrotiri in Cyprus.

Having a large RAF base at Akrotiri was a spot of luck for the British military push. Akrotiri is strategically located almost exactly halfway between the UK and the Gulf. It became the key British staging-post in the massive logistical effort required to move whole squadrons of aircraft, their stores and supplies, and whole regiments of armour and infantry, the 3,000 air miles between the two places. Over the course of the next few months, Akrotiri handled about ten years' worth of normal peacetime air transport traffic.

Typically, John bagged himself just about the only place to lie down in the Herc, on a stretcher, sandwiched in amidst all the baggage and paraphernalia of war, and was quickly snoring his head off. I unfurled a crafty sleeping-bag, and tried to get some rest on the shuddering metal floor. The noise was deafening, the discomfort arse-numbing. There was nothing to do. As for cabin service, it consisted of a white cardboard box with a sandwich in it and a KitKat bar – that was your lot, mate! Military airlines! At least we couldn't hear John snoring.

It was three o'clock in the morning when we reached

Akrotiri; the airfield was pretty quiet. Our second stop, Tabuk, way up in northern Saudi Arabia near the border with Iraq, was anything but quiet. Row upon row of US Air Force F-15s and F-16s stretched away into the distance, shimmering in the heat, along with dozens of Saudi Air Force F-5s, the aircraft in neat serried ranks, all fully armed and fuelled up, just sitting there waiting for the war to begin. Ground-crews were swarming around them. The sight of all these aircraft, confidently lined up, made us suddenly realise the enormous scale of the military operation we were joining, its unprecedented international nature. We refuelled for the last leg to Bahrain.

5

The Hive of War

John Nichol: Bahrain was teeming, a bubbling cauldron of activity. From the air, as we looped down over the city through the morning heat haze, it had looked sleepy, washed out, colourless, the buildings beige against the surrounding sand. Now, as we emerged blinking from the dark interior of the Hercules, there was colour and movement everywhere: aircraft, troops, vehicles and stores.

We stepped out into organised chaos. Every square inch of tarmac on the field was occupied: aside from the big international civilian airliners, the skyline was dominated by more than thirty great grey-painted USAF C-130 aircraft. One of these enormous transports was flying the skull and crossbones, the black-and-white pirate flag fluttering jauntily from its cockpit window. As for the British presence, fourteen Tornados were lined up beak to beak; there was also a squadron of Jaguars, a detachment of Victor tankers, several RAF Hercs, and two more on loan from the New Zealand Air Force. There was a Royal Air Force Regiment squadron, armed with the Rapier anti-aircraft missile system, living in splendid discomfort on a spit of land sticking out into the harbour. There were thousands of US Marines moving through, US Navy and US Marine Corps helicopters shuttling men and stores in and out continuously, trucks, buses and jeeps shuttling troops – it was a hive of war and it was buzzing. There were hardened emplacements all over the airfield already, Triple-A batteries, missile sites, ammo dumps. There were pyramids of spare parts and weapons piled up on wooden pallets, small mountains of JP-233s. Fork-lift trucks scuttled about like busy beetles. It looked like a full dress-rehearsal for Armageddon. The War Operations Centre (WOC), which would be our focus, looked extremely businesslike. It was surrounded by massive walls of sand-filled, sand-coloured oil-drums, towering high in rows two-deep, providing basic protection against air attack.

The moment the Herc's wheels stopped rolling, its crew began the frantic business of unloading, frantic because there was so much pressure on these transport aircraft, with all the equipment to shift to the Gulf. We all mucked in getting our huge quantities of personal kit off, including a bicycle some super-sensible colleague had brought with him. Like myself, JP had taped his kit-bags up with bright red sticky tape, so we were able to rescue them from the mounds of identical baggage pretty quickly.

First thing, we popped into the Operations Wing to take a quick look at our new environment. In our olive-green flying-suits, we felt very much like the new boys in school; everyone else had already switched over into their sand-coloured desert kit, so that they blended in nicely with the scenery. But there were quite a few other things that had not changed. In layout, the Ops Wing was just like home – almost identical to the WOC we had just left behind in Germany: there was an intelligence cell, one of its walls covered in a huge area map, detailing in full our own and the Iraqi military assets, their dispositions and strengths. There were the flying operations boards, which show aircraft and personnel status. And there was a ground-defence cell map, this one showing the layout of Muharraq, our new airfield, perched on the northwest tip of Bahrain. This map detailed Muharraq's communications links and perimeter defences. Then there was COLPRO, or Collective Protection, essentially a giant inflatable rubber bag we would all jump into in the event of chemical or biological attack. Air is pumped continuously into this bag, thus maintaining a positive air pressure outwards, stopping the germs or the chemicals getting in – at least that is the theory. Ready-use gunracks lined the intervening corridors. A flying-clothing room was already set up, with piles of protective Nuclear, Biological and Chemical (NBC) kit, flying gear, water sachets ... Even in the dimmed light, it was so familiar we had no trouble finding our way around.

The next thing, and an absolute priority, was to find out where the post office was. It turned out the mailboxes were in the Squadron crewroom, which was pretty plush by Portakabin standards. It was fully air-conditioned, had fridges full of drinks and chocolate, easychairs around the walls, tables holding up-to-date newspapers and magazines, and piles of 'Blueys' – airmail paper – to write home on. Everywhere you went on base there was the same smell of cold, dry, freshly laundered air, pouring from the air-conditioners, big metal hummingbirds in the ceiling.

Our arrival brief came next. Squadron Leader John Hurrel explained the security arrangements on Bahrain Island, and commented on the threat of attack. The Squadron Boss then arrived, and informed us we were flying that afternoon! We gave the Boss a good listening to, but there was a suppressed groan at this – flying, after eighteen hours on a Hercules! Mutter, mutter, mutter ... In the event, he relented: we were given twenty-four hours off.

They took us to our accommodation; it was quite amazing. We knew it was going to be a large hotel, but we were not quite prepared for its splendiferousness. We drove away from the revetments and the bustle of Muharraq airbase, across the causeway, into Manamah city centre, along the seafront, past the rows of graceful palm trees swaying in the stiff offshore breeze, past the beached dhows, some of them quite new, some quite plainly rotting, their wooden ribs gaping at the sky. On the broad freeway, packed with American, Japanese and British cars, the skyscrapers were coming up thick and fast, as the cityscape grew more sophisticated. The jeep turned into the driveway of the Sheraton International Hotel. Marble floors, marble walls, marble reception desk, imposing cut-crystal chandeliers, a cool and glamorous foyer, a cool and glamorous receptionist behind the desk: *we* were staying *here*? All of a sudden, we were no longer aircrew going to war, we were businessmen; the staff greeted us as such. And, in a way, they were right, we *were* businessmen. We were in the business of war – and, as one Texan officer we met drawled, business was picking up.

John Peters and I would be sharing a twin-bedded room. Oh well, you can't have everything. We set about unpacking. There was about half as much storage space available as we needed. We both seemed to have packed just about everything we possessed in the entire world, just to be on the safe side. We should have listened to Bruce. About three days before we went out, JP got a phone call from the Gulf: Bruce Macdonald, a colleague, wanted to speak to him. JP asked him questions like: How much money will we need? What did he think we should bring, in the way of kit, that he forgot? and so on. He replied, 'Don't worry about any of that. The only thing you need to

38

do is ring Jane [his wife] and get two bikinis from her and a tape of the *Blue Danube*. Oh, and a swim hat; and anything else that might help us with this Christmas revue we're doing.' Receiving so much overwhelming hospitality from the Bahrainis and the expatriate British community, the boys already out there were putting on a comedy revue for them in return. Clearly it was not all going to be war . . .

As it was December, the hot season in Bahrain was over, which meant the weather was like a perfect English summer's day: blue sky, about eighty degrees Fahrenheit, low humidity . . . so we jumped into shorts and went down to swim away the flight fatigue. The pool bar at the Sheraton effectively became the RAF Officers' Mess bar in Bahrain for the duration. What a spot of luck!

In the evening, the eight members of our formation went into Manamah, to the city centre, for a curry. Then we went for a wander around the old market, the *souk*, a wonderland to someone who had never been in one before. Gold- and silversmiths tapped away at their benches, pedlars of every good thing displayed food and leather goods, rugs and spices. The sights, the smells and the sounds were all completely strange and all completely absorbing. Happening upon a cross-legged tailor, an Ali Baba character straight out of a children's picturebook, we had ourselves measured up for desert flying-suits.

John Peters: It was the first time John Nichol had ever used his sunglasses in anger. Without them, the sunlight glaring up off the desert floor could be dazzling once you got airborne. We were starting the serious stuff now. For our first, familiarisation sortie, our four-aircraft formation was led out into the southern Saudi desert by Squadron Leader Steve Randles, from 31 Tornado Squadron, who had been out in the Gulf for some time. He covered air routing in and out of the Muharraq airbase, explained the mysteries of the new 'Havequick' frequency-agile radios we would be using – which took some doing, they were so tricky to operate – talked us through Identification Friend or Foe (IFF), or 'Squawk' procedures, and told us how to contact AWACS, the airborne early-warning aircraft.

Randles also briefed us on the hazards of desert flying. He made sure we took on board the ways in which the sun can deceive and disorientate, and gave us tips on how to fly low, safely, in a flat and featureless environment. He told us to take it carefully at first, not try to get too low too soon. This last was advice we were happy to follow: it really was tricky gauging height under certain combinations of terrain and light. So we kept it careful, to begin with, nothing too gung-ho. But as the days went past, and we got used to the conditions, we began winding the aircraft gradually downwards towards the deck, foot by foot, inch by inch, until we were all hammering along just above the sand, right down at forty feet.

Aside from the danger of flying into the ground, one of the biggest risks was on the ground: simply taxying the Tornado out of the holding pan and onto the runway. There were so many piles of supplies stacked up you had to be very careful not to drive into one. To remedy this shortage of space, the Royal Engineers and their Saudi colleagues were, as somebody put it, 'laying hard standing and asphalt almost as quickly as you can walk across it'.

★

John Nichol: Bahrain is a party island, and this seemed especially true that Christmas before the war. It was just about the only place in the Gulf where you could legally consume alcohol, so people came from all over to slake their desert thirst in the many big hotels and bars. Gulf Air, the big British-run airline, had its air-hostess training school in town, so about 300 young and attractive British women were there, which was just something we were going to have to put up with. The bankers were mostly Brits; there was a Bahrain Rugby Football Club, a Yacht Club, and so on. In short, the island was home to a massive expatriate community, which immediately folded us to its collective bosom. They were fantastic to us. We made friends with everyone from the twenty-five-year-old bankers and their wives, to the older members of the community, including some who had retired to Bahrain for the relaxed way of living and the fine weather. These people treated every member of the Squadron like a long-lost son. The second night we were there, the lead XV Squadron formation could not attend a cocktail party at the British Club, so ours went along instead. The club was packed out. From that moment onward, our social engagements blossomed.

Traditionally, many of the expatriate British gathered at the house of a Bahraini businessman, Sharouk-al-Sharif, for the annual Christmas bash. We were invited to attend, so we put on a little revue for them. The main feature was four of us dressed up in bikinis, doing our synchronised swimming act. Not a pretty sight. Comic sketches and songs followed this aquatic appetiser. We were a bit worried, having seen the size and splendour of the location, the wealth and the glamour of the guests, that they might be expecting a professional cabaret act. They weren't going to get one! But in the event, it all went swimmingly . . . We made many good friends at this party.

We were a little startled to spot most of the top RAF brass in Bahrain in the throng, including our own Squadron Boss, Wing Commander John Broadbent, and the new senior officer taking over as Bahrain Detachment Commander, Group Captain David Henderson. If you are going to make a fool of yourself, it is important to do so in front of the right people . . .

That evening, we had inoculations against biological warfare weapons.

6
Target Practice

John Peters: Operational practices were evolving very quickly, with almost every sortie we flew. We were learning to adapt NATO standard flying practices to the new threat environment – not to mention to the new physical one, the infernal oven, the limitless desert. The main difference was in the sheer scale of the operations we were involved in, a scale impossible to simulate in peacetime. It made Red Flag look like a Sunday-school picnic.

Everybody was travelling along a very steep learning curve. We did a number of joint operations with the US forces, which went well, but a lot of what we did was autonomous, in formation, concentrating on silent procedures, the four Tornados prowling the desert.

We got into a routine: breakfast at the hotel; drive to the airfield, always in civilian clothes so as not to alarm the civilians with our military presence; change at the airfield; then see the 'Squinto' – Squadron Intelligence Officer – for the latest update. We were invariably told, 'No Iraqi attack is expected within the next twenty-four to forty-eight hours.' That day's trip would have already been planned out, most of the details on a tasking sheet, which we checked over as a formation. Next would come the mission brief for the day, followed by individual task checking. Then we went flying. Debrief on return, any lessons learned, mistakes made? Are we having fun yet? Lunch. We would study in the afternoon for a few hours – flying procedures, weapons parameters, enemy aircraft capabilities, and so on – then go back to the hotel for a swim. But we had to stop swimming at Christmas. After Christmas, the Middle East had one of its worst winters on record – very cold, very windy and very rainy.

While it was still sunny enough to lounge about by the pool, and ease the old muscles a bit after flying, John, true to form, found himself a girlfriend. She wasn't much to write home about: only intelligent, blonde, slim, tanned, pretty and fun to be with. The XV Squadron Warrant Officer, Pip Curzon, introduced the two of them. Curzon was a star personality on the Squadron, a father-figure not only to the younger airmen, but also to many of the junior officers theoretically outranking him. All three of them, she, John and Pip, were from the Newcastle area. Bloody Geordie mafia! As usual when he came within a five-mile radius of a desirable woman, John went into auto-witticism mode. They were very soon laughing together, and horsing about in the water. She was an air-hostess and wore a uniform into the bargain, when not in her bikini. I had a strange premonition that sharing a room with John was about to become a problem. Maybe that was why there was all this talk of issuing us with sleeping pills!

There were other excitements. We did some extremely stupendous flying – again, the kind of stuff you join for. Some of the most exhilarating sorties we flew were the practice attacks we made against the US Navy. Along with mines, the sea-skimming missile was the threat that Coalition Navies feared most, and with good reason: the USS *Stark*, a frigate on patrol in the Gulf, had been badly damaged by an Iraqi Exocet in 1987. The Iraqis said it was a mistake, but the loss of life and the injuries had been devastating.

And everybody remembered the British experience of Exocet in the Falklands War. So the US Navy was keen for any chance it could get to exercise its defensive muscles against the Iraqi Mirage F1/Exocet combination.

To carry out practice attacks on the Navy, the Tornados split into pairs. Their instructions were very simple: to sink, 'for exercise', the ship in question. One Tornado acts as the sea-skimming missile, with another acting as the launch aircraft. The 'missile' Tornado tucks itself right up close to the other, until it is sitting just underneath the launch aircraft's wing. Both of us would fly very low, and very close together, as low and as close as we dared . . .

The Combat Air Patrol (CAP) covering the ships ought to nail us first, 100 miles out. It does not. We come on. Fifty miles, forty miles. Onboard the target vessel, deep in the belly of the ship, in the hushed darkness of the Operations Room, the radar operators are watching, watching the rotating radar sweep. Suddenly a blip appears at thirty miles – us.

We are 'popping' to illuminate our target. John switches his radar on. Four sweeps are enough. The ship's electronic listening gear 'hears' our radar and confirms the worst fears of the Anti-Air Warfare Officer. 'Red nine-zero, hostile, closing. Missile attack!'

The nerve centre alerts the ship's defences, the missile launchers swing expectantly in our direction. Suddenly, the uppermost Tornado of the attacking pair pulls up sharply, turning hard away from the ship. Missile away. The 'missile' aircraft engages combat power, glues itself right down onto the surface of the sea, hugging the wavetops, arrowing in even faster and lower at the ship, really low now, bouncing on the pressure wave between the Tornado and the sea. The ship's Ops Room is buzzing like a hornet's nest. Incoming! In combat, anti-missile missiles had not had spectacular results in dealing with sea-skimmers. Their best hope is the ship's Phalanx rotary cannon, its six barrels spitting out 3,000 rounds per minute. But they don't get a minute to shoot the missile down – more like four seconds. The command on board has very little time to make the right decisions, to protect the ship from the sea-skimmer rocketing in. What is fascinating is the way these massive warships can turn virtually on a sixpence, skidding themselves round in the sea until they are nose-to-nose with attacking aircraft like our own.

They fought us almost like an enemy aircraft would in a dogfight. We would be steaming in, with a lovely clear shot at the vessel's big fat broadside, when at the critical moment it would swivel on its axis, spinning suddenly to face the threat, its sharp bows presenting a much smaller, much more difficult target.

We were just flashing over the cruiser, having completed our attack run, when the CAP caught up with us, a pair of Hornets, F-18s, the US Navy's most agile fighter. Oh good. John Nichol spotted them; I was concentrating on avoiding the sea at the time. The crew members on the bridge deck were looking down at us as we wazzed gleefully over their ship. The ship's Captain transmitted over the radio, 'You're clear in, burn the paint off our decks.' The Hornets attacked us in classic style, swooping down out of the sun. It was a spot of luck John had seen them at all. For the next few minutes, all hell broke loose, while I threw the Tornado around the sky to prevent them getting a good missile shot off at us. John got busy with the countermeasures: chaff to confuse their radars, flares to sucker the heat-seeking Sidewinders away from our jet pipes. The Navy pilots hauled their jets around in response, trying to get the kill in. The Top Gun fighter pilot school at Miramar, California must do some good, and not just for Tom Cruise . . . About the best we could expect was to make it difficult for them. We never had a prayer, really. The Hornet is a first-class fighter, one of the best in the world, in a different league to our Tornado where manoeuvrability is concerned. And there were two of them. That's our excuse, anyway, and we're sticking to it. We gave up when one of them got us bang to rights, his gun-sight burning a hole in the back of our canopy . . . tracking, tracking. We parted the best of friends after our little scrap.

Most sorties, we stayed over southern Saudi, or the sea. Sometimes, we did 'trails' down into Oman – flying point-to-point, taking fuel from the tanker at a pre-set time en route. The trick, as usual, was to be there exactly on time and on track. In Oman, the desert throws up spectacular features: jagged hills, gigantic columns of standing stone, which we could practise flying over – or between. Once, though, we were routed up into northern Saudi, swanning around without too much to do for a change, showing the flag for the ground troops. Looking out, an amazing sight met our eyes. Below us in the desert were scores of Allied tanks, simply parked in the sand, huge piles of equipment, tonnes and tonnes of kit, ammunition dumps, supply dumps, fuel bowsers. There were boxes and crates everywhere, piled up high. Mostly, because of the camouflage, it was impossible to tell what was under the netting – vehicles? guns? – there was just an unbelievable amount of it. On the road there was convoy after convoy of armour and supply trucks, the traffic almost continuous, with vehicles chucking up huge dust plumes, Land Rovers billowing rooster tails of sand, petrol tankers rolling along with armoured escorts, motorised infantry, their cavalry flags flying proudly, the red-and-white chequered head-dresses of the Arab troops fluttering in the stiff desert wind . . . Some of this stuff, including dozens of armoured vehicles and tonnes of fuel, was being left *in situ* along the route, as forward re-supply should push come to shove. We were watching the creation of a chain of logistic bases that would soon stretch right across the desert from Riyadh to the Forward Assembly Area, from which 1(BR) Armoured Division would eventually launch its attack. The expected daily needs of this single British division, when the shooting started, were: 1,200 tonnes of ammunition, 500,000 litres of fuel, 400,000 litres of water, 30,000 individual ration packs . . . The colossal scale of the supplies had to be seen to be believed. The rest of the equipment, the stuff that was not staying behind, was headed north and west, towards Iraq.

7

Christmas in the Gulf

John Peters: When the Scud missile alarm went off we were at the Operations Centre, in the flying-clothing room, changing. There was a BBC television crew in there, filming some footage for *Songs of Praise*. As soon as the ear-splitting racket started up, we began running hard for the shelters, clutching our NBC warfare bags. These held the impermeable suit and gasmask that constituted our collective security blanket against the missile coming towards us. The television crew were all but trampled in the rush. Seeing the rest of us scrambling into the gasmasks and chemical warfare protection suits, the BBC people looked totally bewildered, and not a little panic-stricken. They had been issued with the protective clothing all right, but they had left it in their hotel. When they realised this, they looked unforgettably horrified. 'What do we do now, what do we do now?' one of them cried.

To which some wag responded, in passing, 'Die, mate!'

Luckily they didn't – it was a false alarm. We joked about it afterwards. But following this episode, no member of that crew was ever seen more than one foot away from his or her NBC bag. They could be seen touching them superstitiously, every so often, like fetishes, for reassurance. Even during the carol service they were later filming, for the BBC's Christmas Eve *Songs of Praise*, the cameramen had their bags there beside them, well within immediate reach. You live and learn!

I went along to that carol service. It took place in an aircraft hangar, with about 100 people sitting on a Tornado. We were briefed beforehand: 'Don't get too pissed, and do try to sing the right words, otherwise it will look bloody funny on television.' Another comprehensive briefing. But, so far from home, in the simmering heat, the singing seemed empty to me. Despite the fact that his soul was almost certainly in need of some attention, John had decided to miss this particular occasion. That decision was looking pretty sound. I wondered whether the sins of the flesh might have anything to do with his absence. If that was what he was doing, I could only wish him good luck. After all, it might be our last Christmas, ever.

Christmas Day was a normal working day for the Squadron. Our formation was the 'duty planning team', which meant that we were the unfortunates who were stuck on the ground planning the sorties for the next day. There had been a bit of competition as to who would be flying that day: very few aircrew had ever entered 25 December in their flying logbooks!

There was a big fly-past later, with the Victors, Jaguars and Tornados of the RAF detachment flying a superb formation trail over the airfield, which gave the old morale a bit of a lift. In the evening, John and I had arranged a party in the hotel. Everybody turned up, not only all of the aircrew, but the nurses from the Army field hospital, a large contingent from the Gulf Air air-hostess school and a lot of our new-found expatriate friends. The ballroom was looking extremely tinselly; there was good food, fine wines and an excellent band. Suddenly it all felt a lot more like the kind of Christmas our loved ones would be enjoying at home. It was a perfect release from the preceding week's long, hot slog. Next morning we were slogging again.

John Nichol: After Christmas, we had four days' training in Tabuk, way up in northwestern Saudi Arabia near the border with Iraq. This was something else, the obverse of life in Bahrain: here it felt very close to war, and not just geographically. The guys there were not living in nice conditions, they were living eight people to a space that was built for two. The whole place had been thrown up from scratch out of Portakabins and the ubiquitous oil-drum, but despite this it was very impressive. Half of it was semi-buried in the sand, to provide protection. But it was overcrowded. In some cases people were having to sleep on the verandahs, and in winter the desert nights could be very cold indeed – with temperatures frequently dropping below freezing-point. Because of the physical hardships, or perhaps in spite of them, the Tabuk squadrons had a real spirit going: their morale was sky-high, the sense of operational readiness was tremendous. They were living behind the wire, living and working for war twenty-four hours a day. To relieve our guilt about the good time we were having in Bahrain, in our soft and comfortable hotel, we took them over twenty litres of whisky and a few cases of wine – strictly unofficially. They were particularly pleased to hear about the 300 trainee air-hostesses they were missing.

We did some truly excellent flying around Tabuk, through narrow gorges, so narrow JP was continually having to roll the Tornado onto its side, to squeeze through the sheer sandstone cliffs soaring high above us. We flew through the most fantastic rock formations, sculpted by sandstorms. To look at, it was stunning; to fly through, a joy.

We were very well looked after at Tabuk by Squadron Leader Kevin Weeks, a marvellous man and a good friend, who had been with us previously on XV Squadron, before his posting to 16. Tragically, he was soon to be killed, with his pilot, Squadron Leader Gary Lennox, on a combat mission over Iraq. On the last evening we were there, Kev took us out to his favourite local restaurant, a Turkish eatery in Tabuk town. It was already just about full, but we squeezed into a table near the back. They had the news going on the television in the corner.

Tariq Aziz, then Iraqi Foreign Minister, was holding last-ditch talks in Geneva with US Secretary of State James Baker, in another final effort to prevent the war. This, of course, was some weeks after the UN had passed its crucial Resolution 678 on 29 November, calling on Iraq to withdraw from Kuwait by 15 January, and authorising the use of 'all necessary means' to enforce that withdrawal, should Iraq choose to ignore the deadline. There was a tense atmosphere in the restaurant as we waited for Baker to come out of the negotiations: everybody stopped eating for a minute, and laid down their forks. Right across the restaurant, wherever you chose to look, all eyes were glued to the television screen. Despite the tension, there was hardly anybody there who thought the Iraqis would go the distance. Baker had actually taken along to the meeting photographs of the Coalition forces massed and still massing against Iraq, to show Aziz the kind of muscle Iraq would be confronting, just so there was no mistake about it.

Maybe if he had taken a picture of JP eating his kebab to show Aziz, the war would have been averted.

Everyone believed that Saddam Hussein would give way, while he still had the chance. We were all passing comments like: 'Well, this is it, we'll all be back off home soon, the Iraqis are bound to see reason . . . They'll have to pull their troops out of Kuwait now, there is no other option for them . . . Aziz is bound to back down . . . Surely when they realise the enormous scope, the magnitude of the war machine coming at them . . .?' Would Saddam Hussein really topple his country over the abyss into war? He would have to be mad. But then, a lot of people thought he *was* mad. None of us wanted war, but we were rational. Was he?

Baker came out, looking very grave. He told the waiting reporters: 'I have to announce that we have no news. Things do not look good.' He had informed Aziz of the UN deadline, and made clear to him – crystal clear – that if Iraq did not withdraw unilaterally by that date, Coalition hostilities against Iraq might commence at any time. The Iraqis, it seemed, were unmoved by this prospect. We were dumbfounded. Knowing what we knew, seeing what we saw every day, the gathering Armageddon, it seemed inconceivable that the Iraqis would seek to fight. There was just no way we could see them winning, at least not in any military sense of the word: the forces ranged against them were so vast, so varied, and so technologically formidable.

The next day, we returned to Bahrain.

John Peters: To tackle certain targets effectively you need a concentration of forces, so the attacking aircraft have to take fuel – 'tank' – in pairs on the way to their objective. Sometimes, there may be so many aircraft in an attack, they have to wait in a queue to fill up, like cars at a petrol station just before a price hike. When the war was under way, there were aircraft that were not even on the same mission queuing up for fuel behind a single Tristar or a solo VC-10, so enormous was the pressure on the tankers. In this kind of rush-hour traffic, it needed a lot of practising to make it safe.

In early January, our Tornado was one of an eight-aircraft formation attempting to link up with two tankers. The weather was bad. There was a lot of heavy cloud around that night. It is impossible to tank at night in cloud. The Victors try to help by searching continually for clear sky, and steering everybody into that – but it means alterations of the course. The object was to get each Tornado four-ship refuelling from the Victors at the same time and on the same heading. Getting four Tornados onto one tanker under these circumstances – well, just about, maybe, perhaps. But eight Tornados onto two tankers was what you might call a complex scenario: not a bad test of spatial and positional awareness. It was a three-dimensional waltz in the dark, and we were still learning the steps.

The two tankers were supposed to be height-split by a thousand feet, but for some reason they were not, they were much closer together than that. They were meant to be in a specified area – they were not, they were somewhere else entirely. Ninety-nine times out of a hundred, they would be there, bang on the rendez-vous point. But just this once, they were miles off. The Victors, it seemed, had had a bit of a problem with their navigational equipment . . . This was rapidly turning into a very intense and thought-provoking exercise! We had four pairs of aircraft scrabbling around in cloud, at night, to get onto two tankers, in the same little box of airspace – and the tanker they were trying to plug into kept disappearing in the clammy clag ... All this was happening at more than 400 miles per hour. Not to overstate it, it was hairy: it had hairs all over it. All the high-tech stuff, the computers and the radars, suddenly went for very little. We were right back down to basics. Art had replaced science, with pilot and navigator working together to keep the 'big air picture' sufficiently sharp that they did not collide with anything.

The main problem for us was knowing precisely where we were in relation to everybody else, with so few visual clues. What we learned to look for, and we looked very, very hard, was the red glow from the jet engines of the Tornado ahead. It was the only thing there to concentrate on. You just hung on that engine glow. There was one small problem: the jets would not 'glow' at all unless the pilot kept the engines running at above eighty per cent of maximum power. If the revolutions per minute fell below that, those friendly bright orange points in the darkness suddenly disappeared, and you found yourself hurtling through the midnight air scarce feet away from a flying bomb with no idea of its whereabouts.

As a pilot, my capacity was wholly taken up with hanging onto this glow, but the cigartips kept on disappearing, lost in a sudden bank of dense cloud. 'Shit, where is he? I've lost him ... No, there he is ...' It was a bit like driving in fog on a busy motorway at seventy miles per hour, hanging on the tail-lights of the vehicle in front. And we all know where that ends up. My whole being was focused onto one single thing: not being stupid enough to fly into any of the other aircraft.

Although there were standard tanking procedures, each squadron worked out its own techniques for overcoming the likely cock-ups, such as hitting your lead aircraft, that are presented by taking fuel at night, in silence, in a multi-aircraft formation. The method we developed on XV Squadron was to approach the tanker in line astern, form up on its right wing, then slip back behind it in turn until everybody was refuelled.

For my situational awareness, I had to rely on John Nichol, gazing into his radarscope behind me. He talked to me all the time, reassuring me: 'OK, don't worry, the tankers are there, I can see the other four-ship across there . . . Range three miles and closing . . . two-and-a-half miles . . .' I cross-check on the Air-to-Air Tacan range, to confirm his info. 'He is left, three degrees . . . left . . . steady . . . he's on your nose . . .'

As well as guiding us into our little slot in the sky, John watched what everyone else was doing, what they were going to do next: 'The tanker will be turning soon . . . turning now, left, left . . .' This exemplifies the crew concept in modern fast jets. You can pilot a Tornado on your own, but you cannot operate it. For that, you need two people.

When it comes to taking the fuel, the pilot does not actually aim the aircraft's nose-probe into the fuel drogue trailing behind the tanker – the drogue jumps around too much in the airstream, so he would be unlikely to hit it. Instead, he aims the Tornado *at* the tanker, up the line of the drogue. As a pilot, I stick my probe into the trailing drogue basket on the end of the fuel line – but I do it on my navigator's commands.

In the back, John gives me instructions: 'Up and right, up and right, forward, slowly . . .' These instructions will get the probe into the basket. A good team will get it in first time. Every time. You take a tremendous pride in that. The basket has fluorescent pin-points of light on it, and the probe has a little light that can be switched on at the last minute, to help get you in. Once the probe is in the basket, the pilot pushes the Tornado forward, pushing the probe into the fuel line, which engages it and starts the fuel flowing.

All deeply sexual.

John Nichol: About this time, we had the Desert Survival lectures, courtesy of some hardy Special Forces wallahs from the Bahraini Defence Forces. To start with, we failed to take very seriously what the Sergeant-Major in charge was telling us. He had a small menagerie of animals caged up at his feet, including Flopsy Bunny, a furry brown rabbit. It looked like he was staging some kind of pet show. We did not really see ourselves catching rabbits in the forlorn sandy wastes, biting the heads off chickens, or skinning lizards. That was not the business we were in. We were in the business of dropping bombs, and, if necessary, if we got shot down, of hiding in a dune until some big men in a combat helicopter came out to collect us. But we started taking the Sergeant-Major very seriously indeed when he suddenly bent down and chewed the throat out of the rabbit. He simply pulled its throat out with his teeth, before our very eyes. Not the kind of person you would be likely to meet on an animal rights protest march. It took him an eye-blink to kill the bunny, a few seconds to skin it and gut it, a moment more to impale it on a stick for roasting on the fire we would have started in the meantime by rubbing two passing Boy Scouts together. We stared at our implacable instructor, then at the rabbit, so recently alive, now so thoroughly dead. The instructor had our undivided attention. We wondered what he might do to *us* if he caught anybody's attention wandering.

Next in line for the chop was the lizard. The lizard had a marginally better time of it – very marginally. It was an ugly scaly sort of beast, about two feet long and six inches in height, like a miniature dinosaur – but still, it met a sorry fate. Our instructor pulled its tail in the opposite direction to its head, with a swift wrench, parting its backbone in the twinkling of an eye. There was an audible click as the creature's vertebrae separated. He had that skinned, gutted and pierced lengthways with a stick too, ready to turn into lizard kebabs, in about twenty seconds flat. Mmmm . . . Now let's see, three lizards a minute, we could eat quite well, really, although I'd heard one could train the stomach to expect less.

We were less convinced by his assessment of our ability to evade capture in the desert. Despite his best efforts to persuade us to the contrary, we had seen how flat and featureless it was. There was nowhere to hide.

The prospect of war was settling over us now. Very unusually, since JP and I had been good friends for a long time, and got along fine normally, there was a momentary flare of tension between us. I had received a cassette tape from home, which I eventually realised contained a message from my two little nieces: they were saying what Santa Claus had brought them, and recounting their Christmas fun. This was unbearably sweet in the context, and I was feeling pretty choked up about it. Peters kept interrupting me as I was listening to this tape, and I suddenly snapped. I told him to shut up and leave me alone – at least that is the polite version – threw on my tracksuit and went for a long run along the seafront. I sat alone on a rock, for an hour or so, staring out to sea, for all the world like a cliché of romantic fiction. And as I sat there, it suddenly dawned on me, in its full and horrible reality, that I was going off to war. There was no turning back. It had not really hit me before, at that deep level; the message from home had pulled the emotional trigger. But after that, after my sojourn on the rock, I felt better about it – I had come to terms with it.

When I came back I found that JP had been out for a long run too. We didn't talk about what had happened, we had known each other too long for it to matter very much. Instead, we went down to the restaurant for lunch.

8

'I Have a Cunning Plan'

John Nichol: The Squadron decided to go onto a war footing a few days before the UN deadline expired. It was the twelfth of January. The plan was to work shifts, so that combat flying operations could continue around the clock. Our own shift was from midnight until noon the following day. To help us turn our body-clocks round, we were all issued with sleeping tablets. The first night under the new routine, JP and I were both in our room.

'Well, best we get off to sleep then,' said JP. I started collecting my stuff together. We were looking at our tablets, thinking, 'What are we supposed to do with this? Suck it? Chew it?' We popped one pill each, anyway. Nothing happened. Never having taken anything like that before, being good, clean-living boys, we expected the chemical to take effect instantly. It didn't. We were wandering around, ten minutes later, saying, 'Still awake then?'

JP sat down on his bed. 'These don't bloody well . . .' he said.

I looked over at him for the rest of the sentence. 'Work?' I suggested. Still fully clothed, he was fast asleep, dead to the world, flat out, zonked. 'Hmm,' I thought, picking up my book, 'it's all right for you, mate. How am I going to get to sleep?' I sat down for a second. The next thing I knew, the alarm was going off. I was still in the armchair, the book on my lap, lights blazing, and it was eight hours later.

★

John Peters: In modern warfare air power is the dominant and deciding factor. Without air superiority, or better still air supremacy, war is unwinnable. If the enemy has air superiority, you will lose. A primary objective of almost any air force is to establish a 'favourable air situation'. This is achieved primarily by a Counter Air Campaign (CAC). Typical missions in a CAC include:

Offensive Counter Air (OCA) – knocking out hostile airfields and enemy air assets;

Escort – friendly fighters providing cover for the bomber waves and engaging enemy fighters;

Sweep – fighters looking for trade over enemy territory;

SEAD – Suppression of Enemy Air Defences.

OCA missions are designed to reduce the enemy air force sortie rate, i.e., to prevent enemy aircraft taking off, permanently if possible. This is done by closing down runways, knocking out Hardened Aircraft Shelter (HAS) sites, destroying aircraft on the ground, shutting off access routes between the HAS sites and the runways. Alternatively an OCA mission may concentrate on destroying some vital installation on the airfield, such as its Petrol, Oil and Lubricant (POL) facility.

The Tornado's primary conventional role is OCA – the task we had always trained for in Europe. Few modern jets, like the Migs and Mirages operated by the Iraqis, can take off unless they have an unbroken stretch of concrete to operate from – the MOS, or Minimum Operating Strip. Given the size, number and excellence of the Iraqi airfields, denying them these strips in this war was going to be a question of continual, perhaps indefinite, harassment. We would have to crater the concrete and tarmac surfaces with the JP-233s and the iron bombs faster than the Iraqi engineers could repair them.

Most people understand what a bomb is. The JP-233 is more complicated, but it is essentially a very fat, very long canister containing dozens and dozens of bomblets and mines, of varying weights and explosive power. The delivery aircraft, with this weapon slung under it, flies over an enemy runway. The JP-233 spits a hard rain of destruction out over the target area. Some of these munitions detonate on contact, cratering the operating surfaces. Some have delayed-action fuses, timed to go off over the next day or so, to discourage the runway repair parties; for example, they will explode when a bulldozer comes along to help clear up the mess. It is not a friendly weapon. The only snag with it is that for the weapon to be fully effective, the Tornado must overfly a fair stretch of the enemy runway at a steady height. This makes the aircraft vulnerable to ground fire.

Escort assets – your own side's fighters – are often scarce and will only be assigned to valuable or critical attack packages, if at all. An escort formation of, say, Tornado F-3s or F-15s may be assigned in general area support of several OCA attack packages going forward at the same time. The fighters will step in whenever and wherever an opposing air threat shows itself. In this way, one group of fighters can ride shotgun for a whole bunch of different attack packages. This flexibility in the escort's role is made possible by AWACS, which can see the big air picture, far and wide, and keep extremely close tabs on how it is developing.

SEAD includes:

Defence suppression – e.g., F-4G and F-16C aircraft – 'Wild Weasels' – using HARM – High-speed Anti-Radiation Missiles – to knock out enemy missile radars, or iron bombs against enemy air defence network nodes and headquarters;

Communications jamming – carried out by specially equipped aircraft like the C-130 'Compass Call';

Stand-off jamming – EF-111 'Raven' aircraft jamming enemy early-warning radars from long range;

Close-in jamming – EA-6B 'Prowlers' jamming enemy search and tracking radars, and enemy communications, at close quarters.

Before the Gulf War, not everyone, particularly some of the Allied ground commanders, agreed that air power was crucial to success in modern warfare. After it, there was a lot less argument about that fact, summed up by the grudging comment of one senior US Army General: 'Air did good.'

The scepticism about the role of air power before the Gulf conflict was not surprising, given that the high-tech modern air war machine had never been really tested in all its complexity. Many of the weapons, like HARM, ALARM and JP-233, were untried in combat. Launching hundreds of aircraft in sequential, co-ordinated, self-supporting packages from widely dispersed operating bases, incorporating different national air forces, and projecting this air power over a target with split-second timing is hugely complex. It was also hugely untried. Airspace Control – the 'Deconfliction', or avoidance of mid-air collisions between 'blue on blue' or friendly aircraft operating in close proximity – was a major intellectual challenge in its own right. This was before you counted in the enemy's own destructive capabilities. So nobody was sure if it would all really work, when it came right down to it. We began to get an idea of how it might work at the preliminary war briefing. This took place in the Muharraq War Operations Centre on 16 January, the day after the UN deadline ran out. It was attended by the whole Squadron.

This briefing was intense, thorough, and electrifying. We were given our target. Our four-Tornado formation was part of a huge Allied air package, involving eighty-plus aircraft – what the Americans call a 'gorilla'. Our four-Tornado formation would be attacking the Iraqi airbase at Ar Rumaylah. Its mission was, essentially, to harass, as we had thought, and, ideally, to close down the runways. This mission was co-ordinated with an attack by the US warplanes on the Iraqi oil wells near the airfield.

We were part of a gigantic aerial steamroller, its purpose the systematic, clinical and complete demolition of the Iraqi war machine. Packages like our own would be hammering away continually at the Iraqis once the attack began. 'Peeling the Onion' was the metaphor some people in the military used to describe this methodical and cumulative destruction, the stripping away of the successive layers of the Iraqi defences. We were beginning with their early-warning systems, their AWACS and long-range radars: this removed their 'eyes', denying crucial information to their military commanders, increasing the time it would take them to react to incoming threats. At the same time, we would be taking out their 'C3', or Command, Control and Communications assets, severing the brain and nervous system from the body of the Iraqi forces, denying the battlefield and sector commanders the means to co-ordinate their military forces. It was a rolling wave of destruction, kicking down the doors for more and more bombers to go in, to strike at their core assets – like chemical facilities, arms factories – and the Republican Guard that had so savagely invaded Kuwait. But first, the main task of our own offensive was to KO Saddam's air power. This was where we came in. It meant knocking out their airfields and destroying their fighters – cutting off their fists. The big difference in the Gulf War from most preceding wars was that we had the technology to be precise in our attacks: we would be trying very hard not to kill civilians.

The huge scale of the attack we were involved in only became clear during the course of that war briefing. We came out of it silent, slightly stunned, our heads buzzing. There was a lot to think about. If you have to go to war, then this was probably the way to go. It had a certain monolithic style to it. In the words of General Schwarzkopf, Supreme Allied Commander in the Gulf, we were 'the thunder and lightning of Desert Storm'.

We went back to our rooms later to put our affairs in order, which is to say, we prepared for the fact that we might die very soon. It sounds melodramatic, but you have to think this way, it would be wrong to leave it to someone else. Never one to write letters much in the past, I found myself scribbling a lot. My brother, Mark, said that a lot of people in the UK were very gung-ho about 'teaching Saddam Hussein a lesson', but then it was not their little pink bodies in the jets. Over on this side of the world, in the Kuwaiti Theatre of Operations, closet pacifists were suddenly popping their heads up above the parapets!

It was better not to reflect that every letter you sent back home, every letter you received, might be your last, so you didn't. These are two that crossed:

> XV Squadron
> Operation Granby
> BFPO 647
> Bahrain
> 16 January, 1991

Dear Hellie,

Well it looks like this is it. Very close, anyway. We have known our targets for a while, but now we know our package and the 'War Plan', as well. All briefed today, though interrupted by an air-raid warning. Another false alarm, but in the midst of a briefing saying 'You are going to war', it set the pulses racing. We are now basically waiting for the 'go'. Everyone is obviously twitchy, but having finally been told what is going to happen, there is a certain relief.

All I keep thinking of is seeing you, Guy and Toni. I want to go on holiday with you. Anywhere, you name it! We will on my return. Somewhere expensive! Get to know each other again after this time apart.

It could be tomorrow that we start. With what we are involved in, we feel reasonably confident – if it works! I am not going to write any 'goodbye' letter, as I intend to return. You know I love you, and you have made me so happy over the last ten years or so. If it is the worst – enjoy yourself! We are so lucky with Guy and Toni. I look forward to being a proper family for a change.

    All my love,

       John

RAF Laarbruch
BFPO 43
Germany
16 January, 1991

Dear Johnny,

The deadline has expired and everyone here is waiting with bated breath to see what is going to happen. We are all pretty scared, but I am sure nothing like as nervous as you lot. Please pass on my love to everyone, especially John [Nichol], and tell them how much we are thinking of them. Sorry to hear about the jet that went down on Monday, were they based in Bahrain with you?

I got a 10.30 a.m. ferry at Dover and was back in at No. 7 by 5 p.m. German time. Things have already started well. There is a families' happy hour in the Mess on Friday. The Broughs are having a party on Saturday. We ladies have all been invited to a station dining-out night on 8 February, etc., etc. . . .

The kids have settled back to Germany well. Toni is sleeping better and only wakes up twice a night . . . Guy seems fine but still uninterested in his potty!

Please find enclosed your birthday present from kids, and some photos. I have chosen the one to be enlarged, no prizes for which one.

Do try to be as careful as possible, we are all keeping our fingers crossed. Love you lots and miss you all the time,

Helen, Guy and Toni

PS: When you write to your old girlfriends, you want to make sure you give them the correct BFPO!

9
Thunder and Lightning

John Nichol: We woke in the Bahrain Sheraton at midnight, after eight hours of pill-induced oblivion. It was the night of 16–17 January, 1991. At least, JP woke from oblivion – but then, that's his normal state anyway. Several times, well-meaning relatives and friends had woken me, telephoning to see if all was well, to find out what was happening. As far as I knew, the answer to the second question was 'Nothing'. Which just goes to show how wrong you can be. What I did not realise was that just about every TV channel on the planet was running live discussions with 'experts' on the imminence of the air war. Bottoms across the globe were firmly planted on the edges of seats. The Squadron had simply been stood to, but warned the attack could go in any time over the next ten days, so no sweat.

We sat around in the incongruous marbled splendour of the hotel foyer for a bit, chatting idly with the rest of the guys, as they emerged sleepily from the lift. The transport drew up for the three-mile trip to the airfield. As it swung into the hardened squadron revetment, the double rows of sand-filled oil-drums loomed ghostly grey in the narrow headlights. I was the first one suited up.

A wall of sound hit me as I approached the Intelligence Room for the usual evening update. This racket was unusual. What could it mean? If they were singing, that could only mean one thing: they had a mission. A tight little feeling of apprehension grabbed at me. XV

Squadron had been split into two formations, our own formation of four aircraft, and the eight whose crews were briefing now. The door was locked when I tried it. Someone opened it to my knock, and I saw a room full of people, in full war kit, trying very hard to deafen one another. On XV, we had this tradition of singing a ditty made up for us by the Army Ground Liaison Officer (GLO), or 'Glow' as he is known, before every exercise mission. This one was sung to the tune of 'It's a Long Way to Tipperary'. The sixteen aircrew taking part in whatever this briefing was about were singing at the tops of their voices.

When the singing stopped, the GLO said, 'John, give us twenty minutes, we're still briefing.' I knew then, for certain, from his face, the song, and the tone of his voice. I had just been looking at the aircrew on the first RAF attack wave of the Gulf War. As I turned on my heel, I bumped into JP coming along the corridor. Just from my expression, he knew too, but I said it anyway: 'Shit, we're really going to go and do this. I can't believe it; we're really going to go and do it.'

We drifted into the Ops Room, weirdly quiet with all the crews in briefing. Pablo Mason, who would be leading our formation, breezed up. He was wearing a First World War leather flying helmet.

'We're going,' he said cheerily, as if he were talking about a day trip to the seaside. 'We'll have a chat later. But first, let's go and have breakfast at Billy Smart's.' Billy Smart's was what we called the huge mess tent where everybody ate, because it had red-and-white stripes, like the Big Top at the circus. There was no way in the world I wanted breakfast, not at this point. I went off with Gary Stapleton, the lead navigator, to go over our own sortie, while the other two, typical pilots, went off to have steak, egg and chips, leaving the real men to do the work.

It was a pre-planned raid, but some of the details, like the refuelling schedule, still needed sorting out, so Gary and I went through the times for tanker join-up, the final attack, all that kind of thing. We planned it using the Cassette Preparation Ground Station (CPGS). We loaded our mission route into the computer, placing the crosshairs of the glass mouse, or cursor, over the grid square intersection on the map marking our start point, and typing the latitude and longitude readings into the terminal. By moving the cursor over each of the turn points along the route, the computer automatically loaded all these into its memory, too. Having finalised the route to our satisfaction, we could use the electronic brain to juggle times, speeds and headings, on-screen, in real time; we could also print off hard copies of the route, and use these if the Tornado's own onboard computer failed in the air. Switching to a larger-scale map, the navigator repeats the above procedure for the final attack run onto the target.

Some of the guys who weren't flying on our mission took the prepared cassettes out to the waiting aircraft, and loaded them for the outgoing crews. It was their way of showing us support.

This was the big one, the first war sortie. I can't speak for Gary, but I was more than a mite nervous. Because we were on a daylight raid, we would be using bombs instead of JP-233s. We checked and re-checked that we had the safest routes to and from the target, re-plotted the turn points, re-checked the precise timings required to get four aircraft travelling at about 540 knots to drop ordnance onto a target in quick succession and with percussive proximity – this without hitting one another, and giving least advantage to the enemy defences.

For an effective attack, each aircraft must maintain a very accurate time and distance from the others, and stay precisely in position and on track. If it should stray out of its own little space–time slot, the consequences could be disastrous. The Time On Target (TOT) is thus everything, or a great part of everything – the sacred cow of flying a fast ground-attack jet. Miss your Time On Target, and your best mate could be coming up your rear end at a speed of one mile every six seconds. If you are running late you will effectively back into him. Miss your TOT on a real attack, and you might find yourself flying through your best mate's bomb fragments or doing your best to blow up the chaps behind. When the raid is planned, each Tornado is carefully tasked to drop its bombs on the target in such a way that the bomb fragments from one aircraft do not hit the next one coming through – 'fragging your mates', as people say. The dust and debris from a 1,000-pound bomb explosion rise at least 2,000 feet into the air, and can hang there for as much as half a minute. These nice calculations are the bread and butter of the RAF navigator's job: flying in the Tornado, and operating its weaponry, are the jam.

It was very good to be doing something concrete, something I had been through a hundred times before in training, to hit that groove, to think of it as just another mission. On his way back from breakfast, JP later told me he had had one of those gut-wrenching moments that hit you when something terrible and momentous is about to happen, the sudden stab of adrenalin. I had been experiencing similar moments. We were about to find out if we could do it – or be found out.

By now we knew that the TOT for the first mass air attacks on Iraq was going to be at about 0400 Iraq time, after the Tomahawk cruise missiles and the F-117A Stealth bombers had done their preliminary softening up work. We had BBC World Service radio on; sure enough, ever reliable, as the first strikes went in, a clear female voice came over the airwaves, 'I can confirm that Baghdad is under attack, the first bombs are falling now . . .'

This was thrilling, a momentary tingle through the nerves. We were part of this. History was being made. This brief feeling of exhilaration was considerably dampened by the wail of the air-raid sirens. As we attacked them, so they were attacking us. There had been a couple of false alarms earlier that night, but we knew the threat was real this time. There were live Scuds inbound for our heads, and it wasn't funny: it was scary. The siren wail of the air-raid warning went right through you. As it turned out, the Scuds were aimed at Dhahran twenty miles away, but everybody leapt into their chemical warfare suits anyway, donned their gasmasks, and huddled into the air-raid shelter. Eventually, when the all-clear sounded, we went back to the Ops Room for the brief. It was not a small room, but it seemed very crowded. Everybody had guns, helmets, bags, and technical reference books with them: there was stuff everywhere.

The mission briefing was specifically about our own target for the night. It was to be the Ar Rumaylah airfield, in southern Iraq. We were briefed on its layout, its defences, in this case numerous Triple-A, SAM-3 and SAM-6 sites, how we were going to attack it and get out again in one piece, and the air support we could expect. While we were attacking the access taxiways, the tarmac links between the HAS sites and the runways, the US Navy F-18s were trying to hit the HAS sites themselves, and the US Air Force F-111s were taking on the oilfields and military storage sites to the southeast. With all this, unless we were very lucky, the raid was never going to be more than an exercise in harassment.

After the mission brief, we went back into the Ops Room to get our final Intelligence brief from the GLO. He gave us an update on the latest assessment of the defences we could expect to face at and around the target. Then we, too, sang the Squadron going-to-war song. All of a sudden, and from nowhere, I got a huge lump in my throat. It was really difficult to hide this reaction, to continue singing. Singing the song on exercise was one thing. You could have a good laugh about it. Singing it now, on the point of flying into heavily defended territory, with the very real prospect of not coming back, was something entirely different. It occurred to me that I might never see some of the men singing in that room again – ever.

With this rousing chorus, for our formation, Operation Desert Storm got underway.

John Peters: As Squadron Intelligence Officer, one of Janine's tasks was to 'sterilise' all aircrew flying into enemy territory, that is, to make sure we removed everything that might give away to the enemy details of our personal lives: rings, lockets, mementoes, photographs, lucky charms, credit cards ... details that could be used against us under interrogation. Taking off the signet ring my parents had given me for my eighteenth birthday was hard; taking off the wedding ring, and thinking of Helen and the kids while I did it, made me pause for a moment too. Here was my life going into a little plastic bag, to be kept in case I was shot down. We also had to cleanse our flying-suits of anything that might be of military advantage to the Iraqis in the event of our capture. This was no longer make-believe. This was beginning to feel really seriously like grown-up going to war.

Having taken us through our detailed escape and evasion brief – what to do in the event of getting shot down – and handed us the appropriate evasion maps for the area, Janine gave us £1,000 sterling in gold sovereigns, which we were obliged to sign for. She also issued us with our 'Goolie Chits'. A Goolie Chit is a piece of paper on which Her Majesty's Government promises to pay the bearer the sum of £5,000, provided said bearer returns Her Majesty's airman unharmed and in one piece to a place of safety – i.e., with his 'goolies', or testicles, still attached. Being given one of these just before a live combat mission really makes you think. We were also issued with high-tech infra-red light beacons, to summon the Combat Search and Rescue (CSAR) guys in, at night, if we were shot down. Only someone wearing night-vision goggles, like a CSAR chopper pilot, can see these beacons flashing in the darkness: they are invisible to the naked eye. By this time, we were kitted up in full war clothing, pistols strapped round our waists, two magazines apiece, each holding nine rounds. The hardest things to get on were the g-suits, because they were stuffed full of water-filled bags, a shortage of water being the greatest fear in the desert. The g-suit is a system of straps and inflatable bags, a bit like a bondage garment, which blows up automatically when the pilot pulls a hard turn. The inflated bags clamp around your limbs and stop you passing out. If they weren't there, all the blood would rush to your feet at very high speed, starving your brain of oxygen.

Next there came the 'outbrief', a pedantic enforced check that everybody had their maps, film was in their onboard cameras, and so on. Finally, we were signed out for the mission. Every time you go flying in peace-time, you have a specific set mission requirement – air-to-air refuelling, bombing practice, low-level flying or whatever. You have to sign for the aircraft, accepting responsibility for that specific sortie. They don't give them to just anybody. It seemed strange, somehow, though, that we were still signing for the jet in time of war.

As we were about to leave the Ops Room, the eight aircraft out before us on the first wave started to check in over the radios. They were already on their way home. While we had been absorbed in the briefing for our own mission, they had completed theirs. The voice chatter came over loud and clear on the loudspeakers. As the eighth aircraft checked in, the Station Commander broadcast over the Tannoy to the whole station that they were all coming home safely. A massive cheer rippled through the entire base at the news. There had been a lot of worry that the first four days or so of the air war would see heavy losses among Tornado crews, because of the nature and difficulty of the task, and because of Saddam Hussein's huge armoury of weapons. So the news that everyone had come through OK was extremely encouraging.

There wasn't much left to do after that but to walk out to the transport – or rather waddle, what with the immense amount of kit festooned about our bodies. As we walked out, we met the first raid aircrew walking back in. Feeling quite a lot of respect for them, and not a little jealousy, I thought, 'You're lucky, you've proved that you can do it; you're back here, and you've done it. I hope I can prove the same, that I'm not going to wimp out.' While I never really believed I would, the doubt was still in my mind: 'I don't want to let anybody down. I don't want to be the dick that lets everybody down – either by wimping out, or by fouling everything up.' That was the big thing: fear of failure. Deep down, I suppose, I was afraid of my own fear.

The first crew we met was our Flight Commander, Squadron Leader Gordon Buckley, who had led the second four-Tornado formation on the first wave, with his navigator, Flight Lieutenant Paddy Teakle. If anybody ever had an image of a fighter-pilot, Buckley is its archetype – even though he was currently flying a bomber! He's aggressive, confident and capable, and you would never want to compete against him in the air, because he is very, very good. He looked a curious combination of excitement and slight shock; he was obviously hyped-up from the mission, but at the same time had seen something that had not impressed him too much. The pressure and hard work of the sortie they had just flown showed on his face. 'I am,' he said drily, 'stirred but not shaken.'

As for Paddy, he got his cigarettes out, lit up, and, hands shaking just a little, said, 'You should have seen the fucking airfield. It was lit up like a bloody Christmas tree. There was flak everywhere. Tubes of bloody molten metal.' He always did have a way with words. We stared at him.

'But don't worry,' he went on, 'you'll be OK.'

10

Daylight Raid

John Peters: It was just coming up to dawn on the morning of 17 January. We clambered onto the mini-bus that would take us out to the aircraft. Their cockpits glowed an eerie green in the near darkness – just like a movie. We had a team photograph with the ground crew, who had been labouring all night to get the jets ready. The big difference this time was the eight live 1,000-pound bombs strapped under the Tor-nado's long belly. We had never dropped more than one on any training mission before. We had certainly not taken off sitting on top of eight of the buggers. Now we were going to drop the whole live load onto somebody's head, in one big hit. We were also packing two live AIM-9L Sidewinder missiles – 'Limas' – under the wings for self-defence. Again, we had never flown with more than one in training.

The Hughes AIM-9L Sidewinder is the standard close-range air-to-air weapon in use with US and British Air Forces. We were carrying it for self-defence and deterrence. Knowing we had Limas made fighters very wary before they dropped in behind a bomber for a shot of their own. If they had not seen the whole package, there was a good chance that they would be rolling out at perfect missile-firing range in front of somebody – somebody like us. The Lima, the great grandson of the Vietnam War 'Bravo' version, packs 11.4 kg (25 lb) of blast/fragmentation warhead with an active laser proximity fuse. It proved lethal in combination with the Royal Navy's Sea Harrier during the

Falklands conflict: twenty-seven fired for eighteen kills, a sixty-six per cent Probability of Kill (PK). The actual Falklands PK is nearer seventy-five per cent, because three Sidewinders were fired when Royal Navy pilots thought their first shots had missed, or because the target did not go down immediately after the first hit. Having said that, the Argentine aircraft were not carrying infra-red (IR) decoy flares, which might have helped confuse the missile, and most of the engagements in the Falklands War were 'ideal' – the Limas were fired from directly behind the target against a cold background – the Antarctic sea and sky. Very cold.

Under its left wing, the Tornado was carrying a Marconi 'Skyshadow' Electronic Counter Measures (ECM) pod, containing electronic systems that are designed to confuse and drown enemy missile guidance or tracking radars. Under the other wing was a 'Boz' pod: a chaff and flare countermeasures dispenser. Chaff is the word used to describe the little pieces of aluminium foil, much like the cooking foil in your kitchen drawer, that are dropped to confuse enemy radar. The foil, in thousands of little pieces, falls as a cloud, shows up on the enemy radar screens as a big solid object, and, with luck, confuses their tracking systems. Infra-red flares, also dispensed in the aircraft's wake, give out intense heat – the idea being to distract a heat-seeking missile that is homing on the aircraft's engines.

Last, but not least, we were carrying 340 rounds of High-Explosive Armour-Piercing (HEAP) ammunition for the two 27-mm Mauser cannons in the nose, not very much when the rate of fire is 1,700 rounds per minute. This stuff has a nasty habit of decimating anything that gets in its way. You don't need much to turn the average personnel carrier into an armoured colander. The cannon are there as a last resort in air-to-air combat, and otherwise for 'targets of opportunity': a convoy you may happen to meet on the way back from doing something else, a nice juicy row of parked aircraft, or whatever. In short, we had a fully tooled-up Tornado: it felt good – it felt like power.

John mounted up, while I went around doing all the external checks, scrutinising the hydraulic levels, trying movable surfaces like flaps and slats, making sure all the safety pins had been removed from the weapons. I was very slow and pedantic making these checks, especially on the pins. There are two safety pins per bomb. I wanted to make sure that when we wanted to drop the bombs, they were going to come off and go bang. Ditto the Limas. I counted the pins. Time and time again, I checked and counter-checked them with the ground crew. They asked us what we wanted for breakfast when we got back. This was a first: they were going to meet us at the aircraft with breakfast. We must be at war.

We strapped in. After going through the initial checks, I called up the ground crew: 'Clear start APU.' The Auxiliary Power Unit is a small jet engine in the aircraft which is locked in to wind up the main engines.

'Clear to start APU, Sir,' said a voice over the headset.

'Clear. Starting APU.' I pressed the button. Nothing. Zilch. OK, try again. Just make sure you haven't done anything stupid because you are half-nervous, like you haven't checked the power switch is to external power rather than internal power. Nothing. No, I haven't done anything silly; try again. Nothing. You only get three goes on the APU. It was not going to work. This was the last thing we needed. As it happened, we had lots of time, because we had come out early, on purpose, with just this sort of snag in mind. But it was very unsettling, to say the least.

'Shit, shit, shit, shit, shit! Have we got a spare aircraft?' The Tornados were dispersed widely across the airfield, in case of surprise attack, but there was a spare, right on the other side. We bundled out. The aircraft we were leaving was fully set up, all the navigation kit was aligned, the computers were loaded, everything was checked out. We had to shut the bloody thing down, collect all the maps and niff-naff strewn around the cockpit, and get out. Uppermost in our minds was the feeling that we had to get airborne, we had to go. There had been three or four occasions in the past when we had had problems with the aircraft during training flights, and we had turned back: no point in crashing. But the banter from your peers, merciless as always, immediately translated these incidents into a lack of moral fibre (LMF). On exercises there was always a LMF crew, a crew that had been secretly instructed to refuse to fight, to object on moral grounds and generally to cause as much disruption to 'normal ops' as possible over the course of the exercise. It had become a joke that when it came to war, we would be the LMF crew, and sure enough, the sodding jet was broken. The car never starts when you have the most important appointment of your career. But you did not want to be called the LMF crew in this situation. It might just get beyond a joke.

Pulses racing, we grabbed a van, and steamed over to the spare aircraft. My checks were faster on this one – not rushed, just faster. The clock was ticking. We were listening over the radio. Mike Toft and Mark Paisey, who were part of our four-ship, called up to say they had a problem with their CSAS (fly-by-wire) kit. They asked for a specialist to come out. He came out and had a go at it for a few minutes. It still would not work. By this time, the ground crew had fixed the aircraft that we had abandoned – very impressive in so short a time, but this was all getting a teeny bit daft. So Tofty and Mark jumped out and started to wind that one up.

Meanwhile, Chris Lunt and Colin Ayton reported their Skyshadow ECM pod was unserviceable. The ground crew changed the pod. The new one refused to play. Normally it takes an hour to change a pod. The ground crew guys whipped one off another aircraft, and banged it on in record time. But it was getting close to taxi-out time now, and the next thing was that Lunty and Colin's aircraft developed another problem. The Tornado is not usually that unreliable or problematic, as modern fast jets go; the guys were just extremely unlucky. Even so, they wanted to taxi out with us, still trying to get their Skyshadow going, still trying to get everything on line. As the rest of us reached the end of the runway, the formation leader told them to abort; they were forced to acknowledge it themselves: there were just too many things to worry about for the type of environment we were facing. They were staying behind. You could hear the desperation in their voices. It seems strange, but they were heartbroken. By the time you get to the stage of engines running, you have got to go. You are past the sticking point of your courage. You could almost touch the disappointment coming out of their aircraft. They were saying, 'Just hang on, they're putting another pod on, they're putting another pod on.' They did not want to be left out. We felt sorry for them, but at the same time, frankly, we were glad it was them and not us.

Since they would not be coming along, we were now down to a three-ship attack, and I was delegated to lead the back pair of Tornados, with the formation leader and his navigator, Gary Stapleton, out in front on their ownsome. My first lead of a pair, officially, was thus in time of war.

The Victors we would shortly tank with took off in front of us, followed by Squadron Leader Mason, ourselves, then Mark Paisey and Mike Toft. With our extremely heavy take-off weight, a full Tornado war load, we stayed in afterburner until 300 knots, to make sure we were safely off the ground. The initial plan had been: take-off in the night, bomb at dawn, come home. But for operational reasons, which we were never privy to, it had all slipped, things had moved backwards. We would be attacking in broad daylight. Professionally speaking, this was not a good thing. The Tornado attacks at night. Doing so removes much of the defensive fire threat, all the visually-laid Triple-A, all the visually-laid missile systems. It's very simple: in the dark, they cannot see you. Now, they would be able to.

Ours was to be the first, and the last, Tornado low-level daylight bombing mission of the entire war.

There was a little broken cloud at first. We lost sight of the Victors from time to time, then picked them up again as they broke out of the cotton wool. When we had been airborne for about sixty seconds, it looked as though every single friendly missile system in the Gulf locked us up. From the back, as the Radar Homing Warning Receiver (RHWR) blossomed into brilliant points of light, John exclaimed, 'Every bugger's looking at us!'

It was strangely comforting.

If you dick around at all on the tanker, you can foul it up for everybody else behind you, and you are not popular. And it can be bloody dangerous. In this case, there were only three of us, and we had two tankers, so there was no pressure. The formation leader was about three miles ahead, taking juice solo from the first Victor. Our pair of Tornados sidled up to the second tanker together, and we both got our noses firmly into the trailing fuel drogues first time. This was a bit of a kick, no nerves, very relaxed, very quiet, radio silent. It was just like training.

The tanker crew were excellent, real pros. Victors are old aircraft, they have very little in the way of navigational kit, but they let us off the trail at plus six seconds of the time they were meant to, which is exceptional. We stayed plugged into them right until the last second, so we were fully fuelled up. As a bomber, you still want combat fuel. You have a minimum level of fuel calculated, which is the amount you need to get to the target, bomb it, and get back to the tanker again. But you want spare fuel to fight with, if necessary. At that stage, we thought there was a fighter threat, and a very real one at that. On an attack run, you do not want to mess with a Mig-29 unless you absolutely have to. To escape that, or any threat around the target, you want power, which means 'plugging in reheat', afterburners on, which means speed, but it also means massive fuel consumption. At full combat power, afterburners on, the Tornado guzzles 600 kg – 200 gallons – of fuel per minute, instead of the 60 kg it uses at cruising speed.

11

Attack Run

John Peters: It was a gin-clear sky. 'Burning blue'. We dropped away from the Victor about fifty kilometres short of the Iraqi border, diving hard for the deck. At 10,000 feet, a lot of people could see us on radar, including the enemy. As we crossed the border with Iraq, John said quietly from behind me, 'That's it then. No turning back now.'

The three-ship attack we were part of was flying in visual formation, but widely split. The other two aircraft looked extremely vulnerable in the bright sunshine, their canopies winking, an occasional wing flash as one of them manoeuvred. Every Iraqi between here and Baghdad must be able to see us.

Al Badiyah Al Janubiyah, Iraq's southern desert: a barren ocean of sand.

This was nothing like flying in Europe, where there are hills, trees and even buildings to hide behind: there was absolutely no cover, it was completely flat. I wished we were lower: even at sixty feet, we wanted to be lower. At that height, we could see the faces turn skywards in alarm and amazement, as the Tornados roared over Bedouin complexes deep in the desert. This was really strange: here we were going to bomb the shit out of their country, and these people were looking up at us, close enough to spit.

Further inside Iraq, we hit a major north–south highway, teeming with military vehicles, a vast convoy of men and weaponry, a sharp-toothed crocodile, crawling as far as the eye could see. It was our first real sighting of the enemy. It was shocking, a silencer: this was suddenly all real. Down there were several thousand men dedicated to the terminally simple idea of killing us before we could kill them. Our formation leader transmitted: 'OK, quiet boys – let's get to work.' But the few bits of banter that had been exchanged over the secure radios had already dried up.

Obsessively, now, relentlessly, we went through our war checks. We were like a certain kind of married couple, continually nagging and upbraiding one another, making sure, keeping ourselves on our toes. To save myself from the more obvious errors, I had made up my own mnemonic, 'Will the Brits get Aids?' or WILLGBHIV:

Weapons: check the main and reversionary weapons package selection switches;

IFF: switch on until we reached the FLOT, or Forward Line of Own Troops, so our own side did not shoot us down, switch off now, going into enemy territory;

Laser: 'illuminate' targets – give the weapons computer a millimetre-accurate target range;

Lights: all off to minimise detection;

Guns (and Missiles): select both 27-mm Mauser cannons to high-rate, set both AIM-9L Sidewinders to Slave, ready for immediate action; also included under G, we made the Master Arm and Safety (MASS) and the Late Arm switches, so that now I only had to flick the red 'Pickle' button on the sticktop for the weapons to release;

Boz-107 chaff and flare decoy dispenser to manual, Skyshadow ECM pod up and jamming;

Height sensor: make sure we have the radio-altimeter on, now we are down at low level;

Eyes: I always tend to tank with my visor up at night, to reduce unwanted reflections, but you want it down going into combat;

Volume: adjust Radar Homing Warning Receiver (RHWR) volume so we have a nice loud warning of incoming SAMs. Adjust Sidewinder volume so you get a good growl from the missile.

We did these checks *ad nauseam*. We were also monitoring and updating our heading, speed, height, attitude, track to target, Time On Target, time to weapons release, scanning visually all round, all the time, for enemy fighters . . . Checking again.

The Tornado was bouncing hard now in the low-air turbulence as the desert floor warmed up. Out here on our own, with the sun fully up, it was reassuring to know our formation was part of a much larger formation, somewhere near, that we had massive backup in this attempt to knock out one of Saddam's airfields. The opposition's fighters should be showing up about now, if they were going to show up. From time to time, one of the friendly fighters flying the Combat Air Patrol (CAP) for our attack locked us up on its search radar. It was reassuring to know the F-15 was out there, looking – for someone else.

The F-18 radar suppressors had gone in first, the big HARMs strapped under their wings. The HARM offers an enemy a simple choice. He can switch his missile and gun radars on when a raid arrives, in an effort to detect, track and shoot down the incoming aircraft. In this case the HARM locks onto the emitting radar source, flies down its radar beam and kills the radar and everybody near it. Or he can play it safe and leave his radar emitters off – in which case his airfield will be unprotected, his air defence denuded.

Switching the radar on in very short bursts is about the only compromise available, and even that is not safe: if he switches off too late, the HARM's computer may have enough stored information about the emitter's source to score a direct hit on it anyway. Not much of a choice.

Along with the F-18s went an EA-6B Prowler, bristling with electronic jammers. Its task was to jam enemy search radars and tracking radars. AWACS was up there too, Big Brother, the magic eye in the sky, the all-seeing god of air war, telling us where the enemy was, at what height, and what he was doing. Every so often, an operator onboard the AWACS would send out 'Picture Clear' over the radio, a lovely message to hear, sweet as music, meaning there was no enemy air threat. Deeply reassuring.

Our attack profile was 'loft' – throwing eight 1,000-pound bombs apiece onto the airfield's taxiways. With three aircraft, that added up to about eleven tonnes of high-explosive.

The idea of a loft attack is to go in as fast and as low as you can, pull up sharply at a pre-determined distance from the target, and allow the onboard computer to calculate the exact moment at which to release the bombs, 'lofting' them onto the designated aiming point.

In this type of attack, each 1,000-pound high-explosive bomb is released when the forward speed of the aircraft and the tremendous catapulting effect of its sharp upward pull will invest the bomb with maximum energy. As it reaches the top of its graceful ballistic arc, each bomb begins falling to earth, acquiring further kinetic energy from the gravitational pull on its mass. By the time it hits the ground its terminal velocity is enormous, as the bomb drills several feet into the target before sending an explosive pressure-wave rippling upwards and out, buckling tarmac and concrete into long jagged chunks.

The loft attack profile is designed to save the attacking aircraft from overflying the target area, to keep it as far away from the target's point defences as possible, minimising the time an enemy has to react and to shoot it down. Provided, that is, that the enemy defences are not layered out for miles and miles beyond the perimeter of the target airfield. In training, lofting worked very well. This time, it's for real.

Coming up now to the Initial Point (IP), a pre-selected ground feature marking the start of the target run proper: nine miles to pull-up, or one minute exactly. No more. Flat out, at fifty feet, the desert looks close enough to touch, fizzling past like a speeded up film. In the front seat, I am happy with all my parameters for the attack. I had made the MASS and the Late Arm switch, arming the weapons, and the sticktop is 'live'. Position and TOT are both good. The onboard computer is constantly computing the aircraft's speed, its height and the exact distance in feet to the target. I can see the brilliant hair-thin vertical of the bomb-fall line, which shows me where the bombs will strike, if for any reason we have to release them unexpectedly. I can also see the target bars, which will bracket the target for me, either side of the bomb-fall line. The 'time to pull' clock, also in the HUD, also a bright electronic symbol, is running down anti-clockwise, a bit like a gameshow clock. We are flying at good speed. Seven miles – forty-eight seconds – to pull-up. Looking good.

Behind me John is well into his own attack routine. He has set the computer to its attack profile: Fix/

Attack, Radalt (radio-altimeter) selected. He has his head in the radar, looking for the first 'offset', which is coincidentally the IP.

Offsets are topographical features used to update the computer's navigational calculations, fixing the target exactly in space and time relative to the aircraft. There are usually three of them. On a target run John locates each offset in turn on radar, steers his illuminated marker over it on the screen in front of him, and thumbs the button to enter the data. Each offset refines the computer's attack calculations, progressively eliminating any margins of navigational error. Three successfully marked offsets will result in the bombs being planted to within a very few metres of the intended spot. The only problem is that in the desert there are very few features.

John flips on the radar again. He can see something on the display now that should be the IP: it has a couple of masts around it, that is what we are looking for, but it is very difficult to mark exactly. No matter, he knows we are close to where we should be, that the kit is good enough to find the second offset.

'Happy with that,' he calls, 'cancel your offset.' I cancel my own marker. Now we are back into direct target aiming and he can select offset two. Five miles to pull-up, about thirty seconds . . .

'Looking at offset two,' John says. Offset two is a building halfway down the target run. It isn't exactly what we would like, but we can see there is something there, no problem. 'Cancel your offset.'

I thumb the button. 'My offset is cancelled.'

He selects offset three, a corner of the metal fence the Iraqis had thoughtfully built around the airfield perimeter. On the VDU a beautiful corner blossoms up, like the corner of a table: hard-edged, perfect. He can see the double fence, breaking the target out properly from the green and black radar porridge on the screen. He adjusts the gain, adjusts the tilt on the radar, moves the marker over the corner of the fence, inserts, giving the electronic brain a perfect update. In the HUD my target bars jump slightly to the left, straddling the target – exactly where we want the bombs to go. I touch the stick very lightly, easing the aircraft's nose bang onto the updated target position. 'My offset's cancelled.'

'My offset's cancelled.'

Now we are both looking directly at the target on the radar. John can see the HAS sites plainly, he can see all the taxiways; he sticks the marker in the centre of the taxiways so the bombs will spread all around that area. Looking outside, no hostile fighters are watching us, RHWR is quiet, so probably no SAMs are coming up at us so far. John checks the Skyshadow ECM is in the correct mode, jamming the missile systems Intelligence had told us to expect. Fifteen seconds to pull-up. Very near the target now, John punches out chaff to confuse any radar-controlled defences that might be tracking us in.

Heavy Triple-A starts coming up, lazy curving arcs of tracer, dozens of bright points, streaming red droplets like a giant showerhead spraying skywards. The buggers are shooting at us! The shells burst into blossoms of black and white smoke, chucking out shrapnel in every direction. As well as being terrifying to look at, it is weird, because inside the cockpit, with our helmets on, we can hear nothing at all of the gunfire. It is like watching a silent film. The explosions are peppering up in continuous streams, right across the span of sky over the target. They look terminally close. For every glowing tracer ball we can see, there are nine accompanying live gobbets of explosive-tipped lead that we can't. It is the first time we have been under fire. It is horrifying.

Ten seconds to pull-up. Another check round the cockpit to make sure everything is correctly set up, a last glance at the radar screen; the target is still marked exactly where we want it. All the offsets are cleared down, we are in direct target attack mode. Ahead it is flak city now, almost solid with explosions, a box in space holding a wall-to-wall firework display dedicated to us. Adrenalin flooding, heart pumping, seconds to go before pull-up and release. In my headset, John's clear voice says, 'I'm happy with the target, you're clear to commit the attack.'

'Sticktop live.' The time-to-pull clock reaches the end of its travel. The target bars are perfectly aligned.

'Three, two, one, PULL!'

12

Banging Out

John Peters: I eased the stick back on 'One'. My thumb jammed hard down onto the commit button, the red arming switch on the sticktop I must hold down for the bombs to come off, a final chance to ensure we were attacking the correct target. 'Committed,' I said, scanning the HUD for the correct picture.

I was looking for a bright dot of light, generated by the computer – the 'pull-up cue'. My task was to fly the aircraft so as to 'capture' this dot, keeping it bang in the middle of the aircraft symbol in my Head-Up Display. The computer would do the rest. But I could not see it. There was no bright dot to follow. 'Shit, shit, shit . . .' This was a disaster, there was no bloody dot, the bombs would not come off. They must! This was our first attack!

I screamed at John, 'I haven't got a package, I haven't got a package!' I said it in the heat of the moment, it was a mistake; confusion was now king. I was still pulling up, already through 1,500 feet, the bombs had not come off and every bloody Iraqi tracking system for miles around was busily acquiring and shooting at us since we had popped up into general view. John had no idea what had gone wrong – he was feverishly scanning his switches to make sure he had selected the correct weapons package, which was what he naturally assumed I was shouting about. Urgently, he confirmed, 'Eight 1,000-pound bombs at eighty metres' spacing.'

'I haven't got a pull-up!' I shouted. This was much

better, this meant something to him. He looked to see if he had forgotten anything connected with the loft. But by this time we were several seconds through the pull, in very dangerous country: we were high, very heavy, very slow, near to the target and the weapons were still attached. What we should have done at that point was jettison the bombs, regardless of why we had not got the pull-up signal. We didn't.

Because the Tornado is a complex piece of machinery designed to perform a wide variety of tasks, there is a set sequence of switches that should be made for each type of attack. This can mean simply pressing one button, or going through a more complicated routine. If the switches are not made in the correct sequence, the attack will not happen.

John always waited until just before the pull-up to make his attack profile switch, in this case the high-loft switch. He thought maybe he had forgotten to make the high-loft switch.

This would fit. Without that switch, the computer would not know what type of attack profile was required of it, and it would not generate the pull-up signal for the loft. Garbage in, garbage out. He was blaming himself. I was blaming him too – in fact, I was cursing him with every swear word I could think of.

Buttons on the Tornado's consoles are not little soft-touch switches, they are big and solid; you are being thrown around a lot, you have to press hard, to positive-punch that switch. Maybe he just hadn't punched the high-loft button hard enough. He blamed himself. Alternatively, and just as likely, there was a fault in the computer-aiming system. We never knew. We never will.

We were still in trouble. Normally we would top out

at about 1,700 feet after a loft attack, but we were up at almost twice that. I overbanked, whacking the aircraft virtually upside-down, pulling positive g to get us back down and out of there, fast. A phrase from training came back to me: 'A target moving in azimuth, changing in height and under g is very hard to hit.' Let's hope so. I had not forgotten the bombs, but neither had the aircraft. Almost on its back, slow, turning hard and with 8,000 pounds of dead weight under its exposed belly, the Tornado was very slow to recover, to roll out wings level. I was still swearing continuously, a steady stream of obscenities. 'Fucking hell, what a cock-up!'

'Recover, recover, recover!' John screamed.

'I'm trying to!'

I was already on the case, and as he finished speaking the wings finally did roll out level. I dived steeply to pick up speed. We came back under better control.

John said, 'We can't fail here. Let's re-attack.' No one re-attacks. Not ever. It is the biggest sin in the operational rule book. Everybody around the target is ready and waiting, hammers cocked, missiles nicely warmed up. But we sat there thinking about it seriously for a nanosecond: we did not want to go back with 'Failure' written all over our first mission. It might get a bit expensive at the bar. John said, 'Bugger it!' at the same instant as I exclaimed, 'Don't be daft!' We were at about 100 feet now, running away from the target.

'Got to dump the bombs,' said John. For a heartbeat, I hesitated again. Dumping the bombs off would be a very tangible admission of our failure.

'Don't be stupid,' he said, as if reading my thoughts. Both pilot and navigator have a jettison button beside them in the Tornado. He hit his. I felt a huge 'Doosh!' as the bombs came off safely, thudding harmlessly into the desert. Unfused, they would lie there in the sand until the rust – or the locals – got to them. The Tornado lurched upwards as the weight came off.

By now we were way behind the other two aircraft, having spent so much time over the target. They had pressed home their attack and were making good their escape. We had been too busy to respond to calls from the formation leader. His check-in call came again over the radio, much more urgently now.

'Check in!'

'We've had a problem,' John replied.

'Don't worry about it. Get home.'

John was still pushing out chaff and flares like mad, we were still getting flak bursting all around us, but we were running fast away from the target to safety – or so we thought. Inbound, we had spotted a large Iraqi communications site near the IP. Closing on it now, we could see Iraqi soldiers running around the masts, scuttling little khaki specks.

'Strafe the bastards!' John called, hoping to retrieve something, at least to have some gun-camera film to show. But it was a futile call. We were not lined up for it. We decided just to get away from them, out of range of their hand-held missiles, their Triple-A fire. I whacked on sixty degrees of bank, pulling the jet round, well wide of the position. But suddenly there was an almighty 'Whump!' and my teeth rattled. The Tornado jumped across the sky like a scalded cat.

Oh Jesus Christ . . . the right engine's dying, the stick's gone dead, the fire warning is blaring out: we've been hit by a SAM!

In peacetime, a crew would very likely eject from an aircraft with a fire in one engine. In time of war, especially over enemy territory, it can be better to fly on, in the hope that the fire will simply burn itself out. This is not quite as insane as it sounds: each of the Tornado's engines sits inside a titanium shell, which should contain the fire, allowing it to burn out – in theory. And modern aviation fuel is extremely inert: it will not catch fire even if you throw a lit cigarette into it. This is quite true, I had seen it demonstrated in training. The aircraft will fly on its remaining engine. We knew we would never be able to refuel in the air with the problems we had, but we thought we might be able to make it to a reserve airfield or 'bang out' – eject from the aircraft – over friendly Saudi territory.

But this time our luck was out: we were ablaze from stem to stern, the flames fanned bright by the rushing airflow. The whole back of the plane was on fire. And the right wing was on fire, while a plume of grey-white jet fuel was streaming back from the other wing, spilling out into the void.

I said, 'Prepare to eject, prepare to eject.' I was getting good at that: it was the second time in three minutes; I'd already called it when the stick fell lifeless as the missile hit.

For the second time, John told me to wait: 'Whoa! The bullseye point.' He gave me our exact location, with reference to a known position on the map: quite a good idea to know that before jumping out into the middle of a blank, featureless desert. Then we radioed in our present position. Please Lord, and a big Black Hawk Special Forces chopper would be winching us up in a few hours' time, while Apache gunships and fighter cover kept the dogs at bay. John called up the formation leader for the last time: 'We are on fire! We have got to come out. We are ejecting. Ejecting . . .'

Nobody heard him.

I pulled the stick back. The featureless scrub

beneath us disappeared suddenly as the nose came up. Even through the oxygen mask, there came the thick black smell of burning aircraft. I called to John, 'Prepare to eject, prepare to eject . . . Three, two, one. Eject! Eject!'

We both hauled up on the handles between our legs at the same time: there was a faint mechanical thud through the seats. Automatically, straps whipped around me, drawing my arms and legs firmly in against the seat frame to prevent ejection injury.

'Why us?' I asked myself. I closed my eyes, tight. There was a slight delay, for a hundred years, during which nothing happened. 'God it's failed!' Then the rockets fired. A giant grabbed us by the shoulders and ripped us upwards, at thirty times the force of gravity – 30g – rag-dolls tossed high into the air: a massive roaring noise from the seat-rocket motors, a deafening wind-rush, a sensation of tumbling over and over in space. The slipstream was crushing, even through the flying kit, 400 miles per hour strong – try putting your hand out of the car window at seventy miles per hour, then multiply that sensation by a factor of six. There was a feeling of falling, endlessly falling, somersaulting end over end . . . Then the drogue gun fired out a small stabilising parachute, to stop the whirling through the air. Immediately, as the seat came upright, the main parachute deployed. There was a jarring 'crack' as the canopy snapped open, a massive jerk as it caught the weight. My throat tightened. The seat cut free automatically, falling away to earth. I opened my eyes.

I was hanging under the blessed silk of the parachute with a twenty-pound survival pack dangling between my legs, floating down into the deathly silence of enemy territory.

13

Downed in the Desert

John Nichol: 'Shit, this is it,' I muttered to myself on the way down. I looked over and actually saw the Tornado crash. A huge ball of flame went up, followed by a massive pall of black smoke.

'Somebody's going to notice that bugger,' I thought. After the chaos and insanity of the preceding few minutes, it was icy calm.

Landing. There was something I should remember about landing. I tried to collect my thoughts, my head whirling. Since we had baled out at a mere 200 feet or so above the ground, the thought collection had best be rapid.

Not so long before we went to the Gulf, there had been a case where someone had broken both his legs very badly in an ejection. Any extra weight on your lower body, like a pack, is a very bad idea for the amateur parachutist. The drill is to pull the release strap so that the pack falls away, dangling twenty feet or more below and between the legs. That way the extra twenty pounds or so hits the ground first. That was what I had been trying to remember. I started fumbling madly to get at my pack release straps. It fell away just as the ground came rushing up. I landed with a bang, on my backside, winded by the impact.

JP was about 100 yards away; I could see he was dazed, but basically in one piece. I picked up my pack and ran over. As I got near, I started laughing. His matinee-idol good looks were just a teeny bit damaged: he had blood streaming down his face from a big gash over the top of his left eye. He kept touching the source of the blood with a tentative finger.

'You look bloody messy!' I said, to cheer him up.

'What are we going to do now?' he demanded, groggily. A vast stretch of mucky brown plain surrounded us in every direction. Janine's escape and evasion brief, delivered in the calm, orderly safety of the Pilot Briefing Facility, seemed somehow unreal, now we were confronted with this featureless desertscape. Lawrence of Arabia would have come in handy.

'I don't want to worry you,' I said, 'but we're in Iraq. Can you believe it? We're standing in the desert in Iraq!' I looked at him. He really didn't look pretty any more.

We both started chuckling. Suddenly it all seemed desperately funny. We were struck by the absurdity of it all. Once we had started laughing, it was difficult to stop; nervous relief, perhaps.

'Let's get out of here,' I finally said, when we had calmed down a bit. We scrambled to pull ourselves together. I was eyeing the deadly pall of red and black smoke that the Tornado, burning a mile or two away, had become. Hello, Saddam, we're right here: come and get us.

Weighed down by g-suits, water bags, pistols, flying and biological warfare suits, life-jackets, helmets and the packs, we staggered about fifty yards away from the parachutes billowing on the ground. Then we dropped down: must make contact immediately with the Combat Search and Rescue guys. To get our personal locator beacons out, we had to inflate our Dayglo orange life-jackets. Perfect camouflage, of course: about as unnoticeable as a pack of baboons Christmas shopping on Oxford Street. As soon as the beacons came free, I started transmitting: we were both down, both alive, at such and such a bearing and distance from the bullseye point. We could only pray that someone friendly was receiving these signals.

The bright yellow fibreglass survival box holds a dinghy (also Dayglo orange) for ditching in the sea, and a separate haversack with water, food, extra clothing and a survival knife. Great, but the way the kit was always packed meant we had to inflate the dinghies to get the haversacks out. We watched helplessly as the bright orange inflatables careered out of the packs. Very useful in the desert, a Dayglo orange dinghy – and very good target practice for someone, if we were not very careful.

We looked at one another: you really did have to laugh. We could hardly have attracted more attention if there had been a Royal Marines band playing. There we were, standing near a tower of thick smoke, surrounded by bright orange dinghies and yellow fibreglass boxes. A few yards away, the huge orange-and-white parachutes were merrily flapping and billowing over the completely flat and cover-free terrain . . .

A sobering realisation dawned on us both at the same time. The missile that had brought us down must have been hand-held, because there had been no warning on the RHWR before it hit, and because if it had been anything else we would almost certainly have seen it. It would have been swooping down on us, rather than swarming up from behind. This meant only one thing: the guys who shot us down were near – and they were looking for us, now. Somehow, that wasn't quite so funny.

Hurriedly, we stabbed the life-jackets with JP's Swiss Army penknife, and buried them in the sand. The dinghies were more difficult: they are compartmentalised so you can't deflate them by accident. We stabbed and slashed at them, shovelling sand over the deflated bits as best we could. But we wanted to get away from our parachutes as quickly as possible, they were just lying back where we had left them. There was a trail of equipment leading to where we were crouched: parachutes, harnesses, helmets, half-buried life-jackets and life-rafts. It would have taken the rest of the day to conceal it successfully. This was not like training: this was not Europe, where you could hide things in a nice bush.

Perhaps if we moved fast enough, I thought, the stuff would not make much difference as to whether we got caught. I decided we should just run for it. I glanced at JP; he was still looking a bit muzzy from the smack on the head, and he definitely wasn't thinking very straight. But he was the Roger Bannister round here, at home he ran a mean half-marathon. He should be able to outpace me: provided, that is, he could run in a straight line.

We swung the haversacks onto our backs. I told JP to take his pistol out, and make sure it was loaded, with the safety-catch on. We each had two magazines, with nine rounds per mag. The search parties had better come in ones and twos, I thought. The idea was to start jogging. I realised at once that JP's leg, as well as his eye, had been damaged on ejection. Always a danger. Nothing seemed to be broken, the ligaments were probably torn though. He was limping quite badly.

Still, we had to put as much distance between us and the mound of tell-tale litter as possible. We walked for about five or ten minutes, then JP stopped. It was like walking through treacle, the sand deep and slippery around our boots, treacherous. It was searing hot in our flying gear. This wasn't so much making a run for it, as making a shuffle for it.

'We'll have to get down on our hands and knees and crawl,' he said, 'we're leaving tracks.' We looked back, and burst out into another fit of the giggles. There were great big parallel footprints travelling through the sand from the point where we had landed. They read: 'Enemy officers this way.' We pulled ourselves together, continuing westward for a while. I realised it was going to be extremely difficult to judge time or distance in the desert: no landmarks, no nothing.

Another thought struck me: what if we did meet an Iraqi patrol? Were we carrying anything that might be of intelligence value to them? I quizzed JP. He looked at me blankly. His kneepad with the target map in it had been ripped clean off in the course of the ejection, but I was carrying a route map, with the Combat Search and Rescue reference points on it. Shit, that could be very useful to them. I took it out. It definitely had to go; but how, without matches?

I did what they always do in the *Boy's Own* stories: ripped out a bloody great chunk of it, stuffed it in my mouth, and started chomping. For some reason, JP began laughing again. I can't think why the sight of his navigator standing in the middle of the Iraqi desert eating a tasty little map should be so amusing. The rest of the map I buried.

Then it occurred to me: what if we met friendly tribesmen? I asked JP if he had the list of useful Arab phrases on him, that somebody at the British Club in Bahrain had jotted down on a piece of paper for us a few days previously, at the party I now wished fervently we were still enjoying. He dug the paper out of his flying-suit and unfolded it.

The first phrase read: 'I am hurt, can you help me?' This seemed quite useful, so we read on eagerly. Then came 'Pilot, need food, please give me water' and

'May the peace of God be with you'. Better still. But as the list continued, to our amazement the phrases grew increasingly bizarre:

'The red bandana looks lovely on you. Please put it on for me . . .'

'I did enjoy the dried breadcrumbs and water, you really must give me the recipe before I leave . . .'

'Yes, Your Excellency, travelling in the boot of your car would be fine . . .'

Our friend at the party had been having a little joke with us . . . What a wag. There were more laughs, but then right at the bottom, the last phrase read 'Saddam Hussein is a bastard, I hate him'. When JP came to this one he stopped grinning. 'Oh, shit!' We buried that list in the desert, too; I'd eaten enough paper for one day.

After an hour or so at a steady walk, we suddenly got a bad feeling that we had been spotted. We both had this sudden sensation down the backs of our necks that we were being watched. I could feel my neck and scalp prickling. The ground was very, very flat. We tried to crouch down even more. Around us, the odd bit of bush pushed its way up through the sand; for 'bush' read twig with a couple of stalks on it, sprouting a handful of tiny leaves – useless for cover. We tried to move more quietly, quickening the pace.

Then we heard something – vehicles, noises, something was happening away to the right of us. We dropped down immediately, flat against the ground, frozen. Gradually, the noises faded.

We lay there for what seemed hours, convinced we could see somebody over on a slight rise, looking in our direction. It was a horrible feeling: exposed; vulnerable; insecure.

Nothing stirred. Finally we decided we would have

to move, and began leopard-crawling across the ground on our stomachs. Every so often there would be a two-foot rise in the sand. Wriggling over these was a nightmare. It felt like everyone in Iraq must be watching, as we rolled down the reverse slopes. I looked back at JP: his leg was worse, it was stiffening, he was obviously in pain. His left eye was coming up nicely.

Then something really did move, to the south. We lay still. Definitely people, coming this way. We took out our pistols. I checked that we both had a round up the spout. A vehicle moving closer, it sounded like an armoured personnel carrier. Then the real horror: a group of figures shimmered on the horizon, advancing towards us.

We lay perfectly still. There didn't seem much option. I was still hoping against hope, thinking: 'Maybe they won't see us.' As they moved steadily towards us, our only protection was a minuscule twig.

Then we saw a vehicle, a red pickup truck. It drove past our position a couple of times, less than half a mile away. Surely they must have spotted us by now? A volley of shots rang out. 'Bloody hell, what are they firing at? Us?'

Gradually, tantalisingly, the figure-mirage resolved itself: a skirmish line, strung out, advancing purposefully, searching methodically – for us. More shots cracked out, some of them whirring close: they were trying to scare us out of hiding, to flush us out like gamebirds. I remained perfectly still, my heart hammering. I prayed the line would turn, would move away from us.

A loud yell rang out. They had spotted us.

I had never been shot at before at close range. There is nothing more frightening. I wanted to shit, my guts churning, demanding evacuation. They had automatic rifles, AK-47s, the guerilla's friend. Being torn open by one of those is not the way to go.

The noise was unbelievable, endless whipcracks, deafening: crack! crack! crack! crack! The twig we were lying behind was eighteen inches high, tops, but bullets were buzzing through it, swarming angrily over our heads, kicking jets of sand up around our position. In my fear, I found that I was digging a shallow grave in the earth with my elbows, knees, groin, face, everything, driving my whole body down into the sand, the grains in my mouth and nose. Anything, anything to get down below the bullets, to avoid that shattering impact.

The image of the three of us, Helen, myself and John, came back to me, in flashback, that evening before the war, in the living room at Laarbruch, when we had joked about capture, about suicide. I remembered the things we had read that the Ba'ath Party did to prisoners. But did we really want to kill ourselves? Wouldn't that, too, amount to failure, but of a different kind?

I looked at John. Now it came right down to it, I didn't much fancy killing him, in any case. It seemed absurd; we had known each other for a long time. I was much less than sure I could do it. There was another option though.

'Look,' I said. 'They are going to come and get us anyway. Shall we go out with a bang?' I was suggesting that we start shooting back at them, make a fight of it at least. It looked like they were going to kill us anyway.

Dazedly, he looked at the gun I was aiming at the skirmish line. 'No, there's always hope,' he said, with a warmth in his voice I was surprised to hear. I looked over to him, and he smiled, wryly. All of a sudden, I knew he was right. The odds were way too heavily stacked against us. There were at least twelve of them, and they had automatic rifles; there were two of us with pistols, one of us injured. All we could have done is stand up with our little popguns, and fire off a couple of rounds. In return, they would have split our bellies open with the AKs.

We looked at one another. Without a word, we stood up slowly, very slowly, arms raised high into the air.

Never have two people hit the ground again as fast as we did. The whole world was exploding round our ears. We were completely submerged in gunfire, we were drowning in it. The Iraqis were a mass of beige, black and red – a welter of uniforms, wild black hair and beards, gaping mouths. They were charging towards us, screaming, shooting wildly, less than a hundred yards away. Hearts thumping, ears pounding, we tensed ourselves for the kill. This was it.

But the firing stopped. The Iraqis stopped. It was hard to believe, but they had stopped. Very, very slowly, we started getting up again – and again they let loose. It was stupid, but they were scared of us: in the pandemonium, they thought we were shooting at them. At the end of the line, an officer fired his pistol into the air repeatedly, shouting, in English, 'No, no, no, no, stop, give yourself in!' The firing tailed off again. Then, 'It's OK . . . up, up, up!' JP was still clutching his gun, but I had concealed mine, some grand notion of derring-do in my head. We stood up for the third time – extremely slowly! We still expected the worst. I was rock-taut waiting for the bullets to hit. We were both of us trembling visibly.

They came up to us, immediately grabbing JP's gun, and my radio, which was still sticking out of my pocket. There were three Bedouin trackers and a boy of about twelve; the rest, uniformed, were clearly airmen from the base we had just attacked. Great. One of the Bedouins was dressed in traditional robes. His face suffused with rage, he came right up to me, shouting his head off, and started punching me in the face.

We were very lucky the officer was there. Without him, it was as clear as day they would have killed us on the spot. He was shouting at them continuously in Arabic, at the top of his voice, still very worried they might kill us, especially the Bedouins.

He wasn't as worried as we were.

A lieutenant, he strode up to me. 'Where's your gun?' I pointed to my flying-suit. He reached in and pulled it out. So much for the heroics. He gave it to one of the trackers, who raised it and pulled the trigger. One shot rang out, whirring skywards; the second time he fired, the Walther jammed. Good job I hadn't tried anything.

We were quite simply looted: they took all our possessions. As they found things, they just threw them down onto the sand. The Bedouins got very excited by our ballpoint pens and felt markers. Then the one who had punched me in the face found my money, £1,000 in gold sovereigns. He looked at it. The gold glittered back at him. The look on his face . . . It was more than he could reasonably have hoped to earn in five, maybe ten years. He grinned at me, squirrelling it away among his folds. The lieutenant removed my flying watch. 'Don't worry,' he said, 'I'll give this back to you later.' This was a bit like King Herod saying 'Leave the baby, he'll be fine with me.'

'Which one is Peters?' the officer demanded. They had found our flying helmets, with our names on them.

'This,' I thought, 'is definitely not going well.' It felt as though we had wandered onto the set of a very bad movie.

Once they had taken everything, they tied our hands behind us, and prodded us into the back of the pickup with their Kalashnikovs. The little Bedouin boy was beside himself with excitement, bouncing around and waving his hands in the air. The lieutenant said, 'He is very excited: you came from the skies.' The kid had never seen a military aircraft before, let alone anybody who flew one; he was torn between desperately wanting to talk to us and hating us.

The airmen had given our personal locator beacons to the Bedouins, as well as most of the rest of our kit. This was amazing luck, because the Iraqi Army could easily have used them to lure CSAR into a trap. One of the tribesmen turned mine on. A series of beeps came out of it as the locator began working. Whatever anybody said now, the words would go winging back to the Search and Rescue teams. He muttered suspiciously at it. His mate found the other one, and they started speaking to one another, on the back of this truck, the conversation going out all over the airwaves, Arabic voices on our survival beacons. I was suddenly very happy. It meant that someone must know where we were. But could they do anything about it now?

We passed the canopy of the aircraft lying in the sand, blown clear on ejection, then the life-rafts and the parachutes billowing in the wind; one of the respirators had come out of the cockpit. They gave all this to the tribesmen, who slung it into the back of the truck.

It had taken them less than three minutes to drive us from where they had caught us to this scattered wreckage. We had been wandering about for two or three hours in the desert, but we had only moved half a mile or so away from it, even with a compass, so slow had been our progress! The other amazing thing was that they knew exactly where they were, despite the fact that there were no salient features around, just endless flat sand. We drove on a few minutes to where they had left their other vehicles, a white Iraqi military Land Rover and a civilian car, which was evidently the lieutenant's personal vehicle. The Bedouins went off, victorious, in their flatbed truck.

My abiding image of this episode is the bright young face of the little boy, sitting in the back of the truck with a gun in his hand, eyes gleaming black, repeatedly drawing his finger across his throat at me as he disappeared into the distance. It was very encouraging . . .

RAF LAARBRUCH, GERMANY. *Helen Peters:* They were shot down on the Thursday morning. At noon, the Station Commander, Group Captain Neil Buckland, and Maggie Broadbent, the wife of John's Squadron Boss, came to my door. It could only mean bad news. Very bad news. Seeing them there, I immediately thought: the boys are dead. That's what the arrival of the Squadron Commander usually means under these circumstances. But while we were standing in the hall, Maggie put her hand on my shoulder. 'John's plane has failed to return,' she said. 'That's all we know now.' For me, it was the worst moment of the entire war.

On Friday afternoon, the Station Commander came back. I had a few friends round for tea at the time, and they all looked at me in horror as he drew me gently into the kitchen. Gravely, he told me the boys had 'probably' been captured. He said Intelligence sources from inside Iraq, which he was unable to discuss, had reported sighting two captured British airmen. This being day one of the air war, John and John were the only two airmen missing, so it had to be them.

At first, this seemed like the worst thing that could have happened. I knew deep down that they were both afraid of capture more than dying, and I could understand that. They were prepared for death, for the quick death when the missile hits and the world goes white, then black. We were all as prepared for that to happen as anyone can be. They were paid to take that risk. But capture was different. We all expected the Iraqis to use their prisoners horribly. We had the Kurds as an example. In one way, though, I was relieved. At least they hadn't carried out that mad, half-formed suicide pact idea. This was probably just as well. John never was much good at DIY.

This was the only time I cried. At least when somebody you love dies, you know what has happened to them; you can mourn them. Now I was faced with the prospect of not knowing what had happened to John for weeks, months, perhaps for years, perhaps even never knowing.

Any fast-jet aircrew wife with two small children has to be realistic about potential disaster, even in peacetime. So during the long-drawn-out build-up to war, I had vaguely thought about it, vaguely made plans that if he should be killed, I would go back to Birmingham, and buy a house near my parents. I would have to hire a nanny, return to work.

I always knew that John could go out of the front door, any day of the week, and not come back. It happens. It had happened, tragically, to a very good friend of ours. But you come to terms with that, it becomes part of your mental furniture. The trick is to keep it safely stored away somewhere. It is impossible to worry about someone all the time.

One of the worst things was not knowing how to react, after the initial shock. The thing I was confronting was so unusual, so much outside the run of everyday experience. What was I supposed to feel? Was I supposed to be desperate? Keep a stiff upper lip? Did I assume the worst, and grieve for them? Or did I carry on as normal?

I was very conscious of other people expecting me to react in certain ways, and very conscious that I was not always living up to expectations. Maybe I was not weepy enough? Then again, part of me rebelled against this kind of pigeonholing. I am not the sort of person who breaks down twice a minute in tears. But for some reason I'd never faced up to the idea of John suffering.

14

In Enemy Hands

John Peters: They put John Nichol in the front of the Land Rover. I was pushed into the back. One guard had his gun at my head, the other had his gun wedged into Nichol's back. The driver had his pistol out ready on his lap. The officer had already driven off in his car. If ever we were going to make a break for it, now was the time. With a vehicle, we would stand a chance of making it to a rescue pick-up point.

The guards were determined not to let us look up, to see where we were going – as if this mattered in the desert. They kept on tapping our heads down low with their rifle barrels. By this stage my left eye was completely closed; it had puffed right up. Trying to make a sneaky assessment of the alertness and posture of our captors, I got a sharp crack on the skull. But by moving my head very, very slowly, I was able to see exactly how the one covering me was sitting. 'What I need to do is grab this guy's gun, smash my elbow into his nose, shoot the cretin who is threatening John, and at the same time kick the driver in the head.'

My left leg was OK, but there was one small snag: my hands were tied behind my back with rope. Still, they had not done a very good job of it, and as I worked at them the bonds were gradually coming free. While I was having all these wild and wonderful thoughts, another part of my mind was running on a different track: I would be killing a man at very close quarters. This is a much harder thing to do than dropping a bomb on him from far away. If people had to fight their wars hand-to-hand, eyeball-to-eyeball, there would probably be a lot less killing in the world. I thought, 'Can I do it? Yes, I can.' But then something else occurred to me: 'Has the guy got the safety-catch on his gun?' I spent another five minutes or so surreptitiously trying to find out. If I grabbed the pistol, a make I was not familiar with, and the safety-catch was on, or there was no round up the spout, I was going to look pretty stupid when I squeezed the trigger and nothing happened. There would be no time to cock the weapon, and probably not even enough time to release the safety before someone reacted. It was a racing certainty that the guard covering John would pull *his* trigger the moment the action started. Furthermore, John could have no idea what I was planning. To sum up: I had one eye working, one leg working, my buddy was unaware of my scheme, and they had three guns on us. I would have to be James Bond to pull that one off. On balance, it was a bit of a nonstarter. One other factor in reaching this decision was the fuel gauge: the needle was in the red. Even if we successfully took control, how would we make good an escape without a vehicle? They would surely pick us up again. I decided to forget about it, for the time being. We later discovered that they had a reserve tank in the vehicle, when the driver leaned down and operated a switch hidden from sight underneath the dashboard.

John Nichol: I realised immediately we were being taken back to the airfield our formation had just bombed; you didn't have to be a great navigator to work that one out.

'These people are not going to be happy to see us,' I

thought. 'How would our own ground-crew treat an Iraqi pilot who had just dropped an awful lot of high-explosive on them, and killed all their mates?' Answer: a mite roughly.

As we drew nearer to that airfield, we were sneaking looks out of the window when we could. The sheer quantity of the anti-aircraft weaponry around it amazed us. There was Triple-A everywhere. There were, quite literally, hundreds of gun emplacements. It was bloody staggering. One thing Saddam Hussein did not lack was manpower and basic weaponry. There were SAM sites; gunpits dug into the sand with single-, double- and quadruple-barrelled heavy-calibre machine-guns and cannon; tanks with extra machine-guns mounted on them; trenchloads of infantry clutching light-calibre machine-guns, automatic rifles and hand-held missile launchers . . . it was a real rats' nest. And this was just in the one small sector we were in. Nobody on the Intelligence side had foreseen this amount of Triple-A, or if they had, we certainly had not been briefed about it. It would be common knowledge to the Intelligence bods now though, now that the first couple of raids had gone in and been hosed down with lead. There was little wonder we had been hit, overflying this lot . . . If you got anywhere near it, sheer weight of numbers meant that somebody would probably get lucky at your expense.

Driving through these emplacements, our guards began waving their guns out of the window, tooting the horn of the Land Rover and pointing at us. We passed three Iraqi soldiers in a trench. We could clearly recognise the SAM-7 missiles they were holding at the ready from the pictures we had seen pre-war. We drove past a French-built Roland missile battery, sitting on its truck with its radar going, the missiles rotating slowly on their launcher. From down here it looked enormously formidable.

Our captors paraded us around two sides of the huge airfield, tooting and waving, as if we were some sort of travelling sideshow. They drove us through the HAS sites, which were exactly like our own back in Germany. Snug inside, Iraqi Air Force Mig-23 'Floggers' and Mig-29 'Fulcrums' glowered back at us. Although our mission had been only to harass, to deny them the use of their runways, there was clearly quite a bit of work still to be done around here for the rest of the Coalition Air Forces. As they bundled us out of the vehicle, we saw a huge crowd of enlisted men, ordinary airmen and some soldiers, standing around waiting for us. There was hate in their eyes, a burning, intense glare of pure hatred. That was horrible. In Vietnam, it had been known for the locals to kill US aircrew shot down near their village, sometimes slowly, for instance by tying them to a tree and flaying them. The same sort of thing had happened occasionally in the Second World War to Allied aircrew baling out over Germany – death by pitchfork or by spade. These airmen looked angry enough for anything.

Once again, we felt it was the officers who saved us. Speaking good English, many of them trained in Britain, the Iraqi aircrew in charge were professionally curious, and concerned. They treated us exactly as if we were friendly visiting fliers, who had dropped in to overnight at their airbase on a training sortie, instead of an enemy trying to blow it to bits. Noticing JP's injured eye, some of them started asking, 'Who hurt you? Who hit you? Which one of these men hit you?', assuming we had already been beaten up. We kept our silence. Despite their evident friendliness towards us, we did not really feel like establishing friendly relations in return; they were, after all, the enemy. Like any aircrew when we visited a foreign base, the officers were interested, they wanted to know what we flew, how it performed, where we had come from. There was also, and this was surprising, something like a suspicion of awe in their eyes: they respected us.

At that moment the air-raid sirens began to wail. The next raid was incoming. The officers grabbed us, pulling us down with them into the Pilots' Briefing Facility. Unlike our own PBF, this one was underground, a concrete bunker that had been dug deep into the desert. They had to help JP down the steps, as his leg was by now stiff and painful.

Once under cover, the Base Commander, a Colonel, came up and greeted us. A Saddam Hussein lookalike, as were many of the Iraqi senior officers, he was affability personified: 'How are you? How are they treating you? Do you want anything? Coffee?' We held our peace. 'Don't worry,' he said, 'you are safe now. Would you like some water?' We both accepted this, since we could see that the water was the same as they drank themselves. With our hands still tied behind our backs, they had to feed us the water. They brought us dates, cake and oranges with the water, but we refused them. We did not want to risk the chance of being drugged. We were sitting on the stairs, because the bunker was crowded out with Iraqi aircrew. Above our heads, we could hear the Triple-A ripping out incessantly at the incoming raid. The Colonel carried on talking to us as if nothing were happening.

'What were you flying? Were you flying Jaguars?' We gave him name, rank and number, but nothing else. Everybody in the room kept staring at us, as if we were a circus act, but there was no unpleasantness. Overhead, we could hear the distant thud of the bombs exploding.

When the raid was over, the Colonel pointed at JP's leg, and said, 'We are going to take you to the doctor.' They bundled us back up the steps. Outside, there was still a big crowd of airmen hanging around, waiting for the second performance of the pantomime.

'Don't be afraid. Nothing will happen to you here.' Another guard came up. The Colonel took us over to the jeep we had arrived in. 'Look, I am going to put you in this vehicle. You must not try to escape. If you try to get out, this man will shoot you.' He pointed at the guard.

Instead of going to the doctor, we were driven to the main gate, where another guard armed with an AK-47 got in. Both of these guards were great bears of men, not the type one could overpower, except, perhaps, with a bullet. An hour or so later, we saw a highway with the sign 'Baghdad' on it. There was plenty of traffic rolling along this road, but we turned in another direction. After another hour, we arrived at a second airfield, graced at its entrance with an enormous image of Saddam Hussein. We were both thinking, 'This is where the fun starts.'

They kept banging our heads with the rifles, to keep them down, presumably so that we would not see any aircraft or the layout of the base. One of the guards led us into another underground bunker, this one a War Operations Centre (WOC), obviously important to them because they put blindfolds on us first. The atmosphere had suddenly become a lot less friendly. They kept poking us with the guns. Tied back for so long, virtually since the moment of our capture, the muscles of my arms were on fire, the hands numb from the interrupted circulation.

The younger of the two guards prodded us sharply with his pistol. 'Now you are in Iraq!' he shouted. 'Now you are in Iraq!' As if we didn't know.

Once we were right inside the WOC, the Iraqis, still aircrew at this stage, took the blindfolds off. The fluorescent lights gave the room a bluish tinge, sucking the colour from the faces around us. There was no depth to their features, they looked flat and pallid, menacing. They began questioning us again, much more aggressively now, the words shouted in our faces: 'What did you fly? Where are you from? Which base?' They alternated between the two of us. We gave them name, rank and number, as usual, but nothing else.

A doctor appeared, and for some reason decided to take my blood pressure. They had to untie my hands for this. The blood began flowing back into my fingers, but was stemmed to begin with by the cramped tissues; it was agony and relief at the same time, but mostly agony, just like the slow unfreezing after extreme cold. Once they were untied, I could not bring my arms forward, they had seized up, straight out behind my back; the muscles had cramped rigid. I sat there with them sticking out behind me.

The questioning went on and on. Eventually, one of the interrogators said, 'You must answer our questions now, or we'll have to send you to the nasty people. We don't want to send you there. Talk to us now, and we will keep you here.'

We ignored them.

'We are all pilots together,' they said. 'We are friends. Although we are at war, we have the same job to do. Talk to us, it will be better for you.' It was an attractive offer. It was so tempting to say, 'OK, mate', tell them what we knew, and avoid the little physical treats that we were pretty sure lay in store for us. But we did not.

'If you do not tell us we will send you to Baghdad. They will hit you in Baghdad, they will put you on television, you will not like it.'

The words 'on television' rang a big alarm bell. Did that mean we were going to be paraded for propaganda purposes, or would we be held as 'human shield' hostages – as some Britons were after the invasion of Kuwait – at a high-value target, and displayed to reduce the probability of an air raid on the place?

After an hour of this interrogation, angry that we had refused to speak, they untied the ropes and put ratchet handcuffs on our wrists, racking them up tight until they cut further into the rope-reddened flesh. The crêpe bandage blindfolds went back on, cutting into our eyelids. Blindness must be terrible. For us, used to relying absolutely on sight for our jobs, being blindfolded was appalling. We kept looking up, to check if we could see out under the edge of the cloth at all. They guided us back upstairs and into a station-wagon; this one had its windows smeared with mud so that we could not see out. In fact, I could make out a little through the crêpe, but then night fell suddenly, coming as a complete surprise. We had been shot down at 0932 local time, and had already been in Iraq a whole day. It felt like about five minutes. Time flies when you are having fun.

We drove on for hours, both sleeping fitfully. My left hand was once again in agony, it was ballooning, the steel circle cutting into my flesh. I could tell JP's leg was giving him major problems: he kept trying to ease it out straight. When we stopped for fuel, we asked them for something to drink. My mouth was like a dried bone. They refused to allow us any of the water they took themselves.

We buzzed along the tarmac for another hour. Finally the vehicle slowed. As the main gate of a third airfield swam up out of the inky desert blackness, there was a sudden flash of light, brilliant even through the crêpe, followed by an earthquaking explosion that shook the car. The earth erupted around our ears, debris spattering down on the roof. Bombs started exploding all around us. Away to the right, something big exploded, illuminating the horizon. The air-raid sirens started going off, the sky absolutely lit up with Triple-A, while hundreds of guns across the airfield began hammering away; it was a deafening, bludgeoning noise. Heavy-calibre gunfire, when you are near it, unable even to stick your fingers in your ears, numbs all thought, shatters the nerves, rattles the fillings in your teeth. No matter how many times you go through it, you never get used to it. Sitting smack in the middle of this pyrotechnic inferno, we felt extremely small, extremely insignificant and fantastically vulnerable. And scared.

During a slight lull in the attack, they drove the station-wagon in through the gate and parked it next to a concrete blast wall. Immediately, the next wave of aircraft came racketing in, the bombs rippling across the ground, creeping across the airfield towards us, crump after terrifying crump. We were very pleased when they hustled us down into a bunker. Just as we got into the room, we heard the horrible intensifying whine of an incoming bomb. The noise curved across space to meet us, winding up to a furious high-pitched whistle as the bomb winged along its trajectory, louder and louder as it scythed in. Then the whistling suddenly got lower in pitch. Everybody in the room could tell it was going to be a direct hit – on us. They were expressionless with fear. Time slowed right down, unwinding frame by frame. The room had gone death-quiet; we were frozen, waiting. Then, a bullseye, it hit with a shattering roar. The room we were in was pre-fabricated, a substructure built within the concrete shell of the bunker. Its roof fell in, the walls curling in towards us, the grey plastic facings bulging and then splitting under the enormous crunching force of the blast behind. Chunks of concrete protruded through the split plastic, like bones sticking through ruptured flesh. Furniture went flying everywhere, the desks whizzed past, the lights shattered, splinters of glass rained down. As the bomb came screaming in at us, John and I both hit the floor, out of sheer self-preservation. But the Iraqis were extraordinary: they just stood there, screaming curses at the sky and invoking the wrath of Allah. Perhaps they really believed that 'The life beyond is greater . . .', as the Koran promises. It struck me as brave in the extreme.

Through the blindfold, I could see great clouds of dust billowing in the darkened room, lit now by a single emergency bulb. The rank, acrid stench of cordite from the bomb filled the air; broken glass crackled underfoot. His curses tailing off as the dust settled, one of the guards began signalling to his friend, smacking a fist into his cupped palm, then pointing at us. As he strode through the debris towards me, fist drawn back, I flinched away from him, anticipating the blow. He stopped, realising suddenly that I could see him.

'Don't worry,' he said. 'Don't worry.'

'Yes, you bastard,' I thought, 'don't worry is right. I know what you've got in store for us.' He fetched another piece of bandage, and re-tied the blindfold. Now, like JP, I, too, was completely blind.

They took us down a level, further into the bunker. We were standing together in a room, surrounded by a hostile crowd. We had just been dropping bombs on them, now they were going to make sure we paid for it. Then I heard JP being hustled out. I was alone.

15

Name, Rank and Number

John Nichol: No one had asked me any questions. That's the strange thing. But I knew what was coming. There was a horrible presence in the room, an aura of hatred. I could smell the sharp body odour of the surrounding guards; I could feel their enmity. I sensed a gauntlet of hostility – silent, brooding, expectant, savouring my helplessness. It was time.

There was a sudden rush as they fell on me.

The first fist in the mouth is a mind-numbing shock, whatever you have been told to expect in training. I was trying to hold my head down to protect my face, my legs together to protect my balls. A crowd was around me, whipping, kicking, punching, the blows driving in from all angles. I swerved away from the blows; I could feel the skin bruising in their path. The bones felt crunched under the impact of the thudding boots.

The blood spurting from my nose was thick and grimy on my tongue and teeth. I could not protect myself. They had total control; they could do anything they damn well liked to me, and they could take as long as they liked doing it. I'd come from being a significant part of the biggest high-tech military offensive in history to being a speck in a Third World desert. I was surrounded by an implacable enemy population, and there was just me. Talk about coming down to earth with a bang. I twisted away, but it was not much use when there were seven or eight of them, kicking, punching, whipping on all sides, eager men, anxious to please their masters, to show what they could do. When they got tired, they left me curled up in a corner to think about it. There was no sense of time, it was like being in a black vacuum, seamless and endless.

John Peters: It was clear as they led us away from the shattered bunker that the bad stuff was about to begin. This was the place the friendly guys at the first airfield had warned us about. We had to be near Baghdad.

We were taken outside. I felt the air fresh on my skin for a moment. I was sweating with fear. My mouth was dry. When you're blindfolded you start to feel things more intensely. We were led down into yet another bunker, but with more steps, deeper than the one we had left. The corridor twisted and turned. At one point we splashed through a pool of water collecting in this new subterranean labyrinth. The atmosphere was extremely hostile by now. It was at this point they separated us, another clue about the coming punishment, if there were any need for one. I was pushed into a room, alone: a cell of some sort? I blundered around, kicking the walls, trying to work out how big it was, and trying not to think of what was going to happen to me. They left me for a bit, but then the door burst open, and a pack of guards rushed in, grabbing and dragging me into a room nearby.

A couple of seconds later, they jumped at me, using just boots and fists at this stage. It felt like about ten of them were beating me, although it couldn't possibly have been that many. They laughed and joked about it among themselves. The helplessness was a big part of it, humiliating, sordid, degrading.

'No,' I thought, 'I am not the one degraded here.'

Looking back, I realise I must quickly have become punch-drunk. I remember my head rolling uncontrollably, lolling from side to side. But I was trying very hard to stay on top of it mentally. That was the challenge. A boot caught me on my bad knee.

The main thing on my mind was: 'Is there any way I can win? How can I win?' They had total control over me. I would only be able to hold out for so long; therefore, physically, I could not win. 'I must win mentally,' I thought.

But what was there to win, under those circumstances? The answer, and it was the only answer I could come up with, was by not changing in any way, by staying the same person, mentally if not physically. There was no way I was going home a zombie or a basketcase (if I ever got home). It wasn't quite as calculated as this, as cool as this; it was more like scrabbling for some kind of escape route, for a way out.

Some of these thoughts had been half-formed even before reaching the Gulf, some of them were a reaction to what was going on. But the main notion I held onto was: 'Whatever happens, I'm not going to let the bastards change me. I'm going to come through this, and *if* I come through this, I'm going to go home to Helen and Guy and Toni, and I'm going to pick up my ordinary, reasonably happy life and my good job and get on with it, and make it as much like it was before as possible.'

It was an idea, something to hang onto. Humiliation is something that almost everyone has had to go through: try facing a power-mongering boss, or people who put you down socially. How did other people deal with that? Don't let the bastards grind you down, that's what everyone always says. So I decided I had

1. John and Helen on their wedding day, 26 October 1985, at St Peter's Church, Harborne, in Birmingham.

2. John Nichol at RAF Brize Norton, Oxford, in 1983, when he was in his late teens. In those days he was a junior technician providing RAF communication facilities for squadrons deployed in the field.

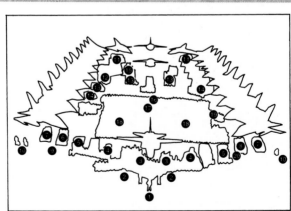

RAF Laarbruch on parade a year before the Gulf War.

KEY: 1. Group Capt. Gordon McRobbie, Station Commander, with his three Wing Commanders. 2. Bombs. 3. Pilots and navigators by Tornado GR1 fitted with wing tanks. 4. Rapier missile launchers with crews. 5. Scorpion light tank, No. 1 Sqn, RAF Regt. 6. Sultan command vehicle. 7. Spartan armoured personnel carrier. 8. Samson recovery vehicle. 9. RAF Regiment gunners. 10. RAF Police dog handlers. 11. Recovery and repair vehicles. 12. Snow-blower and crew. 13. Fire tenders. 14. Ambulances and medics. 15. Bulldozer. 16. Civilian workers, catering and medical staff. 17. Army support units. 18. RAF and WRAF ground staff. 19. RAF Police. 20. Station Adjutant with push-bike.

4. The crews of our four-ship formation gathered outside the Sheraton Hotel in Bahrain. From left: Chris Lunt, Colin Ayton, John Peters, Mark Paisey, Mike Toft, Gary Stapleton, Pablo Mason and John Nichol.

5. Two Tornados take fuel from a VC-10 tanker at 10,000 feet over the Saudi desert; a third waits its turn.

6. Singing the 'Squadron Song' to the tune of 'It's a Long Way to Tipperary' – a custom before all major missions but this time for real. From left: Pablo Mason (in helmet), Chris Lunt, Colin Ayton, John Nichol, John Peters and Mike Toft.

7. The pilot's cockpit, showing the Head-Up Display at the top centre, and the throttle and wing sweep controls at centre left. The pilot's control stick, centre, incorporates the attack buttons; above the control stick is the moving map display.

8. The navigator's cockpit, showing the radar and moving map display in the centre. To the right and left are the computer displays for navigation and weapons attack information. Below the radar screen is the navigator's hand control, and in front of that are the navigation and weapon selection switches.

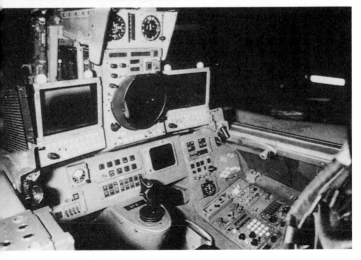

1 Air data probe
2 Radome
3 Lightning conductor strip
4 Terrain following radar antenna
5 Ground mapping radar antenna
6 Radar equipment bay hinged position
7 Radome hinged position
8 IFF aerial
9 Radar antenna tracking mechanism
10 Radar equipment bay
11 UHF/TACAN aerial
12 Laser Ranger and Marked Target Seeker (Ferranti), starboard side
13 Cannon muzzle
14 Ventral Doppler aerial
15 Angle of attack transmitter
16 Canopy emergency release
17 Avionics equipment bay
18 Front pressure bulkhead
19 Windscreen rain dispersal air ducts
20 Windscreen (Lucas-Rotax)
21 Retractable, telescopic, inflight refuelling probe
22 Probe retraction link
23 Windscreen open position, instrument access
24 Head-up display, HUD (Smiths)
25 Instrument panel
26 Radar 'head-down' display
27 Instrument panel shroud
28 Control column
29 Rudder pedals
30 Battery
31 Cannon barrel
32 Nosewheel doors
33 Landing/taxiing lamp
34 Nose undercarriage leg strut (Dowty-Rotol)
35 Torque scissor links
36 Twin forward-retracting nosewheels (Dunlop)
37 Nosewheel steering unit
38 Nosewheel leg door
39 Electrical equipment bay
40 Ejection seat rocket pack
41 Engine throttle levers
42 Wing sweep control lever
43 Radar hand controller
44 Side console panel
45 Pilot's Martin-Baker Mk 10 ejection seat
46 Safety harness
47 Ejection seat headrest
48 Cockpit canopy cover (Kopperschmidt)
49 Canopy centre arch
50 Navigator's radar displays
51 Navigator's instrument panel and weapons control panels
52 Foot rests
53 Canopy external latch
54 Pitot head
55 Mauser 27-mm cannon
56 Ammunition feed chute
57 Cold air unit ram air intake
58 Ammunition tank

59 Liquid oxygen converter
60 Cabin cold air unit
61 Stores management system computer
62 Port engine air intake
63 Intake lip
64 Cockpit framing
65 Navigator's Martin-Baker Mk 10 ejection seat
66 Starboard engine air intake
67 Intake spill duct
68 Canopy jack
69 Canopy hinge point
70 Rear pressure bulkhead
71 Intake ramp actuator linkage
72 Navigation light
73 Two-dimensional variable area intake ramp doors
74 Intake suction relief doors
75 Wing glove Krüger flap
76 Intake bypass air spill ducts
77 Intake ramp hydraulic actuator
78 Forward fuselage fuel tank
79 Wing sweep control screw jack (Microtecnica)
80 Flap and slat control drive shafts
81 Wing sweep, flap and slat central control unit and motor (Microtecnica)
82 Wing pivot box integral fuel tank
83 Air system ducting
84 Anti-collision light
85 UHF aerials
86 Wing pivot box carry-through, electron beam welded titanium structure
87 Starboard wing pivot bearing
88 Flap and slat telescopic drive shafts
89 Starboard wing sweep control screw jack
90 Leading-edge sealing fairing
91 Wing root glove fairing
92 External fuel tank, capacity 330 Imp gal (1500 litres)
93 AIM-9L Sidewinder air-to-air self-defence missile
94 Canopy open position
95 Canopy jettison unit
96 Pilot's rear view mirrors
97 Starboard three-segment leading-edge slat, open
98 Slat screw jacks
99 Slat drive torque shaft
100 Wing pylon swivelling control rod
101 Inboard pylon pivot bearing
102 Starboard wing integral fuel tank

103 Wing fuel system access panels
104 Outboard pylon pivot bearing
105 Marconi 'Sky-Shadow' ECM pod
106 Outboard wing swivelling pylon
107 Starboard navigation and strobe lights
108 Wing tip fairing
109 Double-slotted Fowler-type flaps, down position
110 Flap guide rails
111 Starboard spoilers, open
112 Flap screw jacks
113 External fuel tank tail fins
114 Wing swept position trailing edge housing
115 Dorsal spine fairing
116 Aft fuselage fuel tank
117 Fin root antenna fairing
118 HF aerial
119 Heat exchanger ram air intake
120 Starboard wing fully swept back position
121 Airbrake, open
122 Starboard all-moving tailplane (taileron)
123 Airbrake hydraulic jack
124 Primary heat exchanger
125 Heat exchanger exhaust duct
126 Engine bleed air ducting
127 Fin attachment joint
128 Port airbrake rib construction
129 Fin heat shield
130 Vortex generators
131 Fin integral fuel tank
132 Fuel system vent piping
133 Tailfin structure
134 ILS aerial
135 Fin leading edge
136 Forward passive ECM housing

137 Fuel jettison and vent valve
138 Fin tip antenna fairing
139 VHF aerial
140 Tail navigation light
141 Aft passive ECM housing
142 Obstruction light
143 Fuel jettison
144 Rudder
145 Rudder honeycomb construction
146 Rudder hydraulic actuator (Fairey Hydraulics)
147 Dorsal spine tail fairing
148 Thrust reverser bucket doors, open
149 Variable area afterburner nozzle
150 Nozzle control jacks (four)
151 Thrust reverser door actuator
152 Honeycomb trailing edge construction
153 Port all-moving tailplane (taileron)
154 Tailplane rib construction
155 Leading-edge nose ribs
156 Tailplane pivot bearing
157 Tailplane bearing sealing plates
158 Afterburner duct
159 Airbrake hydraulic jack
160 Turbo-Union R.B.199-34R Mk 101 afterburning turbofan engine

Tailplane hydraulic actuator
Hydraulic system filters
Hydraulic reservoir
(Dowty)
Airbrake hinge point
Intake frame/production
joint
Engine bay ventral access
panels
Engine oil tank
Rear fuselage fuel tank
Wing root pneumatic seal
Engine driven accessory
gearboxes, port and
starboard (KHD), airframe
mounted
Integrated drive generator
(two)
Hydraulic pump (two)
Gearbox interconnecting
shaft
Starboard side Auxiliary
Power Unit, APU (KHD)
Telescopic fuel pipes
Port wing pivot bearing
Flexible wing sealing
plates
Wing skin panelling
Rear spar
Port spoiler housings
Spoiler hydraulic actuators
Flap screw jacks
Flap rib construction

184 Port Fowler-type double-
slotted flaps, down
position
185 Port wing fully swept back
position
186 Wing tip construction
187 Fuel vent
188 Port navigation and strobe
lights
189 Leading-edge slat rib
construction
190 Marconi 'Sky-Shadow'
ECM pod
191 Outboard swivelling pylon
192 Pylon pivot bearing
193 Front spar
194 Port wing integral fuel tank
195 Machined wing skin/
stringer panel
196 Wing rib construction
197 Swivelling pylon control
rod
198 Port leading-edge slat
segments, open
199 Slat guide rails
200 External fuel tank
201 Inboard swivelling pylon
202 Inboard pylon pivot bearing
203 Missile launch rail
204 AIM-9L Sidewinder air-to-
air self-defence missile

205 Port mainwheel (Dunlop),
forward retracting
206 Main undercarriage leg
strut (Dowty-Rotol)
207 Undercarriage leg pivot
bearing
208 Hydraulic retraction jack
209 Leg swivelling control link
210 Telescopic flap and slat
drive torque shafts
211 Leading-edge sealing
fairing
212 Kruger flap hydraulic jack
213 Main undercarriage leg
breaker strut
214 Mainwheel door
215 Landing lamp
216 Hunting JP 233 Airfield
Attack Weapon (two,
side- by-side)

217 Submunitions
compartments (30 SG357
runway penetration bombs
and 215 HB876 area denial
weapons in each JP 233)
218 Port shoulder pylon
219 Fuselage shoulder pylon
220 ML twin stores carriers
221 Hunting BL 755 cluster
bombs (eight)
222 Mk 83 high speed retarded
bomb
223 Mk 13/15 454-kg (1,000-lb)
HE bomb

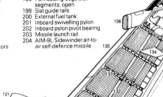

9. The Panavia Tornado GR MK1 cutaway
drawing.

10. Sections of our downed Tornado in the desert. From top to bottom: a Sidewinder missile clearly showing the hole cut by the burning propellant and, on the right, 23-mm shell holes (see numbers 93 and 204 on previous page); the taileron (122 and 153); one of the engines (160); and the shoulder pylon (218 and 219).

. The parade of POWs forced to appear on Iraqi TV. Left to right from top: Jeff
un, Guy Hunter, Cliff Acree, Mohammed Mubarak, John Peters and John Nichol.

12. The POWs on display to the press at the Baghdad Novotel. John Peters is on the far left; Larry Slade is second on the right.

13. John Peters immediately after release on the second leg of the journey home, in the VC-10.

14. Flight Lieutenant Chris Lunt's friendly face was undeniable confirmation for John Peters of his release. This photograph was taken in Amman, Jordan.

15. The Peters family keeping the media happy at RAF Laarbruch with a public reunion after their private meeting.

16. John Nichol with the second batch of released British aircrew, still wearing their yellow POW suits. From left: John Nichol, Bob Ankerson, Rupert Clark, Simon Burgess, Chris Lunt, part of the reception committee, Robbie Stewart and Dave Waddington.

17. John Nichol reunited with his parents at RAF Laarbruch.

. John Nichol with the other RAF aircrew arriving at Riyadh. From top: John ichol, Rupert Clark, Dave Waddington and Robbie Stewart.

19. John Nichol receiving a warm welcome from the children of Collingwood Primary School, North Shields.

20. Another TV appearance, this time in more pleasant circumstances.

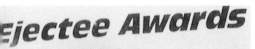

21. Meeting royalty. John Nichol with Princess Diana.

22. John Peters being presented to Her Majesty The Queen at the Gulf War Memorial Service.

23. The first flight together after the war. Back to work as usual.

to depend on my own integrity, at a very basic level: I had to believe in my own worth.

I had to think how they would try to defeat this 'no change' objective. What were my worst fears? Supposing they gang-raped me? Under the circumstances, it seemed only too likely. That might change me: it might well change anyone, male or female. I had to try to believe that they were the ones dragged down by this, not me. Supposing they ripped out my fingernails? My teeth? That would certainly change the way I looked, but it wasn't going to cripple me for the rest of my life, make life unlivable. This was the notion I fixed on.

They might beat me, literally, but in my own way I could at least keep on trying to beat them. There was nothing else to do.

Helen Peters: Staying sane was my priority. Sometimes I would look at a photograph of John, and think, 'I might never see him again . . .' but then I would try and squash the thought. If I thought about it too much, it might come true. There was a suitcase in the corner of the bedroom, which John had left half unpacked, and I just left it. I thought if I moved his clothes, and hung them all back up, it might be unlucky. It seemed to me that the way to keep going was by not thinking too much about the things that might be happening to John. That would only make me feel worse. Having two small children to look after kept me fully occupied, and I tried to concentrate on that. Some of the other wives said they could not sleep until their husbands came home, that they could not do anything, that they just felt desperate. But what could that achieve? Perhaps I had one advantage: I did not really believe that John was dead. I really didn't. I am not a very religious person, but I did believe in something then: I was sure I would feel differently if he had been killed, that somehow I would know.

This feeling, call it superstition if you like, was borne out all the more by the experience of a friend. I went to see her the day her husband had failed to return from his mission. It was awful: the first thing she said to me was, 'I knew he was dead. I woke up at two o'clock this morning, with these awful feelings that something was wrong. I couldn't get back to sleep.' She lay awake, setting conditions for herself: 'if nobody has come knocking by six o'clock, it will be all right.' By 6.15 nobody had come, so she went downstairs and made herself a cup of tea. At seven o'clock, the Station Commander arrived.

'It was all organised,' she said. 'That was the thing. Everything was organised for him not coming back. All the arrangements were taken care of for him not coming back.'

What she told me was frightening and terrible, but at the same time, it helped. It helped because when John was shot down, I had been watching the television late at night, thinking about him in danger, but I had not had any of the feelings she described. Of course I doubted my superstition; something *had* happened, and I had had no premonition of it. But then, I thought, maybe that is because nothing really serious has happened to him. Not yet, anyway. I could hope . . . I could only hope so.

John Nichol: The guards returned, dragged me back outside, collected JP from another cell, and led us down the steps and through the water. This journey was to become horrendously familiar, its end inevitable and routinely horrible. They sat us both down in a brightly lit room, and removed the blindfolds. JP looked wrecked. He looked as though they had just slapped him awake. He did not seem aware of his surroundings, did not appear to be taking much in, as though he had had a very thorough going-over indeed, worse than my own.

Seated behind a long table, an interrogator confronted us. He was flanked by two obese thugs, almost stock villains straight out of Central Casting: greasy-haired, they were wearing brown plastic shoes and brown socks on their feet. Presumably, they were Ba'ath Party interrogators. Both of them were dressed, incongruously, in British flying-suits that were much too tight. Too fat to be airmen, they had put on the flying-suits in an obvious but misguided effort to draw us in, to put us at our ease. The main interrogator stared at us, in silence, for a full minute, like the professional he undoubtedly was. Then he began the questioning, stuff about our mission and any other missions we might have knowledge of. We replied with the stock formula: name, rank and number. Finally, he said something in Arabic, whereupon one of the slugs heaved himself to his feet, and led me out of the room, into another part of the building. We were now clearly entering the classic cycle of interrogation and torture that would culminate either in our death, severe injury, or, most likely, our co-operation. The beatings we had already been through showed that the Iraqis were not likely to compromise in any way. They would escalate the violence if they had to. The continual shifting, the blindfolding and unblindfolding, were all part of the textbook interrogation technique, designed to disorientate, to confuse, and to unsettle. It worked. I had a horrible feeling in the pit of my stomach that it was about to intensify, that it was about to get much worse.

As I was led away, I glanced back at JP, my chum of the last four years, even then being re-blindfolded, surrounded by sadistic bastards. I could tell they were getting ready to start on him again. It was with mixed feelings that I was dragged from the room. What would they do next? Were they going to do it to me afterwards? Would I be able to hear him scream? How much would or could he take? How much could I take?

I was sitting in a cell on my own, thinking, when the guard came back in: 'Do you want to go to the toilet?'

I didn't, but I said yes anyway, just to get the handcuffs off. As soon as he touched my wrists, I jumped back in agony.

'Wait, wait!' he said. He went off, and came back with another guard. The pair of them stood behind me, making concerned noises over the state of my wrists. The cuffs had clamped down onto the protruding knuckles of my wrist bones, working their way gradually down through the flesh. They left large scabs that tore off each time the cuffs were removed or replaced.

'Wait,' he said, 'we're trying to find a key.'

Eventually they found a key that fitted. As soon as he inserted it into the lock, the cuffs sprang off under the pressure. My muscles had seized up, but I managed to drag my arms forward. It was the familiar blissful agony as the blood coursed back into the swollen flesh. They led me along the corridor to the toilet. In broken English, one of the guards asked me how I wanted to go. I pointed to my front.

'OK,' he said, and left me. I leaned my head up against the wall.

When I got back to the room, they did not put the handcuffs back on, but allowed me to sit with my hands on my lap. They showed a touching concern at my pain, which seemed absurd in the context.

John Peters: A fist splitting your lip open is like a stone coming out of a date.

It was a low-tech beating, but the Iraqis had thought about it. They varied between inflicting a sharp, superficial, stinging pain and trying to induce a deeper kind of pain, a pain that was more in the body. When they grabbed me by the hair and threw my head against the wall for a few minutes, it felt terribly flat and cold, my features tried to mould themselves to the flat surface.

All the time I was thinking how to protect myself, how not to give in. When they pulled me up from the floor I doubled over, twisting away from the direction of the blows, arthritic. Hands cuffed behind my back, my front was wide open, intensely vulnerable. One knee came up over the opposite leg, shielding the testicles they were whipping at.

My left eye, gashed on ejection, was extremely squelchy, like a wet sponge, where the face was expanding out. The more it swelled, the more they concentrated on hitting it, smashing down with some sort of pole or cane at my eyes. Absurdly, the thought came that when they hit it, they would do no damage to the eye, because the pulp around it would absorb the shock. The energy would be taken by the cushion of bruised flesh. It's like when you hit a balloon, I thought, the waves will just ripple and roll out across the head. I could feel my face growing: as the eyes came up and the nose swelled at the top, the vision went, the light through the blindfold dimming. It was like slowly putting on a mask.

Even blindfolded, you learn very quickly to distinguish between the instruments of your torture. The thick, plaited rubber strap thwacking across the face, the ear, inflicts a harsh, bitter, penetrating sting, you writhe with it; glowing red weals form with excruciating precision around the point of its impact. A wooden stick or cosh fragments you like crazy-paving, your body resounds with it.

The jarring shock from a wooden bat goes right through to the other side of your head, knocks you flying off the chair, sprawling heavily to the floor. It is hard to believe you have not been knocked out, they seem to have it judged to a nicety. Plenty of practice. They bark and scrabble around you like frenzied dogs over a bone, jostling and pushing one another to get a good angle for the next blow. Hands grab and tear at your hair, wrenching you back up. The atmosphere in the room is intense, narrow, dedicated. The only sounds are the scuffling of boots as they manoeuvre to hit, their grunts as the blows land, the sharp thwack and thud of flesh being hit – your flesh. It is an atmosphere of concentrated, self-contained unreason, the atmosphere of the medieval torture chamber.

Whipping with a rubber hose over the whole extent of the legs and back was a favourite. Number one on their hitlist, I thought, deliriously. This was different again – a sort of matted pain. As with a fist, I could feel the image of it afterwards, the shape of it imprinted on my flesh, growing.

I became detached. My body was being thrashed and hammered, but my mind had moved in on itself, into secret caverns of its own devising. All the time, in this little core of being, I was trying to stay as calm as possible – to assess how they were doing it, how I was doing against them. It was a relief when the beating moved from one area to another – it spread the load, somehow. My nervous system was developing resistance techniques. It tried to reject the pain, to make it abstract, separate. The mind can shut off a vast proportion of the pain in these circumstances, compartmentalise it when you are disorientated, when thought is hanging desperately onto one slim thread: your place in the scheme of things.

The beatings were spaced out, with what felt like twenty minutes or so between each session.

What I feared most at this stage was letting myself and my friends down: 'letting the side down', that old cliché. It's not a bloody game of cricket. But in a strange sort of way, it's all true, the stuff about honour and integrity; I needed it to hold onto. If I did tell them anything, even the limited amount I knew, especially the limited amount I knew, it was my own friends I was dropping in it, it was my squadron mates going out on the next mission. Whatever, the game has some simple rules. You learn fast. Never scream. Grunt, by all means, as the blows land, but never cry out. Once you have cried out, they have got you.

The side of my right knee was grossly distended where it had crumpled on landing, the joint immovably stiff. Just trying to flex it was bloody agony. On the third session, one of the Iraqis noticed this, and began stamping down hard with the edge of his boot onto the swollen spot, chopping karate-style snapkicks with the heel into the meat of the bruise. A massive arch of pain surged up through me in waves, stabbing into my armpit, jabbing up into my head, welling up through the whole side of my body. Again the stamping boot, and again. One pain can submerge the rest.

It was a mistake, letting out that yelp. After that, the kicks became frenzied, hammering down relentlessly onto the football knee. Every time my leg gave way they wrenched me back up onto it, forcing my bodyweight over it, ready for the next bootheel to come smashing down onto the same spot. A question penetrated the mist, the same one I had refused to answer for the past eternity: 'Are you pilot or navigator?'

'Pilot,' I gasped. They dropped me to the floor. I had broken.

Helen Peters: The first shot I fired in the Gulf War was a shot of gin, with a dash of tonic, ice and lemon.

Laarbruch's Station Commander, Group Captain Neil Buckland, decided that with their men away, the wives were allowed to go to the station Happy Hour in the Officers' Mess. This really was a big thing. Tradition still rules in the RAF, and 'girlies' are never ever allowed into the bar on a Friday evening. Happy Hour is a ritual *Boy's Own* drink-up, where the topics of conversation are flying and girls, by all accounts – in that order.

So we were looking forward to penetrating this all-male territory. But the first onslaught was scheduled for the Friday after John and John went missing, so the Station Commander was going to cancel it.

'Don't you dare!' I said when he told me. 'Not only are you not going to cancel it, but I'm going – in fact you can get me the first drink!' Life was going to have to carry on as normally as possible, outwardly, even if it were in fact turned upside-down. Other wives did the same when their husbands went missing, later on in the war: they turned up at the functions and put on a brave face. It had less to do with keeping a stiff upper lip, than avoiding the alternative: sitting miserably on your own at home, brooding.

The bar was packed that night. There was a great spirit on the station, despite all our anxieties, with the squadrons at war. The Station Commander was extremely good. In complete contrast to the Ministry of Defence, he was very candid with me, and gave me and the others tremendous support. This was just as well, because the British tabloid press by now had its teeth sunk firmly into the story.

John has always been my closest friend, as well as my husband. I missed being able to talk to him about what I should do for the best.

John Peters: What is difficult to describe is the sense of utter failure that took hold of me once I had given in. There was an overwhelming sense of shame. I had failed. It was not so much what I had told them. They had asked me a few general questions about the Tornado, mostly what it was carrying when it was shot down. There wasn't much they could have learned of any major value. I knew another target that was going to be attacked, but by now that attack would have gone through, so it no longer mattered. Anyway, they had not asked me that. More seriously, I knew the transmit codes for the Combat Search and Rescue teams, I knew the sequence of signals that you had to give to call in a rescue mission, the stuff John had given me before we baled out. These codes and signals were good for a week. If the Iraqis had found them out, they could have invented a 'rescue mission', with a good English speaker pretending to be a pilot, and simply ambushed it, shot it to pieces. This was one of the few things they could have found out that would have been useful to them, but they hadn't asked it. That did not matter. What mattered was having broken at all – it now seemed only too soon. When I was left on my own again after answering the questions, the most unbearable feeling of desperation and self-loathing swept through me. I kept on and on, reproaching myself. The iron was in my soul all right. Completely isolated, I thought that I was the weak link, the only weak link, that everybody else would have held out for much longer, that I was letting my mates down. I became obsessed by the idea that I was the wimp in the chain, and it was unbearable. There are different kinds of prison.

After that, they took me to another room, which felt far bigger, and interrogated me further. I was feeling pretty hazy still, and I played on this, using the grogginess to stall them. I was still determined to give as little as possible. I spoke very, very slowly, and said I was confused, which was true up to a point, all the time stalling. That day, and over the next day and a half, two days, they asked me nothing that they could not have found out about Tornado, or about Coalition battle plans, from *Warplane* magazine, nothing that the average intelligent twelve-year-old could not have pieced together. It was as if they had no clear idea what to ask me. And that was the best feeling in the world. A wonderful wave of relief flowed through me – but it was not to last very long.

Despite the incompetence of the interrogators, the feeling of failure got a whole lot worse when I spoke to John again, when they briefly threw us back together in the same room.

'I've talked a bit to them, but they could read it all in the papers anyway,' I told him. This was true, there had been quite a few articles in the broadsheets detailing who the Base Commander was at Muharraq, who the Squadron Commander was, that XV Squadron was flying Tornados out of Bahrain.

'Don't worry about it,' he replied.

'Have you said anything yet?' I asked him.

'No.'

I hated him for that. At the same time as not wanting him to speak, to suffer, I wanted the reassurance that in reality I was not the only weak one. But apparently I was. This made it all much worse again.

16

Interrogation

John Nichol: They dragged me back into the room. Silence. But I sensed at least two people, watching. The chair. That's what I learned to fear: backless, tubular steel, vinyl seat. When they held you down on that . . .

My body was tensed for some more of the same, but this time there was a warm, gentle voice. 'It's OK, we don't want to know any information. Don't worry.' They took the blindfold off. The voice turned out to be a mild-looking, middle-aged man, somebody's uncle, a twinkle in his eyes. He offered me food and drink, beside him on the table. I refused. 'Look, it's not drugged, I am eating it.' He asked the Big Four: name, rank, number and date of birth. I told him, that's permitted. This was a style of interrogation I recognised; I'd been warned about it in our combat survival training.

Mr Nice was talking to me again, his warm, reasonable tones filling the room, cosy, warming, lapping gently into my thoughts: 'We don't want to know any information. Here is food, here is drink. Don't worry. Relax.' He started to slip in the odd question. 'What squadron are you from, by the way?'

'I cannot answer that question.'

'Why can't you answer that question?'

'I cannot answer that question.'

And so the tournament began. He wanted me to say something else. That's the game we were playing. I'd given him the Big Four, the only other thing I could properly say now was 'I cannot answer that question.' If I said anything else, I would be striking up a conversation with him, and he'd have got me. I didn't want to do that. He kept on, softly, genteelly. 'Why did you come to bomb my country?'

'I cannot answer that question.'

'Why can't you answer that question?'

'I cannot answer that question.'

'Why have you attacked us? We haven't attacked you.'

'I cannot answer that question.'

This is as difficult as when somebody is beating you and asking you questions. A beating is a very untechnical way of interrogating somebody. Most interrogators will tell you it is not a particularly efficient method of interrogation, because eventually you will start talking in order to stop the pain, and you will tell them what they want to hear, you will say anything, truth or not. The wheedling, the appeals to logic and reason were more subtle, undermining.

My body was still on fire from the last beating, but he was trying to be nice to me, to draw me in, to form a relationship with me. He was going through a list of things that I could actually answer, and not give any information away at all, and I thought, 'I'd love to answer this, I'd love to say something different, but I can't, I've got to keep saying "I cannot answer that question."' It sounded ridiculous, when you kept on repeating it.

He tried a different approach: 'Your friends bombed my family at the airfield tonight. What do you think of that?'

'I cannot answer that question.'

'OK ... Fine. I see you are wearing a chemical warfare suit. Why are you wearing a chemical warfare suit? Is it because you're dropping chemical weapons on my country?'

Now I was thinking, 'Oh no.' I desperately wanted to deny the accusation, but I could not. If I replied 'No', he'd have got me. He realised from the look on my face that he was onto something; he concentrated on that for a while. 'You *are* dropping chemical weapons onto my country, aren't you?'

I blocked again.

'OK. We will talk further. I know that you cannot answer these questions, but *you* know that you *will* answer them. At some point, maybe not today, maybe not tonight . . . tomorrow, maybe, the next day . . . you *will* talk to me. I know you will talk to me, you know you will talk to me.'

I was thinking, 'I know that as well, mate.' But again, I sat and looked stupid; I looked sad, I looked very sad, I tried to get a bit of sympathy from him, but it didn't work. He continued with his questioning.

'OK,' he said, 'if you're not going to talk to me, I'm going to go. Do you want me to go?'

'No, no!' I thought. 'Stay!' But I could not say that. I was thinking, 'I know you're Mr Nice, and you're not going to hurt me.' But again I replied, 'I cannot answer that question.'

'What do you mean, you cannot answer that question? That's stupid. All you have to say is you want me to stay, or you don't want me to stay.' Psychologically, he was trying to get to me. I was desperately trying to fight that as much as I had been trying to fight the pain when they were flogging me.

In the end he decided he was going to go. He stood behind me chatting with someone in Arabic, discussing my case, planning the rest of the evening's entertainment. Mr Nasty came in. He was not a particularly aggressive guy, but he had the threats, he was threatening quite openly: 'If you do not answer my questions, we will hand you over to other people. They will hurt you, and eventually you *will* answer them. Why don't you spare yourself the pain?'

I think to myself, 'Why not spare myself the pain? I know at some point I'm going to tell him what he wants.'

'We will hurt you. People will beat you. You will be taken to a darkened room, it will not be nice like this, people will not offer you food and the drink that we have.'

Mr Nice had attempted to persuade me, attempted to make friends with me, attempted to get me to say something else. Now he was putting his trump cards down on the table. He said, 'I don't need to ask you these questions.'

Now what's coming?

'I can tell you that your name is Flt Lt Nichol.'

That's no problem, I've told him that.

'I can tell you that you are a navigator.'

'Shit,' I thought. 'How does he know that? That could be a guess though; that's not a problem.'

'I can tell you that you are from XV Squadron.'

Now I really was worried. He knew things about me. Where had he got them from? I had a feeling that he got them from John; he could have got them from a newspaper article, but probably not, it had probably come from John. What have they done to him to get it? The same, or worse? Worse, surely. But what? When will I get it? What will it be like? What did they do?

'I know that you are from XV Squadron; I know that you are from Bahrain; I know that you fly with your Victor tankers to bomb me.'

Again this was stuff that he could be guessing, or have read about in the British press. Many people in the Forces had thought that in the run-up to the war the press revealed way too much information that would be of intelligence value to the Iraqis. It was very contentious.

Now Mr Nice said, 'I know that your attack did not work; I know you did not get the bombs off, and that you ditched your bombs in my desert.'

So now I knew. Now a cold feeling ran right through me. John. I thought, 'What the hell has happened to him? Where is he? How is he?' I was worried about him, but even more worried about myself. Deep down, I was glad that whatever had led him to talk had not yet happened to me. The questioning began again; I gave the formulaic reply. But I knew if John had talked, it was only a question of time before I followed suit.

Mr Nice got bored again: he went away, the pattern formed now. The dry mouth and sudden salivas of fear.

Still I refused to talk. In the end they gave up. Now the pain was going to start again. Sure enough, they dragged me off to another room, blindfolding me again. I was waiting, tensed, I knew something very unpleasant was going to happen to me very soon.

They left me standing against a wall in a classic stress position, designed to weaken, to break down resistance. In this position, my forehead was flat against the wall, my feet about twenty inches away from it; I was stretched right up onto my toes, arms handcuffed behind my back. My forehead was supporting my entire bodyweight against the cold surface, a surface flat as purgatory. Every time I tried to move from that position, somebody punched me, whacked me back into it. They left me like that. I tried to move my head, somebody smacked it hard against the wall, a staggering blow. My head must be thicker than I realised, or had I passed out? I tried to move my arms, manacled behind my back now for bloody hours. The handcuffs were still of the ratchet type, tightening automatically if I tried to move. Because of the beating, they were racked up tight to the last notch again, biting into my wrists, a cold, insistent metallic cutting agony. The flesh on the wrists themselves I could feel ballooning up once more over the edges of the cuffs, a two-inch step of swollen flesh, the fingers entirely numb, fluid from the sores flowing out around the steel. My shoulder muscles seized suddenly with the tearing torture of cramp, unbearable, it must be relieved. The arches of my feet were clenched hard with the strain of being on tiptoes, slow rivers of fire burned through the muscle, sinews quivering. Every fibre was shaking now with the impossible effort of maintaining the posture; I had to move, but I knew they were standing, watching, waiting for a twitch, the whip poised, the baton raised. I moved. They beat me to the floor . . .

They dragged me up, walked me around for a little bit to disorientate me, which wasn't difficult, as I was in darkness all the time. Now somebody stood me with my back to another wall in another part of the building – only this time my head was not against the wall, I was standing slightly away from it. I could not see, but I could sense somebody to one side. Suddenly, wham! they smashed my head back hard against the wall. Two seconds later, two hours later, impossible to judge, smash! my head crashed off the wall again. Nobody was asking any questions. Crack! I was thinking, 'Ask me something, ask me something, at least let

me say something, or hit me so I fall unconscious . . .'
Crack! This went on – it could have been thirty times,
it could have been a thousand times, I have no idea.
Nobody asked me anything after this, nothing at all.
Now, dazed, stunned like a chicken before its throat is
cut, I was worried, I had lost track of how they were
going to interrogate me; this was not going by the
book any more. They left me. They put me in a cell
with John, for the first time, but we knew they would
be listening.

He said, 'I've told them something.'

'Don't worry, it's no problem.'

They took me back out of that room, along a corridor,
and attached me to the frame of what was obviously a
bare iron bedstead. At the other end of the room I
could hear someone being questioned. 'Zaun,' he said.
'My name is Zaun.' I wondered who Zaun was. From
his accent, he was obviously American. That meant we
were not alone. He had to be a flyer like ourselves.

They pushed me down onto the bed, but the agony
in my wrists and hands, still ratcheted behind my
back, made me catapult straight back upright again.

'What is it?' asked the guard.

'My arms. My arms.' He uncuffed me, loosened off
the ratchets, and cuffed my wrists back together, but
this time in front. This was absolute heaven, once the
worst of the pain wore off. Utterly exhausted, I curled
up on the bedsprings and fell into a dead sleep. It was
daylight when I awoke. The guard undid my blindfold.
I looked around. I was in what we came to call 'the
dormitory'. Several other beds, some with mattresses,
were dotted around.

'It's OK,' said the guard, 'I'm a friend. How are
you?' Thinking this was another part of the interrogation, or some sort of trick, I shook my head.

'No,' he said. 'Look, I'm trying to help you . . .' He brought out some cigarettes from an inside pocket.

'Do you need to see a doctor, or anything?' he asked.

At this point, I desperately, desperately wanted to say something to this guy, whom I christened 'Ahmed'. Though horribly scarred, his was the first friendly face in what felt already like a long age, a potential soft patch in a particularly unpleasant experience. His was the first friendly voice. But still, at the back of my mind, was the idea that he might be a more subtle form of quizmaster. He was very good though. He brought me some cold lentil soup, and I drank a tiny amount; but despite not having touched anything for twenty-four hours, I was just not interested in food; there were other things to think about.

'Where do you come from?' he asked.

'I cannot answer that question.'

The heavy brigade suddenly came in; Ahmed had my blindfold back on just in time. They began interrogating me there and then. 'Stand up!' Punch, kick. I blocked them with the usual response. They became furious. 'You will be sorry, Nichol, you will be sorry.' A few more blows. They left.

Once they had gone, Ahmed chained me back to the bed by one wrist and took off the blindfold again. My interrogators left me there all that day. And all that day, the air raids came in, the jets screamed overhead, the Triple-A mountings on the roof hammered away, bombs crumped and rattled nearby. During one of these raids, Ahmed was in the room. A bomb went off right next to the building we were in. He looked out of the window, and then said, casually, 'Someone has just been killed down there,' and he pointed. I fell asleep again in the afternoon.

Later, still chained to the bed, a heavy kick in the ribs woke me: 'What's your name? Rank? Number?'

'8204846.'

'Where did you come from?'

'I cannot answer that question.'

'You *will* be sorry, you know that, don't you, Nichol?'

'I cannot answer that question.'

'We will come back for you soon. You will be sorry.'

I know I'm going to be sorry. I'm already bloody sorry.

The psychological terror, the psychological torture, is just as great as the physical torture. You are shit-scared. You desperately want him to come and get you, as soon as possible, to get it over with, so that you can break, so that you can tell him something. But you haven't suffered enough yet, they haven't done enough to you yet to tell them anything. You haven't suffered enough to let anyone down, you haven't suffered enough to let yourself down; but you *do* want it to be over, to reach an end.

In the evening they came for me. They unshackled me, put the blindfold on, hauled me upright, dragged me down the stairs, round the streets, back into the interrogation centre; the familiar journey, almost routine by now. The chair: they threw me down into it. One guy was holding my arm on one side, one on the other. I knew in my heart of hearts that this was the time, I knew that it was going to get really rough now.

I was sitting with the solid fist of my own fear in my stomach.

'What squadron are you from?'

'I cannot answer that . . .'

Bang! somebody punched me in the face. Blood came pouring out of my face onto my lap, dripping. I could feel it warm on my thighs. On my lower half, I was wearing a flying-suit, a chemical-warfare suit, long-johns underneath all that, but I could still feel the blood dripping warm onto the upper part of my legs. Someone was hitting me in the face, over and over again. Question. Then somebody standing just to one side hit me hard across the skull with a solid piece of wood. Thwack! My head rang to the blow like some kind of bell. There were brilliant aching lights flashing behind the blindfold. You really do see stars. I was in the middle of the Milky Way. Question.

'I cannot answer . . .' A kick in the stomach – how he got to my stomach I don't know, they were still holding me down on the chair. I fell over to one side in the chair, my gorge rising; they dragged me up by the hair. Question.

'I cannot . . .' Whack! Someone punched me again, someone hit me with the wood, dazzling bright lights and the sudden downward spiral into blackness. Now I was disorientated, my brain was really starting to shut down, but still I thought, 'It's going to take more than this, it's going to take more than this. I'm not breaking down without good cause.' Somebody dragged my boot off, tearing it away with a furious wrench. 'What on earth? What are they going to do to me now?' Whack! A plastic pipe filled with something hard hit me across the shins. A biting agony across the shins, on and on, biting. Question.

And now, somebody grabs the hair at the nape of my neck, and begins stuffing tissue-paper down the back of my T-shirt. That is appalling. This is terrifying now. I am sitting in a darkened room in the middle of enemy territory, and somebody has just stuffed tissue-paper down the back of my neck. 'What are they doing that for?' I know straightaway what they are doing that for, I can imagine only too well. 'Shit, they are going to set me on fire!' Now I really want him to ask me another question, I *am* sorry, I want to say something, I want to tell him something, anything. But he doesn't ask me a question. He just sets fire to the paper.

I throw my head violently from side to side, to try to escape from the burning, to try to shake the tissue-paper clear of my neck. They are still whacking my shins. Quite soon, mercifully soon, somebody behind me slaps out the flames.

'What squadron are you from?'

'Fifteen.'

I had had enough.

Like JP, I could not get over the simplicity, the naïvety of the questions put. Although they were trained interrogators, who could have extracted what they wanted from us, they did not really know what it was that they wanted to know. And that in itself was a tremendous morale booster. It quickly became apparent to them that none of us knew anything about the big strategic picture, about the Schwarzkopf–Powell–De la Billière masterplan for the total annihilation of the Iraqi Armed Forces. So they concentrated on the weapons we carried.

'What do you carry on the Tornado?'

Anybody could read that in the *Independent* or the *Observer*, but, by making them drag each answer out of me, I could try to spin out the time, delaying the more intelligent and difficult questions that I most feared. We crawled down the list, as slowly as I could manage it.

'What is the main weapon you use against our runways?'

'JP-233,' and then would follow a very laboured and slow explanation.

'What else do you carry?'

'Iron bombs . . .'

'How do you drop them?'

'That depends . . .' Then we could get into the whole business of what bombing might depend on, as vague as I could make it. It took hours, literally, to get through the Tornado war fit alone . . .

'A countermeasures pod.'

'What is the countermeasures pod called?'

'Skyshadow.' Satisfied with the name alone, he failed to ask *what* electronic countermeasures it contained, what systems, what radars its complex electronics could defeat.

Towards the end of a given interrogation session, the Iraqis always waxed philosophical: 'Why have you come to our country?'

'Because we were ordered to do it.'

'Do you agree with this?'

'It does not matter whether we agree or disagree, it is our duty, it is our job.'

This answer, true though it was, invariably enraged them, invariably resulted in another beating. And while they quickly ran out of dumb questions to ask us, they never ever ran out of their enthusiasm for violence.

After a few of these questionings, they drove me somewhere in a vehicle, parked me on a stool in a busy corridor, still handcuffed, still blindfolded. There was a lot of human traffic going up and down. As they walked by, everybody, but everybody, would kick, punch or otherwise knock me about as they drew level. It was almost laughable, like some mad sort of game, Land the Punch on the Airman, like Pin the Tail on the Donkey. Some of them, the bullies and the vindictive ones, were looking to enjoy themselves, to have a little warped fun. One sadistic charmer with time on his hands and a very small brain indeed stood directly behind me. With deliberate slowness he began ripping chunks of my hair out with his fingers, grabbing nice curly tufts and tearing them slowly away from the scalp. Another time, someone walking past casually stubbed his cigarette out on my ear.

To justify this kind of pathetic nastiness, one of the people who had stopped to torment the infidel foreign airman said: 'Your aircraft have just attacked my airfield with JP-233 weapons, which landed on our married quarters. Many of our wives and children have been killed. How do you feel about that?'

I suspected this was untrue, and ignored the question. But there was still some unburned tissue-paper bundled at the back of my neck, so this guy struck a match and set it alight again. Once it was going, he sauntered away. I blundered about like a stuck pig until I had shaken it off.

17
Trial by TV

Helen Peters: There was the odd lighter moment. I decided that while John was missing, I would get Guy potty-trained. If nothing else, at least John could come back home to one of life's minor triumphs, a potty-trained child. But Guy had his own ideas about the process.

Every morning the Station Commander gave a briefing, from about 0945 until 1030, in which he went over as much as he could of what had happened to the squadrons in the course of the previous twenty-four hours. This was very useful, because it brought home to us very sharply how much of what the television and the press were telling us was total guesswork, how much was inspired guesswork, and how much was factual. By comparing the two sources, official and otherwise, we had a much better idea of how the war was really going. The briefings became a ritual for the wives, a very important lifeline: we would have coffee and biscuits, and a bit of a chat afterwards.

The Station Commander had stood up one day, and was just getting into the important bit of the brief, when Guy ran up to him at the lectern. Gazing sweetly up at the speaker, he said, 'Mummy . . .', and made a nice big puddle on the floor, just missing the Station Commander's foot.

John Peters: A man was shrieking in the next cell. It was horrible, almost as bad as being beaten yourself, this extreme noise of another human in violent pain, this fellow prisoner screaming his guts out. It preys on the imagination, works its horror. Whoever it was, he was refusing to speak. The noise went on and on, for what felt like hours. He was an English speaker. Occasionally the screams would flatten out and then rise into an extended repeated wailing 'No-o-o . . .' of punctuated agony. Thinking at first that it was John Nichol, I sent a thoughtwave to him: 'Hang on in there, mate.'

There was another noise underneath the screaming, the sound of a carpet being beaten, exactly that, a dull resounding thudding with a sharper thwack on top.

'Shit,' I thought, 'they must be beating his feet.'

A light came on in my cell, and the dread of that man's agony coming my way next poured adrenalin through my veins. But they put me in a vehicle, and I found myself next to John for a minute or two in a long corridor; so it hadn't been him with the carpetbeaters. Then who? Had somebody else been shot down? As we lay there on the concrete, we pressed our knees together for a fleeting moment, for the comfort that it gave; then I was taken into the little room again for another session.

'Why didn't you tell us about air-to-air refuelling?'

This showed their ignorance, I thought; they knew we had flown from Bahrain, there was no way we could have got there without tanking en route. So I replied, 'You didn't ask me.'

This is where you learn. Under interrogation, you never, ever, get cocky: you never, ever, show open defiance of the interrogator, or show him that you think he is even the slightest bit stupid. This is an obvious piece of commonsense, and there could only have been a tiny hint of contempt in my voice, but it was enough; it was a big mistake. They really let rip. They didn't ask me anything for a good ten or fifteen minutes, concentrating instead on renewing my respect for them by demonstrating their unrivalled prowess at inflicting physical violence. It was mostly the rubber truncheon round the head, the stick across the legs. It was one way of learning a lesson.

After this, they stuck me back in the corridor again, but on my own this time. Someone sidled up to me, I could hear soft footfalls. A match flared, there was the reek of cheap tobacco in my nostrils. Then came a point of burrowing agony in my right wrist, then another; then the same piercing, intense sensation of burning in the other wrist. I wriggled and twisted, wincing with the pain. The Iraqi – I could smell his sweat – was dragging on his cigarette, carefully applying the glowing end of it to my skin, wherever his fancy took him. He wasn't actually stubbing the cigarette out and re-lighting it, just touching the glowing end to the skin and then removing it for another drag, carefully touching it down again. When he got bored of doing this to my wrists, he moved on to the back of my neck.

For the first time, I got really angry. The other stuff, the interrogation beatings, that was different. I was annoyed because this was not an interrogation. This was some sad, sadistic little shit who was taking advantage of my complete helplessness for his own amusement. If I had been free then, I would have killed that bastard – bitten his throat out and made his spine go click.

John Nichol: I must have been unconscious some of the time. The next thing I can remember, I awoke in the dormitory, chained to the bed again. Ahmed the friendly guard materialised suddenly.

'Mr John, are you OK? Do you want something to eat?'

'Yes.'

He brought me some rice, with peas in it, and some bread. It was clear I could trust him. He uncuffed my right arm from the bedframe, removed my blindfold. He disappeared for a minute, and, to my intense surprise, returned leading JP, whose blindfold he also removed. I blew my nose, and a gush of blood poured out. JP said, 'I know what that feels like.'

'Don't talk!' said Ahmed, his eyes growing wide with alarm. 'Don't talk!'

Although we could not talk, just sitting and looking at one another, as we ate the rice, meant that we gained a lot of strength. OK, neither of us looked pretty: we were grubby, ripped, knackered, swollen, and lumpy-faced, escarpments of dried blood were sticking to our battered flesh, but we were both thinking, 'He's not gaga, he's still there.'

There was fight left in the eyes.

Two more guards came in; we realised that this dormitory we were in was their quarters when they were off duty. Like Ahmed, they were both armed with Kalashnikovs; unlike him, they were playing with them, cocking them and pointing them at one another, for all the world like small boys playing Cops and Robbers. Against all the basic rules of military training, this clowning about was not in the least bit enjoyable to watch. Not when we were in the same room as these idiots. People get killed fooling around with guns they think are unloaded. Having convinced us what big macho men they were, the guards stopped showing off, grabbed hold of us, took us to a small side cell, and threw us into it together.

After a few minutes, JP very quietly asked me the question that was burning him up, picking open the half-healed scab in his mind: 'Have you broken yet?'

'I have.'

'What did you tell them?'

'Same as you, probably; stuff they could read in the newspapers. Is that the kind of thing they asked you?'

'Yes. What do you think is going to happen now?' he asked.

'Same as you, I expect; I haven't got a clue.'

'Do you think they are going to shoot us?'

'They could do, but I think it's unlikely; they've got nothing to gain by it. Having said that, there's nothing to stop them taking us round the back and shooting us if they feel like it, is there?'

After this exchange of pleasantries, we fell silent, which is completely out of character for both of us. There was enough said. And we were both exhausted. The room was probably bugged, because after a period of about ten minutes had gone by without either of us speaking, the guards came back in and returned us to the dormitory.

John Peters: They took me down the stairs again, the dreaded journey to the interrogation centre, outside, turn left, left again, do a right, stop. Not again, what on earth could they want now?

But this time it was a slightly different route, down a ramp, deep underground, down into what we realised over the next twenty-four hours was another of those friendly cigarette-end corridors. With our hands handcuffed behind our backs, they sat us against the wall, on the floor, a guard standing over each of us. We were not allowed to move. The concrete was extremely cold. I began to shiver almost immediately. As usual, the shoulders and the lower back became agony, because of the way the handcuffs were done up. After a couple of hours of this, Ahmed – improbable guardian angel; how had he not been shot already for being too nice to captured airmen? – appeared carrying water, unlocked the cuffs and re-fastened them so that our arms were to the front. I took up his offer of a visit to the toilet, which was only allowed when a couple of other guards had been called. These two supported me like a pair of human crutches: after the concentrated attention it had come in for, my leg had become completely immovable, the knee swollen, purplish, ugly, painful, stiff and otherwise totally out of action. Bits of bone and gristly things grated attractively in the knee-joint if I did try to move it. Looking at it in the dormitory, my main worry was whether I would ever fly again. There was also something seriously wrong with my back. What a state! In the toilet was a mirror: since they had released the cuffs, I was able to lift the bandage from my eyes, and catch the first sight of my face since they had captured me.

'Good,' I thought, 'I look like shit, completely terrible, my left eye is a nightmare made human flesh, horrendously swollen and leaking blood; perhaps now the guards will treat me better.' This was pretty silly, seeing as I had just been beaten up for the umpteenth time, but then you cling onto some pretty weird and wonderful hopes in a place like that. Back to the corridor. Despite the massive air-conditioning unit I was parked next to, which sounded like Niagara Falls, I must have dropped off to sleep.

John Nichol: Within a few minutes of being plonked

down in this corridor, the cold began biting up through my backside, spreading through the bones until it had permeated every part of me. But soon I slept: you can sleep anywhere if you've had a full enough day. In my sleep I dreamed, and dreamed I fell into a rubbish tip. I was climbing through a doorway, which opened directly onto a rubbish dump, and at the moment of falling through this doorway into the mound of trash, something hit me squarely in the face, and I woke up. What had actually happened was that somebody had come along and thrown a dirty blanket over me, which was not a dream, but a godsend, because I was freezing. Still, I thought that the dream was a pretty accurate reflection of my circumstances. A little after this, an officer came along. He stood over me, and barked, 'Another blanket for this man!', which was strange, because he said it in English, as if for my benefit. Almost like magic, Ahmed materialised again, spreading a second filthy oblong of wonderful warming rag carefully over my prostrate form. I returned gratefully to the rubbish-dump dream.

In the morning – I assumed it was morning from the increased human traffic passing and kicking, kicking and passing – another officer came up, accompanied by a couple of uniformed soldiers. 'Lieutenant Nichol,' he said, 'do you know that we are going to charge you with war crimes?'

Never at my most genial just after dawn, aching all over, stiff in the limbs, bruised flesh throbbing, etc., I was feeling a bit liverish. I stared blindly up at him: 'Excuse me? I have committed no war crimes.'

'Yes, you have attacked a country you did not declare war on, you have committed war crimes. We are going to execute you.'

There was a short pause while I took in this

interesting information. He was talking to me as though he meant it. I thought, 'Oh well.'

But then he spoke again. 'Right, we can either execute you, or put you on TV.'

I thought about it for something less than a second. A stupid thought flashed into my mind: 'Bring on the make-up girls . . .' Broadcast or die! It was not really a decision, was it? Playing for a little time, I asked him, 'What do you want me to say?'

I had half expected they might want to use us for propaganda purposes at some point, that was their style, we had seen plenty of it, even before the war, with the exploitation of the so-called 'human shield' hostages. Even children had been used. This kind of stunt had backfired on Saddam Hussein then, so I confidently expected it to backfire catastrophically on him again now. I was unwilling to be executed for the sake of a TV appearance, the effect of which would be at least arguable, and would most likely result in another Iraqi public relations disaster. On the other hand, I did not *want* to co-operate, to show the least willingness under any circumstances. These people were the enemy.

'We will ask you a few questions,' said the officer. 'You will answer them, and then you can send a message home.'

'Do what you like,' I thought, 'you are going to shoot yourself right in the foot.'

They picked me up and dragged me off along the corridor, sat me down in a room, removed the blindfold. A crowd of people were swarming around a camera set up in the middle of the space. They gave me a glass of water, and told me to brush back my hair. I ruffled it up, on the quiet. I wanted to look under pressure, under extreme duress.

'OK, we'll rehearse this first,' said someone, and we went through the list of questions, and the responses they wanted out of me: 'What do you think of this war?'

The answer to be given was: 'This war should be over so we can all go home', and so it went on. There were a couple of things in among this farce that were working for me: to begin with, the English was not wholly correct, which would tell anybody listening I was speaking words written by somebody else. Also I spoke very slowly, very deliberately, quite unlike the way I normally talk, for the same reason. When answering the prepared questions, I tried to look away from the camera, to signify disagreement. When I had reached the end of the list, they kept their word and let me send a message home, in return for broadcasting all the answers they had prepared. Now I looked directly into the camera. As I was delivering the message to my Mum and Dad, I thought, 'What must they think of me?', and the emotion started welling up inside me in an unstoppable wave. By the time they laid me back down in the corridor, I was crying, the tears soaking into the blinding crêpe bandage. I was crying for my parents.

John Peters: Kicked into consciousness, which was not my favourite place to be, I found myself surrounded by a gang of guards. They pulled up my blindfold.

'We're going to kill you now,' they said. 'You are a war criminal. We are going to take you out and shoot you, you have killed people.'

'No I haven't,' I replied.

'You are going to go on television.'

'No, I can't do that.'

'We are going to put you on television as a war criminal.'

'No.'

No was not the answer they wanted to hear. They began taking turns slapping me, as hard as they could, across the face. Every sentence we spoke was punctuated by a slap.

'You will never see your wife and children again. Is it worth it? All we are asking is to put you on television. If you do not go, you will never see your wife and children again. We will kill you now.'

'No.'

'You are going to go on television as a war criminal.'

'No.'

'Right. Take him now.'

They grabbed me, picked me up. One of them took out his pistol, cocked it, drew back the hammer, and put the barrel against my temple.

'You are going to die now.'

I was so keyed up, with the pistol butt pressed against my ear, I could have sworn I heard the mechanism inside it creak as he began squeezing the trigger.

'OK, OK, OK,' I mumbled. 'Wait.'

I had tried everything and anything not to co-operate, not to release information, that was the point; but I had reached a stage where the only way to win was to stay alive – where I could only fight them by surviving. They carried me along to the same bright room that, unknown to me, John Nichol had recently starred in. There was a video camera, a single chair in front of it, which they pushed me down into. Someone came and tidied me up a bit.

'Right,' I thought, 'this is good, I look like shit and

I feel like shit, and I'm going to use that; I'm going to misunderstand, I'm going to try to refuse to say what they want me to say.'

As they shouted the questions at me, then the approved answers, they kept whacking me on the head with a pistol butt, because I wasn't speaking up to their satisfaction, because I refused to sit up straight. But I *did* want people to see evidence of the beatings, so I turned my ejection-damaged eye, which they had worked on, deliberately towards the camera. There should be no mistaking the physical abuse. Concerned that I was mumbling, that the message was not getting across, they got some books and propped the microphone up nearer to my face.

To some extent my dumb show succeeded. All those school drama productions were suddenly coming in handy. They obviously saw I was a bad publicity risk, because they cut short the questions we had been through in rehearsal, reducing them to name, rank and number, what I had done (bomb an airfield), how I got shot down (by a missile) . . .

For me, this was the worst thing of all. I *hated* being put on television, with every fibre of every nerve. I thought I would be revealing to the world how weak I had been, how I'd given in too easily; I thought everyone would class me as a traitor. It was the fact of cooperating that hurt. All I could think of was that I was bringing disgrace to my uniform, by conceding to their threats. As with the interrogation, I assumed I was the only one who had agreed to make a broadcast. It never occurred to me that the whole thing might backfire on them.

What did occur to me, as I addressed my family, was that I would never see them again. It brought a huge lump to my throat; I couldn't have spoken clearly if I'd wanted to. As I was saying, 'Helen, Toni and Guy, I love you,' I thought, 'I've done everything they wanted, I've talked, I've done my TV bit; that's it, they don't need anything more out of me, I can be wasted now. I will never see them again.' I tried to continue the message, 'Mother and Father . . .' but I could not go on, it came out stilted: the moment was too much for me.

I was praying that someone else had gone on TV. I couldn't live with the idea of being the one, the only one, to co-operate. The corridor was filling up now with captured flyers. We were not allowed to talk, but I was afraid of finding this out, anyway. This fear of failure was intensified when an officer ordered someone to give me another blanket. Was this some sort of reward for my weakness? It was a relief when he moved up the line giving blankets to the others. Ahmed brought me a piece of cardboard to lie on, with an empty, large-sized baked bean can, which I used as a pillow. I wondered how the war was going.

Helen Peters: That particular day had been horrendous. It was the Monday after the boys had been shot down, 21 January. The Ministry of Defence had confirmed that a third Tornado had been shot down. On the Sunday night there had been reports that captured aircrew, or at least tape-recordings of their voices, had been heard on the radio. I spent most of the day glued to the television, waiting for the news, trying to find out what was going on.

I rang John Nichol's mum. The boys' families and I kept in touch as much as we could all the time, swopping little bits of information, even tiny little things.

As far as she could tell from the voice, it really was her John, she said, although the quality of the recording was very bad. But nobody had heard anything of my John.

It was quite difficult for John Nichol's mum and dad. They didn't know what to say to me. There wasn't much anybody could say. They were incredibly happy to have news of their son, but they were frightened for me. None of my friends or relatives – and I tried them all – had actually heard those tapes. I could get no information, absolutely none. John's brother and sister-in-law, Mark and Sarah, were staying with me at the time, and we got up that morning and went straight to the television. What should we hear but that seven of the POWs had been put on Iraqi TV – but the news networks kept showing only five of them! John Nichol was there, and an Italian pilot, Gian Marco Bellini, but my John was not among them, neither was the Kuwaiti flyer we knew had been shot down. It was like a nightmare. What had happened to them?

That Monday went on for ever. Every time we watched a news broadcast, there was still no sign of John. The newscasters kept referring to seven people, but they only showed five, and they never explained why. Did they not have the time? Did they think that it didn't matter? Or was it something worse? Were they so badly beaten up that they couldn't be shown? Had they already been killed, or what?

Eventually, on the 5.40 evening news, they showed John. Ironically, having sat in front of the set all day, I had just gone upstairs to bathe Guy. Mark and Sarah grabbed for the record button, to start the tape that was always sitting ready in the video recorder. They tried to sit me down. Mark got me a brandy. It was horrible, that rush of different kinds of emotions all at once. John looked terrible, almost unrecognisable. At least it meant he was probably alive. The first thing I had to do was get to the phone, to try to warn John's parents, and my own, that he was on television, and that he didn't look very pretty. But as I stood up, my legs gave way under me.

I remember that the rest of the evening I felt very light-headed. John looked so battered. We kept on playing the tape, looking at it really closely, almost morbidly. I was basically trying to convince myself that a lot of it was injuries from ejection. One good thing was that the children were too young to understand what was going on, though I was worried that Guy, who was two, might just recognise his daddy if he saw the pictures. I kept him well away from the television, just in case.

There had been a nagging fear in my mind that once they went down, they might have gone through with that suicide pact. I'd also worried that they might have got separated, or one of them been badly injured and had to be abandoned by the other: all sorts of things went through my mind. At least now I knew they had both survived the crash.

But I could see they were frightened, that was the terrible thing. John was the only one sitting down, and he was slumped right over to one side, which really upset me. It looked as if his ribs had been broken. Tom King, the British Defence Secretary, said categorically that he suspected torture and coercion had been used to make the downed flyers speak. The idea of torture was there all the time, but I'd have gone mad if I'd allowed myself to dwell on it. Once people had seen John on television, they'd say to me: 'Well at least now you know he's alive.' But that was just what we didn't know. It seemed very difficult to get over to people the idea that the Iraqis could have forced them to make that broadcast, and then simply taken the boys out and shot them.

John Nichol: When they took me back into the corridor after making the TV broadcasts, I realised I was with a whole batch of other captured flyers. There was a comforting feeling of unity. Through the bottom edge of my blindfold I could just make out a pair of standard-issue US flying-boots. Every now and then they would come along and check names. I could hear Guy Hunter, on my left; Guy turned out to be a US Marines Warrant Officer, co-pilot in an OV-10 Bronco spotter plane. He was a veteran of several combat tours in Vietnam. His pilot, Lieutenant Colonel Cliff Acree, USN, was shot down with him. Anybody who flies the unarmed little two-seater Bronco, which hangs around low over enemy lines, spotting and marking targets, has the respect of every other military flier – full stop. It has to be one of the world's most dangerous jobs. Then I heard Jeff Zaun again, the American pilot from the USS *Saratoga*; I could hear Dave Waddington, a Tornado pilot from 27 Squadron, JP, and other people on down the line.

We were still handcuffed, blindfolded, the rifle butts resting on our backs, with the occasional tap on the skull to keep our heads low. They brought tea along for us, hot and sweet, in a glass jam jar. This was amazing. You suddenly realised with a rush of saliva that you had not eaten or drunk anything for about forty-eight hours. They offered some to Jeff Zaun.

'Do you want tea?'

'No, Sir,' he replied emphatically, in that polite tone

Americans reserve for something they detest. Non-plussed, the Iraqi officer stepped back. How could this prisoner who had had no food or drink for two days refuse hot, sweet tea?

'Why do you not want tea? It is OK, there is nothing wrong with it. Look, I will drink some.'

'No, Sir. I cannot drink tea. It's bad for you. It has caffeine in it.'

The Iraqis must have realised then that there was no way they were going to win.

Later that evening, Major Jeff Tice, an American F-16 pilot, was brought down to join our group. He was dumped next to me. Over and over, he was repeating 'Fucking hell, fucking hell, fucking hell,' his voice thick and slurred, as though his jaw was broken. They brought some bread along. They asked him if he wanted anything to eat; he refused. He just kept saying, 'Shit, shit, my teeth, my teeth.'

'What have they done to you?' I asked.

'They've knocked my teeth out, they've knocked my teeth out,' he replied thickly. What they had done was wrap a bare electric cable round his neck and ears and plug it into a car battery. It had blown some of the fillings in his teeth out, and an eardrum in.

The guards went away. Not speaking to anybody in particular, more to himself, he kept repeating, 'I broke too soon, I broke too soon.'

I said, 'What's your name?'

'Jeff.'

I said, 'Jeff, don't feel bad, everybody's done it.'

But he was aggressively pissed off with himself; he had moved right in on himself, he just kept repeating, 'You stupid bastard, you stupid bastard,' over and over again. He was a brave man: he had travelled further down the road to hell than the rest of us, and yet he was the one who was the most upset with himself.

John Peters: Still in the corridor, in the night, the guards returned. Having kicked me awake, one of them started fumbling with my trouser flies, tugging at the zipper. I was very quickly awake, struggling. They pinned me down to the floor. They opened my clothes up, pulled them down, exposing the genitals to full view. Panic. Sheer bloody panic. 'Shit, shit, shit!' Images of electric batteries clipped to my testicles, cattle prods up the anus. One of them had a red felt pen. He lifted up my penis. My mind was racing. 'What the . . .? What is he doing? What's going on here? Why is he drawing on my dick with a red felt pen? He is marking me; they are going to cut along the dotted line.' But the guards moved away, muttering, to the next man up the corridor. Ten minutes after this, I was still shaking, quivering from head to foot, really scared half to death, worse than when they were beating me.

Finally, when I had calmed down a bit, it dawned on me. They were checking to see who was Jewish.

Helen Peters: Hype springs eternal in the tabloid press. Although I was luckily beyond direct reach of the newspapers, inside the station fence, they printed all kinds of rubbish anyway. One example of this was on the Sunday before the boys were shown on TV. The *Mail on Sunday* had the audacity to print in one of its columns that Helen Peters had been desperately trying to contact the newspaper, but had been prevented from doing so by the RAF, 'in case she gave away information that would be of use to the Iraqis'. Nothing, needless to say, could have been farther from the truth. I had not spoken to the *Mail on Sunday* or to any other newspaper. The RAF, as it happened, took a pretty sanguine view of the whole thing – the only advice I did get was to think carefully before talking to the press, if I did. I never did, during this period. What woman would, when her husband's life could be on the line as the result of a misplaced word? Who could predict how the Iraqis would react to an article on the boys' plight? Headlines in some of the other newspapers like 'The Bastards Are Torturing Our Boys' did not seem to me particularly helpful, under the circumstances. Most of the press failed completely during this time to think through the potential consequences of their more extreme stories and statements for the captured airmen. Either that or they thought the story itself, and the subsequent sales, more important.

18

Inside the Baghdad Bungalows

John Nichol: It was the kind of place where they shoot unwanted opinions. There was a rank, putrid smell, a stench of rotting meat and corruption, a clinging stink of death. They had moved us there *en masse*, after the TV broadcasts, all the captured aircrew together, a long drive through the day in the trucks. Arcing my neck right back, I could just make out clay-covered walls, as we rolled to a stop. It looked exactly like a South American prison courtyard, where the only exercise a prisoner ever gets is one very short walk – to face the firing squad.

'That smell is bodies decomposing. We're going to be shot,' I thought. It was very cold. I was pushed through a series of doors, each of which clanged shut behind, then into a cell. They started taking my blindfold off. As I regained my sight, I saw a guard standing in front of me, holding a sputtering, old-fashioned oil-lamp, like Florence Nightingale or something. Then I realised there were at least seven other guards in the tiny cell with me, all wearing red Military Police berets, red Military Police armbands, white webbing belts, white truncheons swinging at their hips, all silent, all watching. Except for their skin colour, they were exact copies of their British counterparts. It looked for all the world as though they had bought a job-lot of uniforms. Even the initials 'MP' were in English.

I thought, 'Eight to one, the usual odds, this is where they have at me again.'

Their leader, a Warrant Officer, said, 'Are you an officer?'

'Yes.'

He turned, his companions following him out like so many goslings. In a little while, the Warrant Officer came back, still with his flock in tow. There is safety in numbers! He was carrying a piece of foam for me to lie on, another to act as a pillow, a couple of blankets, a jug of water, a cup and a metal plate.

'OK,' he said, 'stand up.' He then searched me. I realised that up until then I had never been thoroughly searched – only looted. When he was satisfied that I was not carrying anything I should not be, he removed the handcuffs, told me to lie down on the foam, threw a blanket over me, and went out. This treatment came as a complete surprise. Next day, the light filtering through the barred window revealed a nine-foot square concrete space, completely bare. They took my clothes off me in the course of the morning, replacing them with a new yellow canvas suit, which looked as though it had just been specially run up on the sewing machine, the jacket and trousers roughly stitched, the initials 'PW' stamped attractively in large black letters on the back and chest. With the suit came a pair of black laceless plimsolls. The laces presumably had been removed to prevent us from hanging ourselves. Still, it was the first sign that the Iraqis might have actually heard of prisoners' rights. The way things were improving, the Red Cross would be visiting soon; I'd get a parcel from home.

This was easily the best period of my time in captivity. The Iraqi Army guards, in complete contrast to our Ba'ath Party interrogators, were treating us with decency and even humanity. Somebody up there had at least heard of the Geneva Convention. One superb luxury was that, when the guards weren't around, we could communicate by shouting along the corridor. As the conversations echoed, morale soared.

John Peters: Jeff Tice next door told me about his electrocution torture. Like the rest of us, he had been repeatedly beaten to begin with, but had refused to give in. So they had started using electricity on him. I could hardly hear what he was saying, because his ruptured eardrum made him think he was talking much more loudly than he actually was. He nicknamed the electrical instrument the interrogators had used on him a 'Talkman', because they had wrapped it around his ears, or attached it to them in some way, a bit like a Walkman personal stereo. This little witticism was fairly spirited of him, considering.

After every meal, the Iraqis would come round and retrieve the metal spoons that always arrived with the food. The cells were small solid concrete boxes; did they imagine we were going to dig our way out with the spoons? I asked Jeff what he thought the reason was.

'Well,' he drawled, 'I don't know about that. But I'm building a glider in *my* cell . . .'

As we were chatting, the Iraqis came rushing into my cell; I could hear them bundling into his. A beating looked on the cards. Instead, they took him away, and swapped him for Simon Burgess, another Tornado pilot from 17 (F) Squadron, who had just been shot down. One of his bombs had gone off after release, when it mistook the bomb just underneath it for the ground and fused itself by mistake. The resulting explosion brought down the aircraft: another one downed. I wondered if any of our friends were dead.

When the guards had gone again, Simon Burgess said, 'Who is it?'

'John Peters.'

'John, hello mate. Let me tell you something: you've been on television. I saw you a couple of days ago! Everyone knows you're alive. The world has completely reacted against it. You're bloody lucky, because they can't kill you now!'

So Helen knew I had been captured, and my parents. This was amazing! They had seen me on television! It was strangely comforting. I felt in touch with them. All I had to do now was stay alive, and maybe, one day . . .

The other person I could hear after the Iraqis had shuffled us around was Cliff Acree. He told me that his neck had been badly beaten. He was quiet-spoken and reserved. He sounded like a true gentleman.

My cell window was barred and filled with foam and old newspapers to block out the light. But there was a small hole in the covering. It acted like a lens, throwing an inverted image of the palm trees outside onto the opposite wall. I lay there sometimes, watching the trees swaying upside-down in the sunlight, a topsy-turvy image of freedom. The light-switch was hanging off the wall, its wires exposed. The walls themselves were crumbling, ancient plaster, covered in scratch marks, as though a large animal had been caged up in there at some time. There were nails sticking out of them, whose purpose I could only guess at. Winning the morale war was still my over-riding concern.

An army doctor finally came in and gave me some drops for my damaged eye. I kept the box. One morning, as I was hobbling along to the toilet hole, I noticed an ancient biro pen sitting in the dust on a

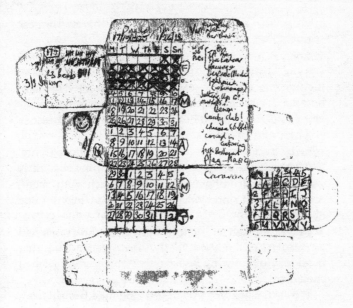

window-ledge. Checking that the guard was looking the other way, I grabbed it and slipped it into my pocket. Up until then I had been carving the date every day on the wall with a nail. It seemed very important not to lose track of time. If time didn't matter, I thought, because one day was the same, exactly the same, as the next, then perhaps life itself would become meaningless. So a pen and paper was a real find. I drew out a crude calendar or 'diary' on the inside of the flattened-out box. Marking down the days I had been in captivity already, I set out tiny rows of boxes to represent the days to come, as many as would reasonably fit on the card. Every box had an X drawn through it, from corner to corner. Every day, according to how my morale was doing, I blocked in a segment of the appropriate X. On good days, I filled in the top segment; on medium days, I filled in the two side segments; and on bad days, I filled in the bottom section. It was a way of standing back from myself, of monitoring my state of mind. Most days, perhaps because I had that little challenge to my feelings, the empty square, in front of me, I filled in the top bit.

There was an old Iraqi newspaper on the windowsill, which I carefully tore into strips, as an alternative to using my hand when I was allowed to the toilet. You were meant to wipe your backside with your hand, always the left one, and then wash your fingers clean afterwards. The right hand is reserved for eating. Washing was out of the question, though, because our air forces had bombed all the water mains. A pretty good way of catching hepatitis, or something like it, I thought.

We christened this prison the 'Baghdad Bungalows'.

John Nichol: Near me was an Italian Tornado pilot, Gian Marco Bellini. Somebody had given him a very bad time, because he had no idea where he was, no idea what was happening to him, no recollection of his capture, nothing. He would not eat; he would not drink. They brought doctors in to see him. He would have yelling fits in his cell. No doubt his problem was severe concussion from his head being hit repeatedly with large chunks of wood – if my own experience was anything to go by.

I glimpsed JP in the courtyard on the second day. Seeing him made me feel we might yet make it, somehow. On the other side of me was Mohammed Mubarak, a Kuwaiti Skyhawk pilot. The Iraqis would have Radio Baghdad on at night, and Mohammed was a godsend, because he could translate for us and relay what was going on. One night he told us, 'The Iraqis claim they have shot down 200 Allied aircraft, they say that they have successfully invaded Saudi Arabia.'

The Iraqis believed this propaganda. All the guards were very excited by the 'news'. They claimed to have assassinated George Bush, and to have killed 250,000 Allied troops. We did not believe it, and we could not credit their naïve belief that they were winning this war. But then, we did not live in a state where every single scrap of information is tightly controlled, where the official 'truth' is the only truth on offer.

Bombing took place with encouragingly monotonous regularity. We would lie there at night, counting the explosions, trying to work out how many aircraft were on the raid, how far away the target was. It beat counting sheep.

As the sun came up, patches of dark discolouration, like rust, appeared eerily on the bare walls. Looking more closely, I could see they were bloodstains. There were curious deep holes and chipped areas in the midst of these marks, as though long steel nails had been hammered into the cement, and then wrenched out again. Or was I looking at bullet holes? Was this an execution cell? Beside these patches on the walls there were little drawings of ships, scratched into the concrete, with messages in Arabic scrawled next to them. Talking to Mohammed at night he told me that there were similar drawings in his cell, and that they were done by the crew of a Kuwaiti oil-tanker who had been captured at the time of the Iraqi invasion, and shut up in this prison. He could not tell me what had happened to them . . .

The days in the Baghdad Bungalows were marked by the evening meals, which varied according to a strict weekly order, ordained by some higher authority: chicken, mutton, mutton, beans, mutton, mutton, mutton. There were no toilets, just pits at the end of the corridor, which quickly overflowed under the pressure of numbers.

Everyone was allowed out into the stinking yard every couple of days, to take exercise. When I had recovered a bit physically, the guards came in and asked if I could play football. I said yes, and was rewarded with extra time outside, which I felt a little guilty about. However, they just wanted me to stand in goal while they took pot-shots.

They would come up to me and shout, 'Kevin Keegan!' I would try to explain that yes, Keegan had been a very famous and successful English footballer, but he was now retired, and they would shout, 'Castle King!', which I eventually deciphered as 'Gascoigne', as in Paul, another England soccer player who is quite well-known, and from my own little corner of the world. They took great delight in saying things to me like 'Maggie Thatcher, how is she? Not so good, eh?' It was useless to attempt to explain that she was no longer the British Prime Minister. For them she was a bogey-woman they loved to hate.

Ten days later, things took a turn for the worse. Mohammed Mubarak had told us we were in Baghdad, but he found out we were about to be moved somewhere closer to the centre; he had heard the guards chatting about going to Baghdad market. Sure enough, that night I started bolt upright as the metal door crashed open. I was instantly wide awake, senses alert, waiting for the shadows to arrive at the cell. What was going on? I had just settled back down into my nice comfortable rabbit-hutch. The last thing I wanted was to be moved. They came in after a minute or so, blindfolded and cuffed me, and manhandled me onto the transport. After a relatively short drive, the bus began spiralling down into what felt like an underground carpark. A fresh set of gaolers kicked, punched and rifle-butted us off the transport. They were wearing civilian clothes, one or two of them were even wearing trainers, and the horrible, brightly coloured nylon 'shell suits' that were fashionable then back home. There was the same atmosphere of icy hostility that had characterised our interrogation centre. We immediately realised, with a sinking feeling, that we were back in the hands of the Ba'ath Party.

John Peters: Two inches thick, the steel cell door of this new prison slammed shut on 31 January. It stayed shut until 10 February. Just before he slammed it, the guard removed the cuffs from around my wrists, and the crêpe from around my eyes.

'British or American?' he demanded.

'British.'

Before I realised what he was doing, he had cleared his throat and launched a great gobbet of spit into my face. Then, as an apparent afterthought, he opened the door again. 1 could almost hear the cogs of his brain turning painfully in his head: 'Oh, I know, I'll let my mate do it, too.' His fellow guard stepped up and gave me another faceful of saliva, just for good measure. It was so absurd, so ridiculously, childishly spiteful, that when they had closed the door again, I burst out laughing.

19

Endless Boredom

John Nichol: Boredom is chocolate brown. I was living in a giant, chocolate-brown urinal. At some point in the past, the Ba'ath Party's Commissioner for Prisons had amused himself as an interior decorator, fitting out the whole of this new prison with chocolate-brown tiles. Icy to the touch, the walls, ceiling, floor, everything was covered in them. It was freezing, shivering cold.

The first few days I spent in exploring the cell, every nook and cranny, tile by tedious tile. I was looking for nails, bits of string, old threads, anything that might be useful. There was no furniture in the cell, not even a strip of foam for a makeshift bed. Instead, there was a hole in one corner that had once been a squat toilet, long since broken and blocked brimful. After a few days of solitary confinement, the hole was overflowing with my own excrement, a foetid mass, a slightly different shade of brown from the surrounding tiles. Apart from the hand, which appeared once a day through the food hatch in the bottom of the door, there was no contact whatsoever with the outside world. There was no sound, the walls were muffle thick.

After a day or two I found myself sitting with my ear pressed up tightly against the door, straining for any kind of sensory input, for the slightest noise. Every morning on waking, I went through a long routine of exercise, and repeated a bucketful of prayers. When I arrived, there had been only one blanket, lying on the floor, with which to combat the intense cold. After about three days, the hand stuffed a second blanket through the hatch. One prayer answered. There were no washing facilities, the only water was delivered by the hand, but I cleaned myself up on a daily basis as much as possible without having access to soap and water. To pass the time after that, I would sit and think of the things back home, of my family, of the other people I had known and loved, of the people that I still loved. High up in one wall was a small metal grille. Too high to look out of comfortably, it was at least a means of telling night from day. And at night, every night, the multi-coloured light show of the Triple-A flickered over the city, in the small patch of sky I could see, punctuated by the brighter flashes of the exploding bombs. Counting down the interval between the bomb flash and the grumbling noise of the explosion gave a rough idea of its distance from the prison. Wherever we were, the bombing was horrendous, virtually non-stop, which most likely meant we were in central Baghdad.

Straining up to this aperture, I was able to prise away from it a thick piece of wire, about two inches long. Using this jagged sliver of metal as a needle, and threads unravelled from the blanket, I fashioned a primitive but very pleasant sleeping-bag for myself, which made all the difference in countering the all-pervasive chill. The floor was as cold as eternity. The activity of sewing took up three whole days of intensive effort: two days for the sleeping-bag, one day for the pillow I also made. They had been right on the RAF's Combat Survival Course: never sit and do nothing. The trouble was finding things to do in an empty box. It is hard to explain how boring it was.

Waking up to find two-inch-long cockroaches

staring into your eyeball was a horrific experience. They stared at me with intelligent expectation, as if they were waiting for me to die. They, too, were brown.

Nobody came into the cell, not ever. They were starving us, slowly and methodically. After a week or so, my bodyweight had fallen dramatically, the stomach hollowing in, the flesh falling away. Once a day, a hand appeared in the small trap that was the only aperture in the thick steel door. Usually it deposited a small piece of pitta bread and some hot greasy water – 'soup'. Once, the hand left a bowl of proper lentil soup – unbelievable, it must have been Saddam's birthday. I went for it, slurping it up in a second or two. Seconds later it came back up, into the faithful corner-hole. Rich stuff, lentil soup, on a shrunken stomach.

The saddest thing was the messages, etched by the fingers of desperation into the hard glazed brown surfaces of the unending tiles. On my ceiling was scratched the inscription 'Patrick Trigg, British Host-age – October 1990'. This meant nothing to me at the time, but Patrick Trigg was a businessman accused by the Iraqis of spying. He has since been released. There was a lot of Arabic script, flowing elegantly across the walls; but there were two further English messages. One read simply: 'God Help Me'; the other, 'God bless Kurdistan'. The second inscription was accompanied by a small drawing of a Christian church. It was mute but moving evidence of the persecution heaped upon the Iraqi Kurds by Saddam's regime. I spent two whole days carefully adding my own potted history to this sorry graffiti, scratching away with the metal splinter: 'Flight Lieutenant John Nichol, Royal Air Force, captured British airman . . .' with the date and so on. It was no surprise to find out later that this prison was the Ba'ath Party's Regional Headquarters in Baghdad.

Even in my sleep, my brain was trying to help me escape the reality of imprisonment. I had a regular dream during these long cold nights: I would be back in the Officers' Mess bar with all my mates, except that this time I would be wearing the yellow POW suit, while they were all in flying clothes. Everybody would be crowding around, asking me how it was, what had happened. It was great to be back, I replied, 'but the only reason they let me out was if I agreed to go back to Iraq later.' Sure enough, the moment 'last orders' was called, I would suddenly wake up, to find myself lying on a freezing floor in Baghdad.

Life narrowed down in the end to a ritual of intermittent but almost continual physical exercise, anything to circulate the blood, anything to stave off the numbing cold, the crippling, chocolate-brown boredom.

The day passes more quickly if you chew very slowly.

John Peters: I had a toilet pan in my cell. Once white china, it was now a slippery mess of green-black fungus, an encrusted nightmare. I was continually expecting something to crawl out from behind it. I hoped if it did it would be friendly, or at least talkative. The water in the bowl was an opaque inky black, with a frothy brown scum festering on the surface, bubbling gently from time to time.

I soon learned to keep back a little piece of the pitta bread that came with the soup poured every evening through the door-hatch into the plastic orange dog-bowl I ate out of. The first evening, I had had to lick this bowl clean, before turning it upside-down to use as a pillow. I became very attached to that bowl.

Normally gregarious, I now had only one form of society – myself. The enforced isolation made me think – not so much deep and meaningful abstractions on the nature of life and death, but more about what I'd done with my time, and what I wanted to do if the chance ever came again. Oddly enough, being locked up twenty-four hours a day provided an opportunity for a bit of constructive thinking.

I thought of Toni, the daughter I hardly knew, and of Helen coping on her own. I could count on her, which was comforting. Guy was just starting to talk when I went away, and I was not going to be there to help him. For the first eleven months of his life I had been doing basic and then flying training. Work was always the priority. I now bitterly regretted not having made more time for him. Would he forget who I was? Sometimes, when aircrew went away on really long exercises abroad, their children started calling every man who came through the door 'Daddy'. Why hadn't I even bought Guy a birthday present? The busy father. Training for war, I had left the whole thing to Helen. He will forget me, I thought. If I get back home in a few years, I will have had no influence on him. This upset me. You want to do the best by your children. I did not want him to know me only as a photograph on the mantelpiece. I must live to see him, I thought; I must live to see them all, even if it takes ten years. It strengthened my resolve.

I thought of other things, of happy times with Helen, and searched back into the past for memories to fill the boredom and emptiness. I've got a lousy memory for names, or for the order in which things have happened to me. So, every morning, after going through my exercises, I made myself a list of things to think about: my school life at Churcher's College, near Petersfield;

holidays; family life; university; the Squadron; flying; people I knew ... I spent whole days trying to remember the names of past friends – the captain of rugby at school: Mark ... A? ... No ... B? ... No, doesn't sound right ... S? ... That was it, Mark Spruce.

I exercised, not wanting my physical condition to deteriorate too much. Every morning, I walked around the cell forty times. Next I did stretching exercises, followed by as many sit-ups as I could, then by as many press-ups. Always, when not asleep, I wore the blanket poncho-style across my shoulders. The real discipline was steeling myself to take it off to get started on the physical jerks. My breath clouded in the freezing air.

I was worried about losing my teeth. I knew that in time the lack of food would make my gums shrink, loosening the teeth. With every sip of water from the small daily ration, I sluiced my mouth out, sloshing the water around and around my gums. I used one of my fingers as a toothbrush, scraping the plaque off my teeth with my fingernails.

I also elaborated projects in my head, the more complicated the better, like planning and building my own house – in the most minute detail. Attempting to formulate a demand/supply curve for my own imaginary business, working the whole thing out in my head, was an intellectual challenge. A lot of the time, I thought about food, especially sweet things that I would not normally eat much, like chocolate cakes. I made up recipes, the weirdest combinations: prawns flambéed in brandy and lemon sauce ... things of that kind. All the time, I was desperately, desperately hungry. I kept coming back to the idea of food, then trying to think of something else. When I ran out of things to think about, I prayed. This surprised me: I call myself an agnostic. I very rarely go to church. But prayer gave me immense strength.

I made well-intentioned resolutions, for the time when I might be released. I would be organised, plan ahead, make concrete goals and attain them. No sooner had I made these airy-fairy plans than I discarded them. I realised, on interrogating myself more closely, that I was never going to be a wonderful new person. The Iraqis might change me, but I wouldn't be able to change or improve myself. Not in that way. As the days went past, in isolation, I was gradually plumbing the depths of my own shallowness.

After a couple of weeks in this sensory quarantine, with just the four walls for company, the guards finally came for me. For once I was glad to see them. One of them was clutching an old metal safety razor. They led me along the corridor, past the rows of cells, to a bucket with a piece of soap beside it. Here, they began shaving me forcibly, the blade blunt and pitted, pulling and snagging. Both water and razor looked like they had been used on about five hundred other prisoners. After about twenty minutes, they got down to the bare skin. If I had to be shaved, I wanted to look different, in case of any more television appearances, so I talked them into leaving me a moustache. When the shaving was completed to their satisfaction, they took me back to the cell.

In the evening, they returned. I asked for some attention to my eye, the one that had been hit. It was still swollen, still aching, still oozing gunge. I was worried about it. I had demanded to see a doctor about it before, mainly in an effort to relieve the boredom – but they always ignored my shouts. They ignored me again now.

'Follow me,' was all the guard would say in reply, as he replaced the blindfold and the handcuffs.

'This doesn't feel right,' I thought. 'Something funny is going on . . .'

When they took the blindfold off, I was in what looked like a business conference room. There were Iraqi soldiers everywhere, arranging things. They had set up a television studio, with a couple of easychairs with screens behind them, in a typical chat-show format. There was a pile of assorted Allied flying-suits in the corner. One of the soldiers grabbed me: 'Are you British or American?'

'British.'

He told me to get into the appropriate flying-suit. I put it on. Because I had lost so much weight, it was hanging off me in loose folds. This meant that the yellow POW jacket was clearly visible underneath – undesirably so, as far as they were concerned. So they carefully pinned the flying-suit together at the back, to make it look as though it fitted, to disguise my evident lack of flesh. They washed my face and brushed my hair. The cold made me shake so much, they had to rig up a huge radiant fire, powered by bottled gas, about six inches from my legs. They waited for a few minutes, until I stopped shivering. I was dressed, but my feet were bare. Eventually the interview began, conducted by a donnish-looking man, who behaved for all the world like an Iraqi Wogan: courteous and professional, with the odd attempt at wit. It was like the BBC Television chat-show, *Wogan*, in format, too, except for the huge guard standing just out of camera-shot; there was a nice low table, comfortable leather-backed chairs, a bowl of fruit, a jug of water with two glasses. The questions were much the same as in the previous broadcast – the rigmarole about my being a 'war criminal', the nonsense about bombing women and children. Again, I tried not to look at the camera, not to admit to the accusations. But this time an Army Major was there, a blocky pit bull terrier of a man. Whenever I tried to look away, or drop my head, or evade a question, this officer thrust his glaring face into mine, shouted at me, and then slapped me across the face, infuriating, stinging slaps, really maddening, until I did answer it. He was quite effective.

I felt the same sense of horrible shame for having co-operated. My hands were cuffed behind me; I was blindfolded. They took me to another room, which was much smaller. I could sense that it was crammed full with men.

'Oh, oh,' I thought, 'here it comes again. Oh God. Haven't I been beaten enough?'

They stood me against the wall. Someone came right up to me. I could hear his breathing, then I felt a hand at my waist, loosening the drawstring on my heavy cotton POW trousers. They pulled them down, then my underpants, leaving me exposed from the waist down, my clothes around my ankles. I could sense the eyes all around me, watching intently. I felt extremely vulnerable. I did not mind if these people got off looking at my dick, but the fear of some kind of violence against my parts made me start to shake. Then someone began prodding me. His hands strayed lower. I flinched away.

'I'm a doctor,' a voice said. 'Don't worry. We are checking because a number of the prisoners have caught sexual diseases.'

'What?' I thought. 'What? How? Not from one another, that's for sure ... sexual diseases! ... God, here it comes. They are going to bugger me.'

His hands went to my penis, lifting and turning it, again as if making a study of some sort. He must have had some trouble finding it, since my genitals were trying to climb back up into my pelvic cavity with the fear of what they might do. But having had his feel, the 'doctor' eventually let me go. They pulled my clothes back up.

Back in my cell, I was still shaking. It could have been the cold. I was watching my hands shake, willing them with all my strength of mind to be still.

'John,' I said to myself, 'you are only doing that because you were scared in there. You know why you are shaking, so stop. Control it. This is silly.'

I found out then that for all the mental strength you may think you have, the body reacts to stress in ways that are completely beyond the mind's control.

I had to learn to accept this.

John Nichol: None of us had washed for six weeks by this stage, though I tried sometimes to save enough drinking water to give my groin and armpits a cursory wash. We were wearing the same underwear and socks we had been shot down in. Everything was horribly soiled. None of us had cleaned our teeth. Most people had a digestive disorder. Our breath reeked. It was only when they took you out, and then returned you to your cell, that you realised how appallingly you stank. The smell had built up and up, but you were not aware of it, since it was in your nostrils every minute of every day. What made you aware of it was coming back upstairs to your landing, and the smell hitting you smack in the face, sickening, like an open sewer on a sweltering hot day. They opened your cell door, and you thought, 'This isn't mine, this person smells disgusting, they've taken me somewhere else.' But suddenly you realised, 'This is what I smell like. I stink.'

One time, I heard them bringing Rupert Clark back to his cell.

'No, no,' he shouted in his unmistakably English voice, as though he were talking to a hotel porter, 'this isn't my cell! I'm in number 10. I want my own cell!'

Bad as it was, your own smell was a lot better than somebody else's.

One of the worst things about this prison was the noises that did sometimes filter through the steel door. One night I woke up with a start to hear the guards dragging an Arab prisoner along the corridor, just outside my cell. It sounded as though they were trying to kill the man with their bare hands. He was screaming oaths, calling to Allah and various prophets. The guards were swearing, cursing and ranting at him as they bundled him along. Over the next few days, the noises seeping through the door alternated between this prisoner's incantations to the heavens, in which he appealed for everything from water to George Bush, and the sound of the guards re-arranging the prison structure with his body. It was horrible having to listen to his suffering, but at least it deflected attention away from ourselves.

One night, when the yelling was at its peak, the door of my cell burst open – terrifying in the middle of all the screaming – and I was led out into the corridor blindfolded. Just outside my cell I tripped over a bundle on the floor. It felt like rags. A soft moan escaped from it, and there was the rattling of chains as it moved under my feet. Looking down through the bottom of my blindfold, I caught a glimpse of a body shackled to the water pipes running along the wall. So that was why I could hear him – they had chained him up in the corridor, right outside my box. The guard leading me giggled. Putting his lips next to my ear, he whispered, 'Don't worry. Just don't look.'

Don't worry. *Don't worry!* What did he mean, 'Don't worry!' What did he expect me to do? The guard told me that this prisoner's name was Salik. I never found out what Salik had done to upset them so much.

20

A Bombing at the Built-More

John Nichol: The Americans nicknamed this new prison the 'Built-More', a pun on the former Biltmore Hotel in New York. Every evening the entertainment was unfailingly provided by the Coalition bombing. It was a man-made thunderstorm, lasting most of the night. There was rarely much of a warning. About five or six minutes after the bombs began exploding, the air-raid sirens would start up, to let people know there was an attack in progress, just in case they had not already been alerted to the fact by having a building fall on their heads. This meant either that the first raids were always delivered by the Stealth bombers, which the Iraqis could not detect, or that Iraq's air defence network had by now been rendered completely ineffective. Lying in my favourite spot on the cell floor, I could see through the air-vent the Triple-A arcing up into the night sky, burning like a witch's oils, green, and blue, and white. I came to rely on the bombing. The noise was comforting, the way the noise of a train passing in the night was comforting when I was very young and safely tucked up in bed.

On 23 February there had been no bombing during the day, nothing but endless clouds, scudding low and grey across the Baghdad sky. But as evening drew on, the sky began to clear. Placing my shoes under my head as a pillow, I had settled down into my home-sewn sleeping-bag, and was lying waiting for the fun to begin. Exceptionally, an air-raid siren went off *before* the raid came in. Perhaps they were guessing. I unhooked my head from the blankets.

'Good,' I thought, watching my patch of sky, 'the hottest show in town's starting . . .'

What I did not know was that tonight we were centre-stage.

There came a low moaning, a rushing through the air, almost human at first, then swelling to a metallic shriek, until the sound of something screaming filled the universe. There was a blinding flash. I normally counted the interval between flash and bang. There was no interval. The whole building shook to its foundations, tottering. The blast-wave from the bomb lifted me bodily off the floor. It took me so long to come back down, that for one moment of terrifying eternity I thought the whole floor had been blown away from under me, that I was falling down through the building.

The noise came again, the same low whining to begin with, then the rushing noise cutting in on top, louder this time even than before, more like an express train, a heavy locomotive, thundering in with its whistle shrieking. It hit. The pressure-wave from 2,000 pounds of high-explosive ripped through the prison, the massive building quivering in its path. Every bone in my body rattled. The smell of burning filled the air, along with a hissing sound, as though a gas-main had ruptured. I noticed that the floor was covered in dust.

'That's two,' I thought. 'How many more?' I scrambled out of the sleeping-bag and into my clothes. I wanted to be ready to run for it if the building came down around my ears. I had carefully saved some water, in a spare bowl I had conned out of the guards, intending the next day to have my first wash in four weeks. Now, I put this next to me, in case a fire broke out. Then I tore a big square of cloth from my blanket, folded it carefully into the larger bowl, and put the whole thing on my head, like a tin helmet, for protection. It was the only thing I could think of doing. I had nothing else to hide under.

Outside, I could hear people banging on their cell doors. Someone was screaming, 'Let me out, let me out, I'm on fire, the walls are coming in . . .'

The next bomb came thundering towards the prison. Three. I remembered books about the Second World War, the kind of book in which someone says: 'It's the one you don't hear that kills you.' It didn't help. It sounded as though a jet was about to crash on us, the noise of the bomb was deafening, its mass disturbing a gigantic volume of air as it rushed towards the end of its trajectory, its kinetic energy enormous. Now the boot was on the other foot: instead of sitting up there ourselves, watching the radar, clinically ticking off the Initial Point of the bombing run, clearing down the offsets, pickling the bombs onto the target, we *were* the target. It was a bloody odd feeling.

This time, part of the ceiling came in. Chunks of plaster fell round my head and shoulders. Bits of chocolate-brown boredom came whizzing around my ears, as the tiles pinged off the walls. I could hear rubble falling, and everybody was yelling now, at the tops of their voices, to be let out. The bombing was more and more accurate. I was petrified, waiting for number four to hit the bullseye – me.

I did not have to wait long. An American shouted the obvious and inevitable: 'Incoming . . .!', the grinding roar of the bomb trucking in swallowing the end of the word. The first three explosions had loosened the building's joints; the fourth blew it apart at the seams.

A moment or two of shocked quiet, then the yelling

started again. The Americans were trying to calm everything down, to formulate a plan of action. 'OK,' said one of them, 'OK, it's all right, it's all right! Let's see if we can sort everything out . . .'

Bizarrely enough, with the walls coming in and the ceilings falling down on top of them, the Brits, as they recognised each other's voices, began chatting manically. With the gaps that had opened up in the masonry, we could hear one another clearly if we shouted. One of the advantages of having a small air force is that you tend to know one another in captivity.

I heard Rupert Clark's voice. This was miraculous. Rupert was a pilot from my own Squadron. He was down, but he was alive.

'Rupert!' I shouted. 'Good to hear you, mate!'

'John Nichol!' he said. 'How are you? We thought you were dead!'

'How's Steve Hicks?' I asked – and then wished I hadn't.

Rupert went quiet. 'Steve's dead . . .' He explained that their Tornado had been hit by two ground-to-air missiles on its bombing run. There was nothing I could say.

Then I heard JP's voice. He sounded as though he were chatting over the garden fence.

'John,' I shouted, 'you OK?'

'Yes,' he said, 'I bet you're not a fat bastard now, then?'

'No, skinny,' I called back. 'I've just shit myself – well, not really – and I'm sitting with my plastic bowl over my head.'

There was a ripple of laughter down the corridor. Then I remembered seeing Simon Burgess in one of the other courtyards.

'Budgie Burgess!' I yelled. 'Are you in there?'

'John Nichol!' he yelled back. 'I haven't seen you since you were pissed at that airshow, running around with a tea-towel on your head.'

'Oh well,' I said, 'I wish I hadn't done that now.'

John Peters: Next to the exhausting days of the interrogations, shrouded in the fog of occasional unconsciousness, that night, the night of 23 February, is the time to which everyone automatically returns, whenever they meet up. The reason for this is very simple – everybody thought they were going to die. Being bombed like we were then is one of the most terrifying things that can happen to anyone.

After the last thunderous bomb-blast, when it was clear that the raid had ended, all the lights went out. People were yelling and screaming, hammering on their cell doors to be set free. The guards, who had mistakenly scurried downstairs to take shelter when the raid started, had apparently been killed. Some of the upper storeys of the prison had collapsed and buried them. We could hear Arab voices, moaning and screaming from the floors below. But miraculously, none of the prisoners seemed to have been harmed. With the Iraqis dead or injured, there was nobody to stop us calling out to one another. Given the utterly shocking experience we had all just been through, the guards could not have stopped us from yelling even if they had survived.

Some of the prisoners had found themselves blown clear out into the corridor: their cell walls had disintegrated before their very eyes. They were wandering around looking for the door keys. This was partly in order to let everybody else out, and partly as a precaution against the fire we all expected to break out momentarily. A second raid would almost certainly come in at any time, we were such a big target. If any more 2,000-pound blockbusters hit the prison . . .

We were thankful now for the thickness of the walls, which we had cursed for their part in our isolation. If that prison had not been so solidly built, we would certainly not have survived. Jeff Zaun was one of the people milling around outside in the corridor, we could hear him shouting to us. Since they were unable to find the keys, they decided to open everybody's food hatches. It was pitch dark, so dark they had to run their fingers along the walls until they could feel the edges of the hatches in our cell doors. Finally they got them open. Now, at least, we could hear one another properly. I could hear Rupert Clark, a neighbour back at Laarbruch, very clearly, he was in the cell opposite me. He told me that Helen was standing up extremely well to the stresses and strains. That was good news all right.

Cliff Acree shouted along the corridor: 'I got so hungry I picked the scabs off my arms and put them in the soup. I needed something to chew . . .' Everybody understood exactly how he felt.

Then we heard a fresh squad of guards picking their way towards us through the rubble of the ruined building.

John Nichol: Somebody yelled that there was a CBS news team in the prison. On cue, a voice said, 'This is Bob Simon.'

Someone who had just been shot down called, 'Bob Simon, the CBS reporter?'

'Yeah,' he said.

There was pandemonium then, complete confusion,

because in their shock a lot of people jumped to the daft conclusion that there was a CBS crew visiting the prison, filming everything.

'We've been set up! We've been bombed by the Iraqis, they did it deliberately ...' came the calls. Someone else yelled, 'Bob, put my name on the TV, make sure my wife knows I'm OK!'

Of course, the CBS crew had been captured in the early days of the war. 'I can't,' he shouted. 'I'm in the same situation you are!'

There was a groan at this. We had all had visions of being filmed for posterity. The CBS crew sounded very scared. 'What do we do if they interrogate us?' shouted one of them.

'Tell the truth!' we yelled back.

We all fell silent when we saw torch beams bobbing along the corridor. For once, we were quite glad to see the guards. The Iraqis were talking excitedly and angrily ... As they reached the landing, one of them suddenly caught sight of Jeff Zaun. Instantly, there was a stutter of weapons being cocked: seeing Jeff free, they immediately assumed he was attempting to escape. Shouts and curses punctuated the dark as they stumbled angrily towards him. In the event, they did not shoot him; they just laid into him with their rifle-butts, knocking him to the ground. When they had finished making an example of Jeff, they turned their attention to the rest of us. With the damage to the building, they had no option but to move us out. The whole place was a shambles. It was so full of holes, you would have been hard put to keep a guinea-pig in there securely, let alone a batch of flyers. They started trying to evacuate us at once, but because all the keys had gone missing in the death and destruction on the lower floors, they had to fetch crowbars to prise open the doors, most of which were jammed in their frames. They were hammering and bashing at the heavy metal and the thick concrete. Each prisoner was treated to a spot of roughening up as he was levered free. A retribution for the bombing, for their dead colleagues, or a reaction to their own shock, whatever the reason for it, these guards were in a cold rage, lashing out at the cell doors, at us lot on the inside when they got to us. You would hardly have expected them to be pleased.

Smashing down my door, one of them shone his torch into the room. The narrow beam barely penetrated the clouds of swirling dust that hung thick in the bomb-shocked air. They grabbed hold of me, gave me a cursory thumping with their boots and fists, then dragged me along the corridor. They dumped me outside another cell door, which they also smashed open, after much cursing and swearing. A guard shone his torch in: there was nothing inside, certainly no sign of any prisoner. The only objects in the cell were two green and white blankets scrunched up into a ball on the floor. The blankets were topped with a small mountain of rubble, in the form of a small pyramid. One of the walls and the whole ceiling had been blown in; the ceiling sagged down diagonally at an alarming angle. The guards poked around inside, kicking at the rubble, eventually deciding that whoever had been in there was no longer alive, and came back out again. We prepared to move off. But they kept up a voluble discussion among themselves, as if they were uncertain what to do. They were clearly bewildered at the lack of a body, or at least of any large body parts, for there certainly had been a prisoner in the room before the bombs had hit. Where had he gone? He could hardly have escaped, they would have met him coming out. One of the Iraqis shone his torch back into the cell,

muttering angrily. Then we saw a very slight movement from under the pile of rubble. Something was
stirring gently, like a small furry animal. A little head,
shrouded in one of the blankets, popped out of the pile
and said, in a strong Italian accent, 'Hello?'

It was Gian Marco Bellini. I almost laughed out
loud. He still looked as though he had no idea what
had happened to him, as though he had just awoken
from a long sleep. He was completely bewildered.
Even the Iraqis by now had realised that Gian Marco
was concussed, so he did not get the rough treatment
handed out to the rest of us. They pulled him to his
feet, showering small lumps of debris, like gigantic
dandruff, from his head and shoulders.

As we continued along the corridor, a sea of cockroaches, smashed out of their nests by the blast, scurried and panicked ahead of us in the gloom. One of
our escort stopped. Shining his torch on a particularly
large specimen, he punched me hard in the face, muttered something in Arabic, and crushed the cockroach
under his foot. 'This,' he shouted, pointing at the
mess, 'is you.'

We were taken outside, into the clean moonlight, pecu-
liarly brilliant after the sepulchral dimness inside. A
group of other prisoners was waiting. We could see
very clearly where the bombs had hit, the enormous
craters excavated by the near-misses, the huge lumps
of reinforced concrete, some of them the size of a small
house, which littered the prison carpark. The whole of
the rear of the prison had simply fallen in. But in the
nature of these things, the building looked almost
undamaged from the other side, its gleaming white
façade intact, except that one complete corner was
missing. As they led us through the carpark, we could

see that most of the vehicles were completely buried under debris from the devastated gaol. The general feeling, and it was almost tangible, was: 'How the hell did I survive that?'

We had had the devil's own luck.

They dragged and kicked us onto a bus they had waiting beyond the scattered wreckage. Having escaped blindfolding, I recognised some of the twenty-five or so POWs sitting inside. Bob Simon, the CBS reporter, was also there; I knew him not from sight, but because he was the only one who did not look at all military: it could not really have been anyone else. Then I noticed that John Peters was missing. Why had they not brought him out with the rest of us? I was sure he was alive, we had exchanged shouts. Once we were installed on the floor of the vehicle, a guard strolled up and down between the seated POWs, casually swiping each one in turn across the head with the butt of his AK-47. He stood over me: 'Where are you from?'

'Britain.'

'Where did you bomb in Iraq?'

'An airfield.'

I was spared the rifle-butt, but he punched me in the face a couple of times and walked on, to the next man up the bus.

'Where are you from?'

'Italy.'

'Why do you come to my country?'

To which Gian Marco replied, a great big smile on his face, 'Ah, you are from Italy as well. That is fantastic! Whereabouts in Italy?' and struck up the most unlikely one-sided conversation with this unpleasant thug, who had no idea how to respond. Peering at Gian Marco, to see if he were being ridiculed, the

Iraqi could make no sense of what was being said to him: there was none. In the end, he punched Gian Marco in the face anyway, and wandered off, muttering darkly to himself.

Before we set off, they dragged Mohammed Mubarak, the Kuwaiti A-4 Skyhawk pilot, onto the bus, and threw him crashing to the floor. The Iraqis hated Mohammed, because they blamed Kuwait, and therefore him personally, for everything that had happened to Iraq. Five of them stood around him in a circle, smashing down at him with their Kalashnikovs, over and over again. He was in bad shape. They turned their attention away from him, though, when Salik was brought onto the bus. Salik they really loathed, more than any Coalition pilot who had bombed their country and killed their people. They threw him to the floor in the aisle and set about beating him for his unspecified crimes. Robbie Stewart was sitting nearby. His leg had been broken in several places on ejection, and he had to walk with the aid of a crutch. When the Iraqis got tired of thumping Salik with boring old boots and rifles, one of them snatched hold of Robbie's crutch and laid into Salik with that. After one particularly vicious whack, the crutch snapped clean in half, so we had to help Robbie walk. As we were not allowed to talk to him, nobody could help Salik.

John Peters: As the dust was settling, I could hear other people being taken out of their cells. They reached me, but there was no way they could get my door open. Although several of them were straining and hacking at the doorframe, they could not even begin to budge it. Eventually they left, saying they would come back the next morning. There were six other prisoners wedged into their ruined cells; someone was howling and howling. Like the Iraqis, we were completely desperate to get out, we were all expecting a second wave of bombs to hit the prison at any time, to finish the job off, if it needed finishing. The whole place was crumbling around our ears, anyway. I could not believe the guards would simply leave us overnight in that wrecked hole.

Simon Burgess, from 17 (F) Squadron, was along the corridor, calling out. In the eerie silence of the ruined shell, only the dust sifting down between our words, the debris slowly trickling, he sounded near to tears. Simon was still suffering massive after-effects of shock.

'My toilet is smashed,' he said, 'all the shit's across the floor . . .' I told him mine was too.

I felt a sudden surge of empathy for him. There is no good age to die, but I was twenty-nine, and had known Helen for ten years, we'd had happy days together, and we had two children. I had left something behind. Simon was much younger, and had been married for only four months. For some reason, the idea he might die that night hit me really hard. He hadn't really had a chance. I felt pretty much the same for Rupert Clark, whose wife Sue had just moved to live in Germany with him, immediately after she had become pregnant. What was she going to feel if her husband got killed? Perhaps the way I felt about these two mates helped me deal with my own anxiety, transferring it to someone else. Perhaps I was repressing it. I did not think about whether I was going to get killed, but whether they were. In the end, I lay down among the rubble, to try to sleep, on the grounds that if the bombs did hit I would know less about it, and if I woke up at all it would be a bonus. The second wave never came.

Early next morning, squinting through the food hatch, I could just make out the empty corridor, knee-deep in smashed glass and rubble. As they had promised, the Iraqis returned, and began struggling once again to open the door. They failed. A number of them then climbed up onto the roof, where they started trying to crowbar open my cell window from the outside, again without success. They even passed me a crowbar, so that I could work at it from the inside. Finally, completely frustrated, they fetched sledge-hammers, smashing them against the metal door, in a deafening tattoo. I sat with my hands pressed firmly over my ears, while the hammer-blows resounded around the room, but even so it was excruciating.

It was obvious they were getting very angry. I had managed to get hold of a small woven mat. I wrapped this around my middle, inside the yellow suit, to provide padding against the inevitable beating, and for warmth. In the end it became quite comic: the guards called in the Baghdad fire brigade, who turned up, strangely enough, looking very much like their Los Angeles counterparts, in black coal-scuttle hats and all the gear. The leader looked like Steve McQueen in *The Towering Inferno*. More practised in such emergencies, the firemen managed to break down the steel doors. I was the last prisoner freed. They hauled me downstairs to the basement. Here, a stinking lake of water mixed with petrol from ruptured fuel tanks lay ankle deep. I sploshed through it in the laceless plimsolls they had issued along with the yellow POW suits back at the Baghdad Bungalows. It was a miracle there had been no fire. As we emerged on the far side of this subterranean garage, I sneaked a look back at the prison. It was like the end of the world. There were huge slabs of concrete lying together crazily, great mounds of rubble, more glistening puddles of petrol and oil. Some were ablaze, billowing acrid black smoke. But for the scale of the destruction, it could have been contrived; it looked like a film-set. The guts of the building were hanging out into the carpark. At the far end of the open space, at the edge of the carpark, a group of prisoners was sitting on the ground. Simon Burgess was among them, swathed in blankets. I sat beside him, and the guards let us chat for a little while. Then one of them, who had been watching us, sauntered across. He looked admiringly at Simon's dark hair gleaming in the bright sun. He had his thumbs hooked into the front of his belt. Standing over Simon, the guard smiled winsomely down at him: 'You very pretty boy,' he said, nodding and winking at his fellow guards.

Simon was pale anyway, but he turned a shade paler. You did not have to be a genius to guess what the Iraqi was after. 'No,' said Simon hurriedly, 'I'm married. I've got a wife.' The other guards were laughing and pointing, they found this attempt to chat up Simon vastly amusing. He didn't quite see the joke. The last thing we wanted at this stage was the Iraqis gang-banging us. The guard moved closer, and sat down next to us on the hard ground.

At that moment the air-raid sirens went off.

They pushed us at a fast trot out of the carpark, straight onto what we realised were the streets of Baghdad. Through a hole in the blankets they made us put over our heads, I could see we were walking among the crowds, in the centre of a busy teeming city, in the bright sunshine, in our yellow uniforms. People began staring and pointing at us, muttering angrily. It was as if the guards were showing us, and themselves, off, as if they were proud to be the ones who were in charge of us. We felt extremely vulnerable. We were outside the prison, which was definitely a welcome change, but being outside meant we were at the mercy of these people, whose city had been massively bombed. They must already have lost most of their essential services, electricity, piped water . . . So it was a huge relief when we arrived in a relatively quiet street, at a small, very ordinary-looking, detached civilian house, where they pushed us down into the front garden. Having learned that Allied aircraft would not strike at civilian targets, the military were occupying residential buildings, evicting their rightful owners. After the all-clear had sounded, we were pushed and prodded at a fast trot back through the streets, to some kind of small headquarters building. Here, they loaded us into a Range Rover. We passed blue-painted mosques, with tall beautiful minarets, gleaming in the strong sun, and the much less beautiful pictures of Saddam Hussein plastered up on giant hoardings by the roadside, which seemed to come up every five minutes. Then we filtered onto the Baghdad ring-road. Heading northwest and then west, judging by the position of the sun and the time of day, we sped past a Triple-A site by the side of the dual carriageway, its gun-barrels angled up at sixty degrees. Here we turned off, bumping along the perimeter of a rubbish tip. Black birds were scavenging among the plastic bottles, polythene bags billowing in the stiff breeze. Some dogs were fighting and snarling over a scrap of food. We had arrived at 'Joliet'. The guards dumped us down in the same courtyard where the others were waiting. I spotted John Nichol immediately. He looked about half his original bodyweight. He winked at me. I muttered something to the man next to me. A guard immediately came up and whacked me twice over the head with his rifle, for daring to speak without permission. To stop us communicating, we were spread out at wide intervals in the huge courtyard. Just to make sure, everyone had to put his blanket over his head again. We were sitting there cross-legged, like little human pyramids, some shivering in the deep dark shadow cast by the prison walls, some sweating in the bright sun. Through the hole in my blanket, I was inching my head round to see what was going on. But whenever the vigilant guards saw the slightest movement anywhere, they came and smacked the offending head back down. I picked up some pebbles, and a tiny seashell, lying in the dirt at my feet. Later, I played Fivestones with them in the cell, the game coming back to me from my childhood. I also found a slender sliver of wood, about three inches long, which converted into a brilliant needle for sewing up the holes in my blanket, using thread teased out from the frayed ends.

When we had all been sitting there most of the day, a guard came up. 'You,' he said, 'are going for a little walk.'

They led me inside, where it was freezing. The room was like a small outhouse, its walls lined incongruously with farmyard implements. In the corner was a cast-iron toilet cistern, built sometime while Pontius was in Pilate training. But the thing that I found myself staring at was the black vinyl chair, backless, with a tubular metal frame, identical to the one I had been forced to sit in during the interrogations. The sight of it made my stomach lurch and turn over with fear. The chair. But it turned out they were not beating people this time. They gave me the same interrogation I later discovered everyone else had been through, about the plans for the ground offensive. Like everyone else, I could tell them nothing, even under threat of death.

When they had questioned everyone, they banged us all up for the night. I got immense strength from the fact that during the short walk into the prison I was in a shuffling crocodile made up of all my fellow countrymen and mates. I was part of a group again, even though I was going back into solitary. You don't have to talk, always, to communicate.

After a couple of days on my own, I was moved into a cell with Jeff Zaun, who was in the grip of a vicious stomach bug. Most of the Americans had the most tremendous squits: perhaps the water supply on their floor had been contaminated. Although we were allowed out to relieve ourselves three times a day, Jeff had to go more often – much more often. He tore a large section off the plastic window-covering, and shat into that. He would then place the resulting package on the windowsill, in an effort to keep down the stink. Memorably, horribly, it still stank, festering away as the hours went by. He would keep it like this, and carry it to the toilet hole whenever we were allowed out. There was nothing else he could do. At night, when there was no one to see, he simply pissed out through the window grille. Because of his sickness, he had not eaten all the bread they had given him – he'd hoarded a small pile of hard crusty stale pieces in the corner next to him. I really wanted that bread; I would have gobbled it up in a flash. At night, when it was really cold, we tried to warm one another – but it always ended up that the one against the cell wall got warm, while the other, sleeping on the outside, got freezing cold. So we finished up sleeping separately, and both of us froze.

21

The Blues Brothers

John Nichol: We drove across Baghdad for an hour, until the bus stopped outside another prison which the Americans immediately christened 'Joliet', after the penitentiary John Belushi is released from in *The Blues Brothers*. According to them, this new place looked just like the prison in that film. Each cell measured about six feet by ten, and was freezing cold, as usual, and fetchingly carpeted throughout in birdshit. No blankets. They crammed six or seven of us into each little cubicle. This might seem bad, but it was bliss. This was the first time I had really been with anyone on the same side as me since being shot down. I actually knew some of the people in the room there with me; it was like being at a very small, very crowded party.

After an hour or so, we were allowed to visit the toilet. A couple of us helped Robbie Stewart, who was still without his crutch, to pay a visit. Mohammed Mubarak was with us, heavily bruised, but full of stories culled from the radio and the overheard chatter of the Iraqis. He said that the Allied ground offensive had begun on 21 February.

The luxury of communication. We stayed up all night, chatting, telling stories, even laughing. Everyone was suffering from the same feeling of sensory deprivation: they were bursting to talk, to recount, above all, their experiences of interrogation. It was the one dominant topic. Sitting in solitary confinement, everyone had reached the same conclusion: that they had given in too readily, that they should have held out much longer. The relief of learning that we had *all* given in, at pretty much the same stage, was immense. The burden of self-reproach and guilt was, for the moment at least, lifted. We were in prison, beaten to shit, we still didn't know if we were going to survive, but we were on a fantastic high.

We slept for perhaps twenty minutes that night, no more, until a bright winter sun came slithering up the walls. When I woke, there was cacophony. We were in an old, nineteenth-century prison, but for a moment I thought I was on a crowded platform on the London Underground: thousands and thousands of voices, twittering and chirping like a huge flock of human sparrows, resounded in the corridors and courtyards of this aged gaol. There were two floors, the cells giving out onto internal balconies running right round the building on each floor. Guards patrolled this inner space. Through the bars in the cell door, we could see an endless tide of humanity, ebbing and flowing. It was like something out of Charles Dickens. There were thousands and thousands of these prisoners.

After a couple of weeks of Ba'ath Party hospitality, featuring nothing for breakfast, nothing for lunch and a bowl of gruel for tea, we were all extremely skinny, mere skeletons, as you might say, of our former selves. But now, the door clattered open, and lo! Food! A couple of trusties brought in a small amount of bread, a plastic washing-up bowl with steaming lentil soup slopping around in it (steaming!) and another washing-up bowl filled with hot sweet tea. We were suddenly very keen to stay in this lovely prison where we got our first hot food for weeks; but later that same morning they took us out, and sat us down in the prison court-yard, where we remained all day, under the blazing sun.

As if they had nothing better to do, the men detailed to watch us armed themselves with rubber truncheons, and passed the time walking among us, whacking people when the urge took them. JP turned up in the afternoon.

As the day wore on, they took us off one by one, for another round of questioning. All the interrogators wanted to know from us was: what could we tell them about the ground offensive? Where would the main Allied thrust come? Would there be a seaborne landing, a frontal assault on Kuwait City itself? Where would the paratroopers be used, would the US Marines be used? The interrogator went on and on, but of course I knew nothing. Finally, he said to me, 'Nichol, I am giving you one chance to save your life now.'

'What?'

'I am giving you one chance only to save your life. Tell me something I will save your life for.'

'What do you want me to tell you?'

'Tell me something about the ground offensive that will help me save your life.'

I was trying quite hard to think of something I *could* tell him, since he seemed perfectly serious, but there was nothing, nothing at all. My ignorance must have been blindingly obvious to him.

He let me go.

As I was being led back into the courtyard, I passed JP, seated on one side. He looked wasted, as if he had been shrunk a couple of sizes in the wash. Wearing a horrible spade-shaped beard, he was hard to recognise as the same person.

They split us up into two groups, British and Americans, and marched us off in separate crocodiles, as if we were very small school-children. We each had to place one hand on the shoulder of the man in front, and keep our eyes fixed on the ground. JP and I manoeuvred ourselves next to one another. I put my right hand on his shoulder, and squeezed. JP reached his own hand up to cover mine, pressing firmly down on it. That touch was very important. It was a little moment of warmth; nothing more than an instant of human contact. But it made a difference; after the lonely horrors of the beatings and the solitary incarceration, the hatred of the surrounding Iraqis, I felt a surge of morale flooding back, and I could feel the same thing in JP.

'We're still here,' I thought. 'Still alive . . .'

The Iraqis were not, as it turned out, moving us to another prison, but to a different wing of the same one, where they could lock us up individually again.

Because they did not let us out to the toilets very often, disposing of excrement became a recurring problem. Other cells had the same difficulty, I realised. I knew this because every so often a sprinkling of urine hit me as another prisoner on an upper floor emptied a bootful out through the mesh of his air-grille, to prevent the shitpool in his own room from growing bigger. The splashes hit me if I happened to be sitting near the tiny metal grille in my own cell.

Salik had been locked up somewhere near us in this new wing, seemingly attached to our group, though he was definitely a civilian prisoner. We decided he must have spoken out against Saddam, or done whatever is the greatest crime under that obscene regime. The Iraqis still had it in for him. All night long, which meant for eight solid hours at a stretch, his screams echoed and rolled around the prison. It sounded as though they had either driven him mad with the constant beatings, or he was mad to begin with. The cries were unearthly, lingering agonised banshee wailings, interspersed by sharp yaps of pain. At first, I lay there feeling extremely sorry for him – no one could deserve that much beating. But after an hour or two, I was surprised to find myself feeling selfishly venomous towards him, because the noise was rasping continually on the edges of the nerves. It was impossible to sleep.

The next day, the screams continued, intermittently, only this time they came spiralling up from the prison courtyard, ringing around its harsh exterior walls. Levering myself up to the air-grille in my cell wall, I could just make out what they were doing to him. The Iraqis had invented a new and very unpleasant form of volleyball. There was no ball, and the sides were what you could only call uneven. There were six or seven men on one team, but only one on the other: Salik. They had handcuffed him to the volleyball net that stood in the middle of the yard, so that he was spread-eagled against it. The Ba'ath Party guards were standing around him clutching short lengths of their favourite instrument of torture, the thick, whippy rubber hose. They were taking it in turns to beat him, really swinging their arms back, laying into him, whipping him as hard as they could. Dressed in nothing more than a raggedy pair of thin old pyjama bottoms, the man's skin was blistered all over with thick red welts, the contusions visible even through the sickening crusting of vomit, food and excrement that coated him. His whole body was swelling as the unending blows rained down on him. Unbearable.

At about mid-day, the rubber-hose squad went off for lunch, leaving Salik sagging on the net. I was still watching him, transfixed and appalled. Next to him were a couple of huge metal containers, holding the drinking-water for the prison. The water-mains had long since been bombed. Then Salik started wriggling his pyjama bottoms down. This did not seem like a wise move. He really must be mad. Eventually, he stood naked in the sun, pyjamas round his ankles. Twisting his body towards the vats of water, he urinated carefully onto the sandy ground, until there was a substantial puddle of his own piss in front of him. Then, with great deliberation, he stepped free of his pyjamas and paddled his right foot thoroughly around in the resulting mixture of urine and dirt, until he had gathered a good load of it up around his toes and on the sole of his foot. Cocking his leg high into the air, like a dog at a lamp-post, he dunked the contaminated foot into the water, swilling it carefully to and fro. This process he repeated several times.

As an example of human defiance and the will to revenge, it was hard to beat. Especially after what he had been through.

'Go on, mate,' I muttered, 'give them some!'

Shortly after this, the guards returned. One of them took up a ladle and dipped it into the urn. They all began drinking eagerly . . .

After a few days in solitary confinement, they moved us out of the single cells, putting one British POW in with one American. The cells were slightly larger, with barred windows. I was paired up with Larry Slade, a US Navy Lieutenant, a Tomcat backseater from the aircraft carrier USS *Saratoga*. He has since become a good friend. We were chatting away, when we made a big mistake: we looked out of the window. Over on the other side of the prison, but down a floor, there were three Arab inmates. They waved up at us, so naturally we waved back. One of them began miming, counting on his fingers. He meant, 'How many of you are there?'

'Twenty-eight,' we mimed back. We had counted one another in the courtyard. Then they made signs to indicate an aircraft dropping its bombs.

'Yes,' we nodded back.

At this, the three of them began cheering, though we could not hear the cheers, and gleefully waving victory signs. Then they did something incomprehensible, pointing at us, then pointing at the side of the building we were in, but lower down. They were trying to indicate that there were more captured aircrew, or at least more Caucasian faces, maybe even the British civilian captives, Douglas Brand and Ian Richter, in that section of the prison.

A yell rang up from the courtyard below. Looking down, we saw a dozen or so of the Ba'ath Party guards gesticulating furiously in our direction. We immediately dived back down out of sight. Inside a minute, we could hear the guards banging furiously on the main door to be let into our wing.

'Shit,' said Larry, 'they're coming to get us . . .'

In order to see out of the cell, we had removed the sheet of opaque plastic that normally covered its barred window. Feverishly, we struggled to replace this polythene. Now we could hear the awful clatter of boots on the stairs as the guards pounded along the corridor. They flung open the cell door, seven of them pouring into the small space. They stared up at the window. We had just managed to replace the covering in time.

'Were you looking out of the window?' one of them shouted.

'No, no. Not us,' we chimed in unison.

They ran out, burst into the neighbouring cell, where Rupert Clark was being held. We could hear them shouting out of his window. Someone must have signalled up to them that it was in fact the next cell, our cell, that held the guilty parties, because they came thundering back again. It would have been funny if it had not been so bloody frightening. They were really beside themselves now. They advanced slowly towards us, their eyes fixed on ours.

They started on Larry first, punching him to the ground. It was as bad, if not worse, than anything in the interrogation. They almost literally kicked the shit out of him. I was watching from the corner, frozen with horror. It was a concerted, merciless avalanche of furious blows and thudding kicks. There was no escape. When he stopped moving, they kicked him viciously hard a few more times for good measure, and then it was my turn. They punched and kicked me until I fell, then started kicking me in the face. I could feel the blood streaming down over my cheeks and mouth in a hot torrent, could dimly see it dripping onto the floor of the cell. I remember lying there as the kicks came in, watching the bright red drops spattering down onto the dull grey concrete. They hauled me upright. I was staggering, close to losing consciousness, reeling drunkenly. The walls and floor seemed to be heaving, it was like being at sea in a heavy swell. I was falling, falling . . . They punched and kicked me horizontal, then somebody dragged me up again; this went on and on. I was trying to cover my face with my hands.

'Keep your hands down!' one of them screamed. 'I'm going to break your face!'

My flinching attempts to protect myself seemed to infuriate this particular guard. He became frenzied, lashing out wildly at my features. Finally, it stopped. I could hear them breathing heavily. Through the dense grey mist that surrounded me, I heard one of them ask, 'What were you signalling?'

'We were just waving,' mumbled Larry, through his mashed lips.

'Right,' said a guard, 'you're dead.'

He took his pistol out, snapping the slide sharply back and releasing it, to charge the weapon.

'You two stand together.'

They hauled me over next to Larry. The guard pointed his pistol at us.

'You are now going to die,' he said. He moved closer, until Larry could see down the barrel of the gun. For a number of seconds, for a long lifetime, the Iraqi just stood like that, quivering with rage, the knuckles of his fingers white, the slack taken right up on the trigger. We were a heart's beat away from death. He pulled the trigger. Click!

It turned out he had removed the weapon's magazine before this mock execution – so there had been no bullet in the chamber all along. He sneered at the expression on our faces, and walked out, laughing.

Later, in the evening, they came back. This time they were clutching the rubber truncheons in their fists.

'Oh no,' I thought, 'not again.'

They asked us one more time: who had been waving to us from the other side of the prison? We did not want to answer. One of them whacked his length of hose against the wall. It gave a sharp crack. I looked at Larry. We felt terrible. With a burning sense of shame, we told them which cell it was. And with that they were gone. About ten minutes later, the screams and the yells started floating up from the other side of the prison . . .

That was a very low time for us, Larry and me: we were responsible for those screams. But we had had enough for one day.

★

John Peters: Sound dominates your life when you are alone in a prison cell. One of the hardest things to get used to is the ceaseless clanging of the cell doors. After the aching silence of the previous prison, where I had strained to catch the merest whisper of activity, there was now nothing but din in this new gaol.

So I was always listening. It was just about the only way of getting information, and the sound of approaching trouble was the very first thing I learned to recognise. There were two sounds which were particularly strange. They took a while to identify: one a plastic shuffle, which turned out to be Dave Waddington, who had plastic bags for shoes, making his way along the corridor; the other sound was a kind of drag and click, which was the sound of Robbie Stewart limping along with the aid of a makeshift crutch. But the overwhelming sound, that filled my mind and that I learned to hate, was the continuous, never-ending, ceaseless, horrible screaming of Salik. I kept hoping they would knock him unconscious, anything to switch off that noise.

On the second or third day I was in with Jeff, we heard the sound that all prisoners dread: the guards' heavy boots clanging up the stairs, the echo turning the footsteps into a clattering roar: trouble coming. We were in for it. The two of us crouched down in the small angle of the cell that could not be overlooked by the guards. We were sitting on our bums, hugging our legs with our arms, like small frightened children, our hands clenched together, knuckles white, fingers stuffed against our noses, pressing up against the nostrils, desperately praying that this trouble, whatever it was, which sounded like a real beating, would not come along the corridor to our cell. John Nichol's voice rang out in alarm, followed by the harsher bark of a guard's shouted command: 'Raise your arms!' I heard an explosive 'Uuuph!' of expelled air as the guards thumped John in the stomach. Then came the unmistakable sound of flesh being hit. That sound went on for a very long time.

'Hang on in there,' I thought. But then again, my main feeling, to tell the absolute truth, was a feeling of relief that it was not me on the end of it.

John Nichol: That night, the night of 27 February, was one of the worst for air raids during our entire time in the hands of the Iraqis. It was like no other night of the war. It sounded as though every military jet in the world was using our cell as the starting point for its bomb run. There was a continuous scream of engines overhead. The sonic booms the aircraft made as they increased speed to escape after bombing was as loud as the bombing itself. Explosion after explosion crumped incessantly nearby, until the air itself felt exhausted. I had grown accustomed to the bombing, and would miss it when it did not come. But this was different. It was terrifying, lying there huddled up with Larry, both of us still covered in dried blood from our bit of fun earlier. The bomb-blasts seemed to be getting closer and closer. This prison, unlike the last, was jerry-built: it looked as though someone had dumped a load of plaster on the ground and then it had rained for a couple of days. There was no way it would withstand a direct hit, or even a near miss. The noise of the bombing went on all through the night. Strangely, there was very little sign of opposition, no sign of tracer in the sky, hardly any sound of opposing Iraqi ground fire. Then, at first light, there was gun-fire, a tumultuous crackle breaking across the city in a wave: small arms, Triple-A, heavier guns, it sounded like a pitched battle was going on in the streets just outside the prison walls. Despite the constant air raids, which had inured us to the sound of gunfire, we had never heard anything like this before. The attacking jets had gone home.

I turned to Larry: 'What the hell's going on?'

'One of three things,' he replied. 'One of our guys has been shot down close by and they've got hold of him, they're celebrating; or there's a battle going on outside – somebody, some of our Special Forces or whatever, is coming in to get us out; or the war has finished.'

Over the rest of that day, there was sporadic gunfire, again most of it small arms, as if people were firing wildly into the air. There was a lot of movement around the prison. Later in the afternoon, a huge Iraqi soldier came around, a good six feet seven inches in height, with a physique to match. He and his entourage began taking names. From time to time, this smiling giant, for he had a fixed smile on his face, would thump one of us, hard, in the stomach or on the head, almost as if in play. We were quite pleased we hadn't come across him before. It was like being swatted playfully by a full-grown grizzly bear. When they had verified everyone's identity, they moved us again.

There was a bus outside, with its engine running, its curtains tightly drawn. 'Do not look out of the windows,' they said. As they were driving us through the streets, the guards were coming round the bus, wrenching at our hair with their fingers, casually kicking us.

If you had been standing at a little distance from that bus, you would have seen the prayers coming out of it, wraith-like, rising up to the heavens. Everybody, even the heathenest heathen, was praying like a bastard. If the Iraqis really had lost the war, what was to stop them getting rid of us? The transport drew up at a grim-looking army camp. We hadn't the faintest idea what was going on. As our names were called in turn, we were blindfolded and led off the bus one by one. This was definitely not looking promising. Just for good measure, I was punched and kicked along a gauntlet of soldiers on the way down the corridor. As they removed my blindfold at the cell door, I could see they were paratroopers, busily knocking lumps off the next man in line, and warming to the work. Inside, the cell was one of the dankest, the most dismal I had been in so far. I was back in solitary confinement. Great. The floor was wet, there was very little light and no window. Screams and shouts and kicks and punches filtered through the slit in the door that provided the only light.

On the wall, somebody had scratched 750 ticks, to mark the passage of his days in captivity. They were in blocks of five, and divisions of 100. I wondered how that prisoner had stood it in that dark hole, and what had happened to him in the end. I thought I would not last as long, and prayed I would not have to.

That night, a senior Iraqi Army officer came around. Blinking in the sudden glare, I stood up.

'How are you?' he enquired politely, as if we were in a holiday camp. When he had gone, a private threw in a couple of blankets. For the first time in many nights, there were no air raids. It was obvious something crucial was about to happen. A peculiar pall of calm hung over the prison.

About an hour after dawn, a guard came round clutching a large sack. Like a magician producing a rabbit, he triumphantly withdrew three freshly baked wholemeal rolls, holding them out to me with a big grin on his face. I stared at him, then at the rolls. A couple of them reeked, as though they had been soaked in petrol. They tasted that way too, but I ate them anyway.

'Would you like more?' he enquired, politely, interpreting my amazement as hunger. He stuffed another three rolls into my hands. In his wake appeared another Iraqi, an officer, younger, his hair a brilliant black. He was clutching yet more blankets.

'Would you like more blankets? How many?' He began doling them out, counting, his teeth flashing whitely at me in the gloom, 'One, two, three . . .' All of a sudden, it was like Christmas Day. The extra blankets were heaven, because now I could fashion a mattress. My hips were covered in thick pads of calloused skin, where I had been lying on concrete floors for six weeks.

I thought, 'We are back with the military, perhaps we will be treated like prisoners of war – professional aircrew, not prisoners of conscience, who are treated like animals.'

Sure enough, over the next two days, food began arriving with unusual regularity, things we had never had before, like cold rice and chicken, at least once a day. On the third day, a suave civilian in a smart grey designer suit appeared. He looked utterly out of place in the bleak surroundings, but he seemed quite at ease, although wreathed in apologies.

'Do make yourself comfortable,' he began, greasily, a note of something very like apology in his voice, looking about my cell as though it were a hotel room, as if the blood of its many dozens of previous inmates was not spattered across its walls.

'Now, if there is anything you would like, anything

at all, do let me know. My staff is here to help you. If you want to visit the toilet just knock on the door, they will take you along to the toilet; if you would like some food, just ask. Anything we can do to help, just let us know . . .'

It was bizarre. Laughable. Surreal. 'My staff . . .!' Here we were, filthy, stinking and starving, and here was this character behaving like a fond uncle on a school visit. His staff? Now, would they be the same paratroopers who had beaten us up on the way in? Or had they been replaced by uniformed maids, and bellboys?

Something definitely was up.

Naturally, the immediate thought was that they were being nice to us in preparation for release. I felt a wild surge of hope and optimism, followed by an equal rush of caution. 'No, I am not raising my hopes too high . . .'

Deep down, I knew I was going to get out; but superstitiously, I did not want to acknowledge this feeling, to let it surface. One of the biggest weapons any interrogator has is the weapon of emotional manipulation: raising your hopes to the skies, and then dashing them.

Delicious cheese, marmalade and baked beans appeared for breakfast, along with the rolls. The guards built an open fire, in the courtyard, cooking plain but wonderful barbecued chicken on it. The only problem was that my digestion went on strike, and a bout of diarrhoea came bucketing through my system. Quite a few of the others also found the sudden arrival of food too much: I knew because the guards were kept busy escorting people on numerous toilet trips.

★

John Peters: We were moved again. Every time they move you is the worst time. Every new cell, every new place, you sit and listen, trying to establish the routine of the new prison. Is it going to be good, or bad? This new place was bad, the whole floor was awash with water. I played a negative versus positive thinking game. What was positive about it? Well, there was a small dry patch in the corner, where I could park my bum. Positive. There was very little light, but there was some. Positive. I sat and waited, listening, listening, trying to work out the routine of the place from the sounds. To pass the time, I watched the light from the tiny grille in the door work its way around the cell. It grew from a small spot on the cell wall, extending and thinning slowly – around four o'clock in the afternoon – moving gradually round the room and then dying out as night fell, at about half-past six in the evening.

On 3 March, they shaved me again. They had a little pot filled with scummy cold water, awash as usual with the scrapings of other beards. The razor was half-blunt, caked with hair and the crude soap they were using. I insisted that I shave myself, but the guards held my face tight, scraping away. I managed to persuade them to leave the spade-like beard I'd grown, fearing that they would put us on television yet again. I suppose because it was thick, and looked quite Arab-like, the Iraqis let me keep it. After the shave, they took me along to a concrete cubicle, like a shower cubicle. It had a bright red plastic dustbin in it, brimming with lukewarm water, a creamy-grey colour from the washings of my fellow inmates. The guard gesticulated that I, too, should wash in this filthy muck. I took my clothes off, readily now because the atmosphere was much less intimidating in this new gaol.

There was a bright green plastic jug. I dipped this in the water, and threw it over my head. The scum didn't matter. It was a marvellous feeling after weeks of grime just to feel the warm water coursing down my body. When they took away the dirty yellow canvas suit, and issued a fresh one, it felt almost like being clean again.

On 4 March, my dreams came true: they gave me laces for my plimsolls. This could only mean one thing: we were due for release. A large party of senior officers began touring the prison. I heard them going into the next-door cell.

'What's your name?'

'Lawrence Randolph Slade.' Larry, I later discovered, had been in with John Nichol.

'Do you know the war is over?'

22

Baghdad in the Rearview Mirror

John Peters: There was a silence. It was the first confirmation I'd had of the secretly hoped-for fact. There it was, they had said it, it was undeniable. And it was tremendous. A rush of emotion and relief ran through me. I had no thoughts of whether we had won or lost – only the thought of going home.

'In twenty minutes,' continued the unseen officer next door, 'you will be going home to your family.'

My family. I could hardly bear to think about them. I had schooled my feelings so efficiently, screwed them down so tightly, I had almost expected never to feel things like love and closeness again.

The Iraqi Lieutenant came into my cell. 'You are going home in ten minutes,' he said.

I looked at him dazedly, incapable of taking it in. I began shuffling round the cell, gathering together the bits of string, the biro and the piece of cardboard, the scraps of cloth, the nail, all those little oddments that made up my most precious possessions, objects I had become obsessively attached to as a prisoner. The pen and my diary, that I had kept carefully hidden down my sock, that had helped me chart the days and my fluctuating morale, were my most carefully guarded things. Then the reality of what was happening seeped through to me. I no longer needed all this stuff. Soon, in a matter of days perhaps, I would be seeing Helen and the children, my Mum and Dad, and the rest of my family. I would be home. It was as much as I could do to contain my feelings.

They led me outside; the dazzling sunshine made me blink. Food was laid out on a small table. Over the past forty-eight hours, we had had more food than in the previous two weeks. The ten of us who were being released had pitta bread, good cheese, and, best of all, tomatoes, with salt. I recognised none of the others, they were all Americans. Why was John Nichol not coming with us?

It was all very civilised. An elderly gentleman in glasses bumbled about, wringing his hands, as we gobbled down the food. He was like some sort of holiday tour operator, chatting amicably, holding a clipboard. 'Your trip has been delayed, Sir.' Then, when the transport arrived, 'For your own protection, please do not look out of the coach.'

Despite this new cordiality, the guards still kept coming round and tapping our skulls from time to time; old habits die hard ... We set off. Our 'courier' was chatting to us as we drove along, quite as if we were on a sightseeing trip of Baghdad, telling us about how he had lived in the US for several years, in Baltimore, which he loved. 'Is New York still as dirty and horrible?' he asked. He had travelled widely throughout Europe, and was a cultured and even courtly gentleman. Giving us our release schedule, he was chatting to us, skeletons that we were, as if none of the recent events had taken place. I could feel no resentment, now that the ordeal was almost over, towards him or any other Iraqi.

The bus pulled up in front of the Baghdad Novotel. An amazing sight met our eyes: in front of the hotel, in packed ranks a dozen deep, the serried legions of the world's media were ranged to receive us. It was awesome. We were totally unprepared for it.

They were like a football crowd, heaving and

shoving, jostling and pushing one another, frantically brandishing their cameras and their tape recorders in our direction. It was a fantastic shock to realise that it was us they were after. Looking at this sweltering multitude, I felt a wave of tiredness and nausea sweep over me. For this, I was just not ready. All I wanted was to get home, I was exhausted. My guts were still churning wildly from the unaccustomed food. I felt like getting under the seat of the bus, just lying down and curling up, in the hope that it would all go away. Getting off the bus was a nightmare. The media surged forward, elbowing and shouting, engulfing us and the guards in a welter of insane energy. Reporters screamed questions into our ears, in a hundred languages at once. It was impossible to answer, even to hear a coherent sentence in that scrum. On all sides, cameras clicked and whirred. To clear a path through this mayhem, the Iraqis began shoving everybody back, forcibly; it was, after all, what they were good at.

Inside the hotel, which we reached only after a struggle, was a Red Cross welcoming committee. It was set up at some tables in the centre of what looked like a ballroom, all done out in damask and chandeliers. At least it was relatively quiet, and there were chairs to sink down into. But even in here the noise of the crowd outside penetrated through to us. They were climbing up the windows, clinging on wherever they could, buzzing up against the glass, like human flies. The Red Cross officials hurried to close the curtains, plunging the room into gloom. They were apologising; there had been no warning, they said, it had all been done at the last minute. The Red Cross had been trying to get access to us for weeks, without the least success. And then suddenly we were there. They gave us an initial, if cursory, medical examination, to make sure we could all travel safely out of Iraq, questioning us about any current physical problems. The doctor, a Swiss, had huge flowing black moustaches and a copious beard. They offered us coffee, Coca-Cola and buns with a great dollop of greasy lamb in the middle, a truly horrible sight given my tender guts. 'Here I am,' I thought, 'in a hotel of international repute, I am starving hungry and I cannot bring myself to eat the food!' The Red Cross had known absolutely nothing of our release until that very morning, but they were whistling around, trying to get organised, doing their level best. Our reception had been cobbled together at the last minute. Still, it was miles better than anything we could have imagined. They asked us what we wanted. Almost to a man, we replied, 'Chocolate.' More than anything in the world, we wanted chocolate. Preferably Swiss chocolate! They went rushing around the hotel until they found a chocolate machine, brought us the little squares, and we wolfed them down with orange juice and Pepsi-Cola. Not the best thing for a queasy stomach. Predictably, I had to visit the toilet in a very few minutes.

As I turned into the corridor outside the reception room, I saw a woman. Being in captivity had put a complete stop to any feelings of desire: sexuality had been suspended for the duration. Now, it returned with a rush. For the whole time in prison, I realised, I had hardly thought once about sex. Now, it was like a switch flicking back to On, none of that stuff about psychiatric readjustment, and the need to take things easy, there it was, Bang! Straightforward lust, fully-formed (well, forming), instantaneous and crude as ever. Stupid, really, I thought. I looked at myself in the bathroom mirror. I was a sight. My hair was matted and standing on end; I looked hollow to the core, cheeks, eyes, body; I stank. It was clearly going to be some time before any woman returned the compliment of finding me desirable.

Back in the main room, the Red Cross said there was no way the press would let us out, or even let us sleep, unless we granted them a photo-call, at the very least. Most of us just wanted to lie down for a bit! To keep them happy we agreed to be photographed, but we all refused to say anything: we were still serving military officers. The Red Cross officials said, 'What we'll do is put you all on a long table, we'll let the reporters in in groups of ten, and they can have thirty seconds apiece.'

We sat in there, while outside the journalists fought among one another for precedence. There were two other released British POWs in my group as we waited for the doors to open, and they were definitely not aircrew.

'Just don't smile,' they told me, 'don't attract attention to yourself.'

What they meant was, 'Don't attract attention to *us*.'

The first group of reporters came rushing in. 'Hi!' yelled the one at the head of the queue, at the top of his voice, though the room was quiet. 'I'm from NBC, I'm from California. Is anybody here American?' Nobody responded.

The reporter behind shouted, 'Hi! Would anybody like to be on the cover of *Time* magazine?'

That did it. 'Yeah!' cried what seemed like all the Americans at once. 'Here! Over here!'

As for the instruction not to smile, it was difficult not to laugh out loud. With so little time allocated to them, these first ten reporters moved frenetically along the line of POWs. They were festooned with cameras, shoving the lenses into our faces, snapping continuously, motor-winds whirring, shutters clicking. I suddenly realised they were much more apprehensive about the whole deal than we were. Almost without exception, they were trembling visibly, shaking, in some cases, from head to foot. These were obviously career photographs for them, this was big-time stuff. I almost felt sorry for them. Almost. Up to this point, I don't think any of us, least of all John Nichol and me, had had any inkling of the interest in the POWs. Even though we knew we had appeared on television, several weeks had gone by, and in any case we had not realised the extent of the impact it had had. After all, we had not seen the pictures. The journalists' and photographers' nervousness made me realise, for the first time, how firmly we were all fixed in the public eye. Little did I realise quite how firmly.

All these power journalists were eager-beavering, with their power-drives, their shoulder-padded egos, their TV lights, trailing clouds of cables and high-technology, when in wandered a diminutive African reporter, wearing a shabby grey suit and a checked shirt. He was clutching a crumpled camera bag. Oblivious to the scrum, as his fellow cameramen wrestled to replace spent films, he stopped calmly in front of us. He took a very old, very battered Leica camera out of his bag, followed by an equally ancient light-meter. Twenty-eight of his allotted thirty seconds he spent fiddling with this meter, holding it up to our faces, stepping back, then forward again, adjusting the f-stop ring, focusing the lens. Finally, he stepped back, and pressed the shutter release. Nothing happened. He had forgotten to advance the fresh film! He wound on, carefully, once, twice, then re-focused. Click! He took the one shot, smiled at us gravely, bowed and retired. His serene dignity was utterly incongruous in that context, but he endeared himself to us because of it.

When the media's thirst had been slaked, the Red Cross officials suddenly took off their jackets and offered them to us. Some of these jackets were expensive, rich leather. What on earth was going on? The idea, it turned out, was to disguise our very obvious, bright yellow prisoner-of-war suits, on the way out of the hotel. We were leaving Iraq.

'We're sorry,' they said. 'We are going to have to drive you into Jordan. There is no aircraft available. It's a ten-hour trip. But don't worry, we've got loads of stuff in the jeeps, food and everything. And these will keep you warm.'

Sorry! I could not care if I roller-skated out, as long as I got out, and soon. On the way back out of the hotel, our captors became our protectors again. The press were still hanging around, doing their job, bugging us. But the guards shouldered through with a will. After they had forced a passage for us back through the manic multitude, we scrambled onto the long-wheelbase jeeps, the new ships of the desert. Emblazoned with the bright red markings of the International Red Cross, they were our transport to Jordan. We were travelling in a three-vehicle convoy, the armed Iraqi escort taking the lead. We set off through the streets of Baghdad.

Baghdad. It was a ruined city, but it was ruined in a fantastically impressive way. A radio mast had been sited in the middle of a housing cluster. The radio mast itself had been blasted to a pile of twisted metal, its jagged ends clutching skywards, but the surrounding homes were quite untouched. We passed target after target that had been specifically taken out. It was extraordinary. Although in prison we had been on the end of many a bombload ourselves, here was first-hand evidence that the precision bombing had, in fact, been just that: precise.

We came to a small town on the other side of the capital. Some of the key buildings in the centre had been destroyed, along with a new bridge, its spans lying drunkenly in the wide river. The jeeps had to pick their way very cautiously over the old bridge, which was itself quite badly damaged. We lurched to a stop. Everyone in town seemed to be carrying a rifle, except for the street vendors, who were brandishing grilled meat on sticks instead, making their sales pitch. The meat smelled delicious, but it wasn't worth staying for. The townspeople were staring at us, gathering silently until there was a big crowd. There was no love in those stares. Some people began fingering their weapons. We were glad of the Iraqi escort.

It was a relief to emerge into open desert. Straight as an arrow, the tarmac ribbon of the road shimmered and wavered in the heat haze. There were continual reminders of the war. Every twenty kilometres, the otherwise featureless landscape was punctuated by a radio transmitter, housed in a small building by the side of the road – or rather, an ex-radio transmitter. Every single one of these links in the Iraqi communications chain had been obliterated, blasted into oblivion. Not one had been left out, all the way from Baghdad to the border. They were gruesome milestones, blackened and deserted. As well as these ruins, large trucks and fuel tankers, bombed off the road, lay twisted and broken along the route, like scrap. We stopped occasionally; some of the others still had bowel problems, and needed to relieve themselves with monotonous regularity, squatting in the sand by the side of the road.

During these intervals, we sipped heavenly iced tea, from thermos flasks provided by the Red Cross.

Never quiet and retiring anyway, I now found myself unable to stop talking. For the whole ten-hour trip, I talked and talked, to anyone who would listen, and even to anyone who would not. It was my reaction to solitary confinement, to the fact that there had been so few opportunities to talk in the past seven weeks. I had missed, among other things, the sheer pleasure of conversation, the joy of communicating with my fellow human beings. Goodness knows if anybody took any notice of my endless wittering, but it did me good. Underneath the chatter, I realised we were not yet free. Despite the red crosses on our vehicles, we were still inside Iraq. But the wide desert and the sunlight were intoxicating after the narrow horror of the cells. It was enough that there were people there who wished us well.

Happiness is the Iraqi desert in the rearview mirror.

John Nichol: Designer Suit, as I called him, the smooth-talking, important-looking Iraqi civilian, came into my cell. He stared intently at the side of my face, still swollen and discoloured from the kicking the guards had given me when they had caught Larry and me at the window.

'Did somebody hit you?' he asked, as if this were something unheard of in Iraq.

'Yes,' I replied, resentfully. This was a bit rich.

'An Iraqi?'

Most of Iraq, I thought, has had a go, at one time or another.

'Yes.'

'Never. That is impossible. None of my people

would hit you. We are Arabs. We do not hit unarmed men.'

Not half, you don't, I thought, but the guy was sincere. He really believed that our captors had behaved with honour. It was almost a shame to disillusion him.

When he had gone, I heard the Lieutenant say to Larry next door, 'You will be going home soon.'

I could hardly bring myself to believe it. Iraq is a society that is fantastically insulated from the rest of the world, because of the iron grip that the all-pervasive, Orwellian agents of Saddam Hussein, the torture-happy Ba'ath Party, have on information. But this time, it was the truth.

Twenty minutes later, a line of ten prisoners, including JP, filed past my door. I was pressed up against it, my face tight against the bars. I was appalled. They were leaving me behind! Then I heard other captured fliers banging on the walls, realised that this was just the first batch, and the fear turned to joy. It would be my turn next. But the minutes dragged on, and then the hours, and no one came. They were keeping us in overnight! So close to freedom, that hurt. It was personal.

To make things worse, the various air forces of the Coalition cut sonic booms across the sky above the prison during the night, the F-15s and F-16s rolling in victory across Baghdad. 'Please, no,' I thought. 'Don't provoke them. Don't let it start again. I know I'm going to get out of here soon.' But there was no Triple-A to greet the display, so I hung onto the idea that all would be well, that the next day would see my release.

And so it proved twenty-four hours later. They came in, and offered me the chance to clean up a bit. I had a quick sluice down in tepid water. This provided only partial relief from the engrained filth. I was infested with body-lice by this time, tiny crabs that burrowed deep into the groin, itching horribly, a form of company that was impervious to anything but specialised treatment. After the wash, the guards served up a half-decent breakfast, and said, 'You will be going home in twenty minutes.'

Upon hearing this I knelt on the floor of my cell, and offered up a prayer of thanks. Prayer had helped sustain me throughout the ordeal. In this I was no exception: everyone had turned to something, to God, or whatever it was they believed in in place of God, many times during those hard days. The others I had talked to nearly all mentioned praying. And the mere fact of our survival, that was almost enough to make me believe in a guiding spirit of some sort, which had seen us through. It was a miracle we had survived the missile, the horrendous fire, a miracle we had survived the hail of bullets during capture, a miracle we had survived the relentless bombing, a miracle we had survived . . . But we *had* survived.

23

No-Man's-Land

John Peters: At the border with Jordan we crossed a wide strip of no-man's-land. Here, out in the middle of nowhere, pollution covered everything. There were boxes strewn across the sand, aged trucks without tyres, burned-out vehicles – all kinds of rubbish. It was like a scene from a futuristic film: *Mad Max* or something.

It was very cold. By the time we reached the checkpoint it was pitch dark, and we could only just make out the Jordanian soldiers in the glow of the headlights. This was the moment of maximum tension. This was where it could all go wrong. Were they going to change their minds and take us back? We had been treated like puppets for so long, we were afraid. A twitch on the string could haul us back to Baghdad.

There was a suffocating silence. But all of a sudden we were through, waved across the border into Jordan. A squad of soldiers advanced into the headlights to meet us, to act as our new escort. They told us there were helicopters somewhere, waiting to lift us out. This was extremely good news. They were kids, for the most part, and really jumpy. They had general purpose machine-guns mounted on the backs of their open jeeps, automatic rifles, red-chequered headdresses. Their nervousness was not surprising, given the weeks of phenomenal bombardment that had been going on just across the border. But looking at them, I really felt that I would not be safe, nor properly 'released', until I felt the firm and friendly grip of a

British hand on my arm. In the interim, it looked like anything might happen. The Jordanians were particularly nervous of our Iraqi guards, eyeing them at once with dislike and fear. Scared themselves, they were frightening. What eventually happened was that the Iraqis, aggressive to the last, handed us over with curt formality, turned their vehicles around, and raced back along the highway the way we had come. It was the most incredible relief to see the back of them.

Once they had gone, our new guards drove us very fast along a very bumpy road. Rounding a corner, we were blinded by bright white lights, as a motorcycle outrider pulled up alongside to escort us. We drove through this wall of light, emerging into a sort of compound on the other side. Inside this space was what looked like the other half of the world's journalists, the half we had not met in Baghdad. It was their camera lights, blazing in the desert night, that had blinded us temporarily. There was the same huge sweltering crowd of people. We had not expected this, not in Jordan.

The British and American Ambassadors to Jordan, along with several high-ranking US, Jordanian and British military officers came forward to meet us. The media were only about twenty metres away, corralled behind flimsy temporary fencing. With a sudden roar, they broke through it, charging across the intervening space, shoving and elbowing the VIPs out of the way to get at the POWs, fighting for the best camera-angles. I saw the British Ambassador, a man who was the soul of courtesy, elbowed in the face by a cameraman. As he was recovering from that, another cameraman pushed his head to one side, to get a clearer shot at us. The diplomats, used to more delicate negotiations, turned to confront them, to protect us, to hold back the tide. They may as well have tried to hold back the sea. It was complete mayhem.

Finally, we made it into a closed tent. The scene inside was straight out of *M.A.S.H.*, with olive-green stretcher-beds laid out in neat rows. Processed cheese, bread and cans of Fanta orange drink were set out on a table. The Red Cross had organised a second medical inspection, the standard once-over. A doctor took everybody's pulse and blood pressure, examined everyone's eyes. After this, there was the inevitable bureaucracy to satisfy, forms to be filled in in triplicate, before the Jordanians would hand us over to our respective welcoming committees. We were all determined to hang onto our yellow POW overalls for those fancy-dress parties in happier days to come. The last badges of our imprisonment, it was good to get them off. Western business corporations had donated all kinds of things to the POWs, including clothes, mostly sweat-shirts and the like. The powers that be told us to put these clothes on inside-out, because they did not want us used as free human advertising billboards, with great big logos screaming from our backs. They even told us to wear the baseball caps, courtesy of NBC News, inside-out. With all the seams showing on our clothing, we must have looked like complete half-wits.

We eventually managed to reach the cars that were meant to drive us the short distance to the waiting helicopters. But as soon as we had climbed inside them and shut the doors, the vehicles were engulfed by reporters and cameramen, and we were unable to move a centimetre in any direction. At a conservative estimate there were between one and two hundred news people swarming around the vehicles, sticking lenses up against the windows, shouting incomprehensible questions, banging on the bodywork to attract our attention. Then, when the Jordanians finally did open up a gap, it turned out that in all the excitement our driver had forgotten the ignition keys! At last, we inched ourselves free . . .

It was a fantastic relief when the helicopter rotors started turning, when we lifted clear of the crowd down below. In the helicopter, we ate chocolate-chip cookies, baked for us personally by the US Ambassador's wife.

We touched down in Amman. Officials quickly separated off the American POWs, so they could be processed by their own people. I was left on my own. Seeing me shivering in the cold air, one of the British reception team, a Wing Commander, draped his combat jacket round my shoulders. This sort of casual kindness was getting to me. But as we walked inside, although all kinds of conflicting feelings sloshed around inside me, I was still in control, still feeling fine, thinking, 'Well, here I am released then . . .', until I saw a familiar face walking towards me along the corridor. It was Chris Lunt, from our own squadron – part of the crew that had not managed to get airborne on that first fateful attack. Was it only seven weeks ago? He bounded towards me.

'John!' he exclaimed. All the pent-up emotions of the past weeks came crashing to the fore. It was like a dam bursting: I fell into his arms, crying like a baby. As I was blubbing, I was desperately annoyed at myself, trying to turn off the waterworks, shouting silently at myself: 'No! Stop . . .' But I could not stop. I was completely overcome. I must have sobbed quietly there for about five minutes, while everybody looked at their toes, or discovered bits of fluff on their clothing. When I had finally regained my composure, I stepped back and shook Lunty by the hand. One of the senior officers nearby remarked, 'Well, it probably was quite a good idea to have someone he knew come along, then!', which made us all laugh.

'Has someone got a handkerchief?' I asked, my eyes and nose still streaming. The officer who had spoken handed over a large square of white linen, which I filled with the most tremendous blast from my engorged hooter. When I had emptied most of my sinus cavities into it, I offered it back to him.

'No, no,' he said, recoiling from it in horror, 'that's quite all right; you hang onto it!', which made us all laugh again.

I was desperate to know whether John Nichol and all the others had been released, but Lunty interrupted me: 'Look, I'm sorry about this, but we need to know . . .' They all thought maybe, if they were really lucky, there would be one other missing RAF pilot or navigator still alive, but only one at the very most. Because they hadn't heard anything about the others since the broadcast, they had assumed the worst.

'Is John Nichol alive?' asked Chris.

'Yes, he's fine.'

'That's fantastic news. But . . . is that it? I mean, are there any more?' I could hear the tension in his voice.

'Yes,' I was happy to reply, 'there's Rupert Clark, Simon Burgess, David Waddington . . .'

He was bowled over. Nobody could quite believe it. Gathering round, they kept saying, 'Are you sure, are you sure?'

'Yes,' I said, 'I'm sure. I saw them all not twenty-four hours ago. They're all alive. Some of them are a bit smashed up, but they are basically OK. They should all be over soon, tomorrow probably . . .'

'That's fantastic!'

They had been convinced that Rupert was dead,

and in fact his navigator, Steve Hicks, had been killed. But no one knew for sure. True to form, the Iraqis had not released any names of captured aircrew.

The RAF had a VC-10 outside, waiting to whisk us off to Cyprus. I said goodbye to Chris, who was staying to meet the next batch of released POWs. Flight Lieutenant Rob Woods, from my squadron and my next-door neighbour at Laarbruch, turned up to escort me home, which was excellent. His brief had been to smooth my passage back to Laarbruch. They could not have chosen a better bloke for the job. What wasn't so excellent was that as we walked towards the aircraft, I kept farting. I suddenly noticed my fellow passengers were sagging away from me in their seats, frantically waving away the fumes. Johnny Fartpants or what? Lunty had brought with him a big biscuit tin, filled with chocolates and my favourite sweeties, Liquorice Allsorts. It was the liquorice on top of everything else that had done it. As if I did not smell bad enough already.

They gave me some food in the VC-10, but I was still jammed on transmit, chattering wildly to the crew. They must have been glad when I disappeared for a while, to shave off my beard in the toilet, an act that I'd looked forward to, a symbolic act, an act of freedom.

At RAF Akrotiri, in Cyprus, there was an ambulance waiting for us, which took us straight to hospital, to begin the process of rehabilitation. We wandered into the empty ward. The first thing I wanted to do was to telephone Helen. As we walked in, Rob and I started pleading with the nurse for a beer. She was all kindness, starch and cleanliness. I was trying to be charming in my rank dishevelment, but it wasn't working.

'No,' she said, 'certainly not, it's against the rules.' But a few minutes later, she returned with a six-pack of the local brew.

'Don't tell anybody I gave it to you,' she smiled.

It was about three o'clock in the morning, German time. But I was certain Helen would be up. She should know by now I was on my way home and would probably be celebrating. A male voice I immediately recognised as 'Tadge' – Flying Officer Martin Entwisle, one of the Squadron's single men – answered the telephone.

We instantly engaged banter mode: 'What are you doing with my wife at three o'clock in the morning?' I demanded.

He laughed. He said that Squadron Leader John Deane was there as well, with quite a few other people – everybody was toasting my release. Having wished me all the best, he went off to find Helen.

'Hello,' I said, 'it's me.'

'John, have you still got your balls?' she said immediately. She sounded great. It was fantastic to hear her voice again.

'Yes,' I said, 'I'm OK. Good to hear my wife is still a true English rose!'

'Well, we did all think the Iraqis might cut them off at one time, didn't we? Where are you?' she asked.

'Cyprus. I'll be here for a couple of days, then I'll be coming home.'

'Everybody's been round,' she said. 'We've got through twenty-one bottles of champagne! You'd better come home and join us.' Helen was . . . Helen! – pragmatic and funny. It was a very good feeling, talking to her.

Helen told me that nobody on the station had confirmation of who was alive. So she was delighted to learn that John Nichol, Simon Burgess, Robbie Stewart and Dave Waddington were all fine. But there was one more piece of amazingly good news, which was that Rupert Clark was alive and coming home. Virtually everyone on the base was convinced that Rupert had been killed. She dashed off after ten minutes to ring the Station Commander with the news. I put the telephone down. I was sorry the children were asleep.

I called my mother and father. My brother picked up the phone.

'I can't be too bad,' I said, in answer to Mark's droll questioning, 'I must be sane. The last time I was in Cyprus, Keo beer tasted like shit. I haven't had a beer for seven weeks, and it still tastes like shit.'

Rob Woods lunged over and grabbed the phone from me. 'Mark,' he said to my brother, 'don't worry about John. He's exactly the same, I can't shut the bastard up!'

I had been up for over twenty-four hours by now, but still did not want to sleep. At about nine o'clock, I decided to give Rob a break (he was bored rigid), and went off for a bath. The attention since being freed had been gratifying, but at the same time it had annoyed me slightly: you survive prison on your force of mind – all this fussing made me feel I was weak. I took my clothes off voluntarily for the first time in seven weeks. In the mirror, I saw a stick insect. I realised why they had been fussing: they were looking at a total weakling. Normally weighing in at around 160 lb, I was now less than 130 lb. There were salt-cellars where my collar-bones used to be, my stomach was hollow; my legs were so spindly you could distinguish every detail of the knee-joints. I examined my eye and the remaining bruises on my body. None of the damage looked very permanent, except possibly for the knee injury.

I climbed into the bath, my first proper bath for forty-seven days, and began soaping myself down. I did it thoroughly twice. That was just for starters. It took four heavy applications of the industrial strength medicated hospital shampoo to get the thick grime and grease out of my matted hair. After this first scrubbing, I let out all the dirty bath-water and cleaned the scum from the sides of the tub. Drawing a fresh bath, I lay back, lazing in the luxury of the steaming hot water. Bliss. Then I climbed into the cool, crisp, blue cotton hospital pyjamas. I felt almost clean.

When I got back to the ward, Rob was sitting in the middle of a pile of national newspapers, spread out around him on the bed. I stood stock still in the middle of the room when I saw what was on all the front pages. My own face was looking back at me. It must have been taken off the first Iraqi television broadcast, I realised, looking more closely. 'Crikey!' I thought. It was flattering that our story was 'news'. But the feeling of excitement wore off as the days went by. Over the next few weeks that attention would become more and more worrying.

The rest of this day was taken up with more medical examinations. Spinal X-rays revealed 'wedging' – two of my vertebrae had been crushed together, an injury they thought I had probably sustained during ejection from the Tornado. But the long-term prognosis, and the good news, was that I would be OK after intensive physiotherapy on my leg and back. The damaged knee, which was still giving me gyp, would return to normal use in time. I should certainly be able to fly again. This was a major weight off my mind.

Having reassured me on these points, one of the doctors, a man in his mid-fifties, then demonstrated the lung capacity test he wanted me to do next. 'You'll have no trouble beating an old codger like me on this one,' he said, 'a young man like yourself.' When he had registered his own mark, he handed me the machine. I took an enormous breath, and blew out with all my strength into the mouthpiece. It registered less than eighty per cent of his score. What a wimp! I was so used to my condition that I had come to accept it as normal and healthy. It wasn't.

The medics wanted everything – we had to give them stool samples, in a special tray they provided. I don't normally inspect my excrement, but I was surprised to discover that it was creamy white!

When the doctors had run out of tests, the Intelligence team took over. There were two of them. They didn't want much, just everything, from the moment we pulled the ejector handle over the desert, to getting out of the helicopter in Amman. Where were you and when? How do you know? What did it sound like? What did they do to you? Where did it happen? What did that interrogator look like? Did he have a moustache? What did the prison smell like? What colour was the paint on the walls? Who said what to you? How did they speak? Some of the questioning seemed trivial. But every apparently insignificant detail was cross-referenced with everybody else's answers, so that they could build up 'the big picture'. I had total recall, for the most part, which surprised me.

I was desperately tired after that. I had been up for forty hours. Severe stomach cramps meant that I had to excuse myself politely from time to time during the intensive debrief. At last, I returned to the ward and climbed into bed. Incredibly, it was hard to sleep. After so much time sleeping on a concrete floor it was uncomfortably comfortable. Used to being freezing cold, my body refused to adjust to the warmth, and for weeks afterwards the bedclothes were wet with my own sweat when I woke in the morning.

Everyone was impossibly kind and generous. But I behaved like a selfish squirrel. I took everything, and hoarded it, even if I didn't need it. I could not stop myself. In solitary confinement, there is no one but yourself to think of, and much of the time that is all you think about. Self-centredness had become a habit. Also, having been deprived for so long of material possessions, I wanted *things*; I wanted lots and lots of things around me that I could look at, own and touch. After a couple of days, I caught myself doing this, and apologised to people.

The same medical team that would later treat the British hostages released from Lebanon, including John McCarthy, was looking after us during this period, holding us carefully by the hand as we took our first tottering steps back to normality. This team was highly professional. Wing Commander Gordon Turnbull, who was in overall charge, had been involved in stress therapy for some time, and had counselled the victims and the rescuers after the Lockerbie bombing. Turnbull was not at all like the popular conception of a psychiatrist – far too plain-speaking and down-to-earth!

He sat us down and told us that Post-Traumatic Stress Syndrome is a universal human reaction: that people of all races, all ages and all walks of life undergo it; that it affects the body as well as the mind. After his initial lecture on post-traumatic stress, I found myself thinking, 'I'm all right, I don't really need all this.' But I also thought it was good we had people available to us, in case any of us needed it. 'Sharing our experiences' was not something we were used to in military life! There were various things we were supposed to do, designed to help us along the road to emotional rehabilitation. To begin with, two psychological social workers formed all us aviators into a circle for a group therapy session.

'What we'll do is introduce ourselves,' said the first woman, 'so that we all get to know one another . . .'

'Oh no,' I thought. 'Therapy for head cases, or what!'

Inevitably, when they thought the social workers were not looking, some of the guys started pulling ridiculous faces, aping about, scratching their armpits and generally pretending to be mad.

What I found most therapeutic at this stage were the unofficial things, the simple chats I had with Rob Woods. I needed to talk about what had happened frankly and calmly with a friend. It really helped.

Helen Peters: The morning after that first telephone call from John, I had to appear at a press pool briefing. How did I feel? Ecstatic, I said. Relieved, hugely thankful. But it was weird telling all these strangers about it. The main thing they wanted to know was what we first said to each other. What was it like talking to someone who a few weeks ago you thought might be dead? What did you say? I couldn't tell them very much, since 'Have you still got your balls?' was not exactly a question I wanted all over the front pages.

Some of the other stuff we talked about was classified for military reasons: for example, one or two of the other Squadron guys John had confirmed were alive had not yet been released; we did not want to foul things up for them. The press got quite frustrated, quite quickly. Some of the reporters obviously thought, from my apparent inability to answer their nice, simple questions, that I was either partially insane, or just plain stupid. I did manage one answer that made them laugh – and me blush.

One of the cheeky buggers asked, 'How will you pick up your love life again, after everything you've both been through?'

Without thinking, I replied, 'Oh, I expect we'll just slip back into it!'

24

Escape Committee

John Nichol: By the time they got around to the second batch of released POWs, a day later, the Red Cross had things much better organised at the Baghdad Novotel. Although the media were still camped outside its doors in strength, there was a path cleared to the hotel. We were whisked up a number of floors, out of reach of even the most intrepid drainpipe-climber. There was a suite set aside for us. A magnificent buffet met our eyes as we filed in through the doors: baked salmon, roast potatoes, cauliflower – fantastic, mouth-watering. Real food. The sight and smell of it! Proper, fresh, nourishing, well-cooked food. It was a forgotten luxury we were extremely happy to remember. Just breathing in the smells was a major digestive event. Schooled by the first batch of POWs, the Red Cross had provided another source of nourishment: boxes and boxes of Swiss chocolate. We gobbled up all this lovely grub.

There was a US Army medic with us called Rhonda, who had also just been released. Watching us stuffing our faces, she commented, 'Your enzyme co-factors X, Y and Z won't be able to handle all this food at once. You'll be sorry!' We all pooh-poohed this. She was absolutely right. Within the hour, my guts and everybody else's had gone completely berserk!

When we had finished eating for the moment, we all began chatting frantically, exchanging stories, catching up on what had happened in the war. Then came some bad news. 'Look, we're sorry,' said the Red Cross people, 'it's too windy, you can't fly out tonight. You will have to stay here. We'll fly you out in the morning.' This announcement was met with predictable gloom. But the delay wasn't our only worry. Out of the windows, we could see crowds gathering and advancing on the hotel, for all the world like a huge lynch-mob. What on earth was happening? It was not beyond Saddam Hussein to stage a 'spontaneous' popular demonstration, releasing the anger of the oppressed Iraqi people, with unfortunate consequences for us.

'Who's protecting us?' I asked.

'We are,' replied an official, a woman of about twenty-eight.

'And who's protecting you?'

'Our Red Cross will protect us,' she answered, pointing at her badge. This was courageous if unconvincing.

Nobody wanted to sleep that night. We split into small groups, gathering in various bedrooms, with people coming and going all the time. We could not stop ourselves talking. We had to keep telling our stories, over and over again. For breakfast we had wonderful hot croissants, aromatic coffee, honey, jam and marmalade, boiled eggs.

A message came through to say that all of the British POWs must cover their faces with blankets when they left the hotel. This was presumably to prevent the waiting press identifying the POW being released. The Iraqi mob was outside too. They were curious to see these people who had wreaked havoc on their country. We had to fight our way past them. Keeping our faces hidden, even with the blankets, was a tricky business. Photographers thrust their cameras up against the windows of the bus at all angles, and we had to crouch down low between the seats to avoid being filmed. We got onto the bus all right, but once on it we sat in the carpark for an hour. We were stuck. The news people would not move back; the Iraqi crowd would not move back. Eventually an armed escort was called; we edged free.

On the way to the airport, we had a guided tour of Baghdad. One of the Iraqi escorts showed us the main points of interest, only in this case they were not the usual tourist sites, but the results of the Coalition bombing. He seemed almost proud of them. We passed the remains of the telephone exchange, a blackened mass of twisted girders, nothing more. Amazingly – and when you were on the ground close by, it was absolutely amazing – this ruin was flanked on either side by substantial department stores, neither of which showed the slightest damage. A power-station was next, similarly flattened, the surrounding buildings untouched. It was just as striking to see the *un*damaged parts of the city. The centre of Baghdad was much like any cosmopolitan city anywhere: there were the stand-ard, large luxury stores, some of them bearing signs in English, and the international hotels, like the one we had just been in. It was a complete contrast to the Iraq we had seen up until then.

Regular Iraqi troops were swarming all around Saddam Hussein International when we got there, but the airport's doors were firmly bolted against us. We sat outside, for what seemed like hours, until the doors suddenly swung open, and wave after wave of return-ing Iraqi prisoners of war started streaming out. They must have been among the first to come home. We thought they might even be returning in exchange for ourselves. After an age, when this flood had dried up to a trickle, they let our group go through. Then all at once we were on the plane, with the stewards making the doors safe, and the cheerful Swiss pilots chatting over the intercom. We settled back in our seats, relaxing in the naïve belief that we were safe at last. But the Iraqis had reserved one more little treat for us, and a most terrifying, skin-crawling and horrifying one it was.

Looking out across the airfield, we had noticed that every single hangar, every single Hardened Aircraft Shelter, all the major installations had been blown to bits. Only the terminal remained intact, an exception that must have been a deliberate decision on some Allied planner's part, given the thoroughness of the destruction everywhere else. What had also survived were the dozens of Triple-A sites that littered the airfield. As we began taxying out of the holding bay, all the Iraqi soldiers who had been loitering around doing nothing much were suddenly galvanised into action. They started running towards these gun-emplacements. Only there was no raid. As if at a signal, the gunners trained the barrels of their weapons directly at our civilian airliner.

It may have been no more than an empty gesture of defiance, but a graveyard hush settled over the interior of that aircraft. We were so vulnerable.

'No, they wouldn't dare . . .'

'They can't be . . .' and less optimistically, 'What have they got to lose?'

The long black barrels swung with our progress along the taxiway. The Iraqis were having fun, we told ourselves, they were snapping their fingers in our face. It was an empty threat. But it was a very sick kind of fun when you saw those guns sighted up on you. Rolling down that runway for take-off, we all had our heads down. You could hear the prayers go up. As the aircraft's wheels came unstuck from the tarmac, the most tremendous resounding spontaneous cheer went up, ringing out as we soared clear of the Iraqi guns. The blankets and coffee the Swissair staff brought round immediately after this were extremely welcome – we were in need of a little warmth after the shock. But they were nowhere near as welcome as the two F-15s that came out to meet us while we were still in Iraqi airspace. Pulling slow victory rolls as they approached, the fighters pulled up alongside us, until they were sitting very close on our wings. Brilliant infra-red flares began streaming out behind the fighters, the pilots releasing them as a victory symbol, a celebration of our liberty. One of the pilots took his mask off, and began punching the air with his fist, in the American victory sign. Strangely, we were all having difficulty with our vision. It was a very emotional moment.

Not to be outdone, two RAF Tornado F3s turned up next, the Tornado air defence variant, a 'stretched' version of our own GR1. In the context, they were a truly beautiful sight. In proper British style, the pilots contented themselves with waving at us – but it was enthusiastic waving! I was up in the cockpit with a headset on. It was very, very moving speaking to one of the F3 pilots over the radio. Somehow the sight of those friendly aircraft, shepherding us home, brought our freedom into sharp focus.

Keying the mike, I said, 'It's fantastic to see you . . . I never thought I would be glad to see an air defence guy on my wing . . .' (As bomber crews, we normally hate fighter jocks!) The four fighters, two British, two American, escorted us into Saudi airspace. There was another resounding cheer as we crossed the border, leaving Iraqi airspace for ever – we hoped. Now we really were beyond reach.

As we came in to land at the huge Saudi military airbase in Riyadh, home for the duration to a large percentage of the Allied Air Forces, we could see a huge reception lined up for us on the tarmac below. Every Allied Air Force person who could get away was there to greet us; there were thousands and thousands of them. The Americans were lined up, clapping and cheering, but what brought a prickling of tears to the eyes was the British crews. They were formed up, in the thirty-degree heat, in uniform, standing rigidly to attention in our honour. It was like a scene from *The Bridge on the River Kwai*. That brought a lump to my throat all right. It was important not to let rip with the waterworks just then, however; there was too large an audience!

As we taxied up to the red carpet that had been rolled out for us, we were staring out of the windows, overwhelmed by the sight outside. Somebody shouted, 'Hey, there's Schwarzkopf!' We had just come from the desolation of Baghdad, and now this! We stumbled down the steps of the aircraft, dazzled by the bright sun. We met 'Stormin' Norman', General Norman Schwarzkopf.

'Welcome home, you guys,' he said. 'You've done a great job.' He was flanked by the Air Commander British Forces, Air Vice-Marshal Bill Wratten, and the British Ambassador to Saudi Arabia. Saudi Arabia was represented by the Prince Regent. This was amazing and brilliant, and quite unexpected. We were extremely pleased to meet Stormin' Norman, it was an honour; he had grown almost legendary in a matter of months, even before the war started. But ... just beyond General Schwarzkopf, just beyond the collection of VIPs clustered around him, were our aircrew mates, including the familiar face of my mate Flight

Lieutenant Chris Lunt, from XV Squadron! I had not expected to see anyone I knew, let alone a friend. Seeing Lunty, my resolve to keep a stiff upper lip was shattered. I ran over to him. His friendly face had the same effect on me as I later learned it had had on JP. We had a bawl!

Following this tearful reunion, we were all whisked off to a waiting Hercules. I settled down for the short hop to King Khaled Military City (KKMC) airfield, where we would pick up a second plane for the trip to Cyprus.

One of the Hercules' crew came up to me: 'Flight Lieutenant Nichol, I think you should see this . . .' He was holding out a British newspaper report from the early days of the war, which stated that John Peters and myself had been tortured and killed . . . Then there was a second newspaper article, again front page, giving the news of our release. It showed JP arriving in Cyprus, and had a picture of Helen, Guy and Toni at home. There was also a picture of me, the one that had been taken off the Iraqi television broadcast. It wasn't this picture that got to me, though that was bad enough: it was the report itself, which said that my parents were battened down behind closed doors. They were prisoners of the press. The story said that they did not know I was alive! The news was shattering. It was appalling. I could see my parents sitting in the dark, the house shuttered up like a bunker while the press, eager as ever to sensationalise, prowled about outside. It was more than I could take. I found it hard to control myself.

Squadron Leader Gordon Buckley was waiting to greet the aircraft at KKMC. Normally my Flight Commander on the Squadron, he was to be my personal escort home. I could not have wished for a better one. We hugged each other a bit, then he stepped back and said, 'Nichol, you stink. You need to get rid of that stuff you're wearing.' He handed me over a clean flying-suit. He also gave me a goodie-bag: by the time I was released, the powers that be had realised that the POWs had nothing other than the disgusting clothes they stood up in. And no one, after all, knew what to expect, or even how many of us would be coming out. The goodie-bag was an Aladdin's cave. It held a Walkman personal stereo, fluffy white clean towels, soap (soap!), entire galaxies of mouth-watering chocolate . . . it was good to be back, bang in the middle of consumer capitalism. But despite the distractions of alcoholic drink, and my favourite meal, chicken tikka and all the trimmings, some of the flight to Cyprus passed in a blur, as the anxiety about my parents kept on bubbling up.

Still, by the end of it I was feeling better, laughing and joking with Gordon. We drove over to the hospital. As I walked through the entrance, the first person I saw was John, John Peters, striding towards me. He looked squeaky clean, but skeletal, definitely not as large as life. We had a couple of victory hugs. It was absolutely fantastic to see him. We had come through, and that was ecstasy.

As with JP and all the other released POWs, Wing Commander Gordon Turnbull, a superb man, was overseeing my rehabilitation. He strode into the meeting-room.

'What do you guys want?' he asked. What did I want? I was desperate, desperate, desperate to get to a telephone. The thought that my parents still had no idea whether I was alive or dead, and were worrying themselves sick, was consuming me.

Some of the hospital staff appeared, wanting us to go through some medical checks, but I was adamant: 'A telephone,' I said. 'That's what I want! Get me a telephone now!' I got my telephone. But I did not get my parents – at least not immediately.

Instead, a voice said, 'Caller, what number are you trying to get?'

'What?' I replied, in outrage. I had dialled my home number – so what was happening?

What was happening was that my parents had been so harassed by the media that their telephone calls were being intercepted. On top of that, the operator could hardly hear me, the line was so bad. After so long, after so much heartache, it was incredibly frustrating: I screamed down the telephone, 'Put me through, put me through! I'm John Nichol! I'm their son.'

The operator kept replying, in a cool Newcastle voice, 'What number are you calling?' I must have sounded just like a frustrated journalist.

I slammed the telephone down. Grabbing another phone card, I rang my elder brother's home, in Welwyn Garden City. No sooner did I hear Paul's voice than I broke down in tears. He started crying too; my sister-in-law, Angela, came to the telephone, she was weeping for joy. It was her birthday. There was not a lot of coherent conversation, but there were plenty of long pauses.

'Calm down,' Paul managed to say eventually. 'Give me your number.' I gave it to him. He called my sister Teresa, who lives around the corner from my parents. Teresa dashed round to them with my number; they then telephoned me in Cyprus.

My breakdown on the phone to Paul was as nothing to the tear-floods now. The first sound of my dear mother's voice was enough.

I was dimly aware of John Peters coming into the room. Despite the fact I had not spoken to him for so long, I was utterly unable to speak to him then. Immediately recognising what was happening, he simply bent down, gave me a quick hug, and went out again. Through the haze, I remember him saying, as he went through the door, 'Don't worry, everyone has reacted like that.'

I wasn't worried.

The next thing on the agenda was a recuperative beer. As far as I could make out, there was none to be had in the immediate vicinity – I had already checked the bedside cabinet. Considering that we hadn't had a beer for a couple of months, this looked like something of an oversight. Rupert Clark and I had been released together, and he felt pretty much about the beer shortage as I did. All psychological rehabilitation programmes should invariably include beer, we decided; it was an essential lubricant in easing the old emotional springs. We diagnosed one another as being sadly lacking in carbohydrates and in real need of some liquid sustenance. So we became the first Allied POWs to form an escape committee! We managed to convince one of the medical team to drive us down to the bar in the Officers' Mess – only for one quiet beer, of course. We did have the one quiet beer, but it was rapidly followed by about ten extremely noisy ones! What could be better therapy, we asked ourselves, than to be back in a RAF bar with a few beers and a fair sprinkling of attractive women? The President of the Mess invited us to drink at the Mess's expense for as long as we liked – we needed no second bidding! – prison breath and all. With the huge number of aircrew passing through Akrotiri, the atmosphere was extremely convivial: there were friends there I had trained with and had not seen for years. What we did not realise in our cups was that there had been a terrorist alert in Cyprus on that very same day, and the whole island was in a state of high security. So within a moment or so of our disappearing from our hospital beds, there was a general assumption we had been kidnapped, with the resulting rumpus. The Officers' Mess bar was the last place they thought of looking for us: too obvious. We returned to the hospital a little the worse for wear and a bit ashamed at having caused the people who were looking after us such trouble. 'Twas good fun though!

25

Homeward Bound

John Nichol: Like JP, I had Gordon Turnbull to help me get back onto the straight and narrow path of sanity. He began with a mini-lecture. Post-Traumatic Stress Disorder (PTSD) is not a disease, he said, but a syndrome; it can and does affect anyone, and there is nothing 'unmanly' about experiencing it. There are many symptoms:

Violent outbursts
Unwillingness to talk about experiences
Unexplained changes in character
Self-loathing for surviving when others did not
Self-isolation
Inability to readjust to normal life
Inability to communicate with loved ones, or to reciprocate love
The desire to be with others undergoing it, who 'understand'
Flashbacks and nightmares brought on by reminders of the trauma.

Turnbull told us the danger is that when the symptoms appear, and in most people they invariably do, the sufferer thinks that he or she is going 'mad' or has a psychiatric problem. That person then tries to ignore or hide the problem, which can lead to more trouble, and can sometimes become very damaging.

He said the most important thing was to talk about our experience and not to bottle it up or ignore the feelings. In the weeks, months and years to come, it was possible that some of the features of PTSD would appear. He asked us to bear in mind that expert help would always be available. We spent a number of sessions going over the whole affair and how we felt about our captors and ourselves, if we harboured any hatred towards them for our torture. Being military aircrew, we were sceptical about baring our souls. But in retrospect, everyone agrees that the whole thing was necessary.

John Peters: During the rehabilitation programme, they told me that if I needed more time, or if they found anything wrong with me, they would fly Helen out to join me.

'Gibber a bit at the medics,' Rob joked, 'and we can all get a free holiday in Cyprus!' Unfortunately, I was pronounced physically and mentally fit enough to return home.

When it did come to going back home, there were some major surprises in store. One of the biggest was the HS125 jet laid on by the RAF as my personal transport to Laarbruch. This just doesn't happen to junior Flight Lieutenants. The Base Commander at RAF Akrotiri was there to bid me goodbye. He shook my hand. As I mounted the aircraft steps, the RAF Corporal on the door snapped to attention, executing a textbook salute. That doesn't happen to the likes of me very often, either!

On the flight to Germany, with the whole plane to ourselves, Rob Woods and I were like a couple of small kids in their Daddy's new car, working the seat mechanisms to see how far we could recline, clicking the ashtrays, badgering the indulgent steward for extra goodies.

When we reached RAF Laarbruch, there was another shock: Air Marshal Sir Roger Palin, Commander-in-Chief, RAF Germany, and the Station Commander, Group Captain Neil Buckland, were waiting for me. The latter looked as though he had been in the wars himself: he was supporting a broken ankle. They were saying things like 'Whatever you want, we will organise it . . .'

'The press are after you,' they told me, 'but we will attempt to keep them at arm's length. What do you need?'

One great advantage to living inside the perimeter of a front-line military base like Laarbruch is that the media can, if necessary, be kept firmly outside, or at least controlled when they are allowed in. We walked towards the cavalcade of black cars. Rob had done the hard work of seeing me through virtually the whole process of release and return, and had been forced to listen to my endless chatter all the way back home. Now we parted company. It struck me that certain people are singled out and hyped to the skies, regardless of their worth; others, perhaps more deserving, are ignored.

We reached the car. There, the Station Warrant Officer, Mr Hogan, saluted me, holding open the car door and shaking my hand firmly. He made me feel very proud.

On the way to the Ops Wing where Helen was waiting, the Station Commander said, 'When you've had half an hour, or however long you want, with Helen, would you mind if we came and shared some champagne with you? We'd like to celebrate your release.'

Having gone through the long emotional reunion with Chris Lunt, and having already spoken to Helen on the phone, I assumed I would be fine. But as I walked up the path that led to the Operations Wing, the ground began to quiver and dissolve. I looked up. Helen was there, at the top of the steps, holding Toni in her arms. Guy came toddling out from behind her, down the stairs towards me, his thick mop of hair shining.

'Daddy!' he shouted. I gathered him into my arms, hugged him a long, long hug. I had worried so much in prison that he might have forgotten me, it was fantastic that he still recognised me. In his busy little world, where everything was new all the time, I might have been gone for only a few days. I was overwhelmed.

Then Helen was in my arms and we held one another, long and close. It felt like forever since we had parted. In a little while, we went inside together. Toni, who had been only two months old when I left, a little baby, now looked completely different, a diminutive grown-up, her character emerging. She looked completely adorable, so pretty. My happiness at being with them again was almost unbearable. Helen and I chatted for a while, about this and that, keeping it light, then there was a knock on the door. A woman came in, very well dressed and very friendly. I had never seen her before.

'Hello,' she said, smiling. 'How lovely to see you. Shall we have a little champagne?' This was Lady Palin, Sir Roger's wife. When the champagne had been drunk and we were all feeling bubbly we climbed back into the car to go and meet the press. They shouted questions, endless questions, which I could never have answered. There was nothing I felt up to saying. But they took a library of photographs. When they had finished snapping, we drove round to the base married quarter that had been our family home for the past two years, one in a street full of identical houses. The whole community had turned out to meet us, all our friends. Balloons and banners with the words 'Welcome home John', 'Welcome home Rob' were everywhere, along with a huge crowd of people. It looked like half the base was there. It was incredibly moving. Lots of people were crying; we were all hugging one another. Disregarding the suggestions that we would want to be alone, we went straight on to Rob's house, next door, and began a party. We wanted to put ourselves back on the map. Having a drink on base with friends and family, that was when it began to feel like being back home. I felt very much a part of it all again – the Squadron, the Air Force.

Helen Peters: I didn't actually see John coming down the steps of the aircraft. The RAF didn't want John and me to have this big meeting at the foot of the runway in front of the world's press, like we were Humphrey Bogart and Ingrid Bergman or something. We didn't want that either. Some things have to remain private. Still, it was odd to be told that the C-in-C Germany and Station Commander would be welcoming John back publicly, but that I would not. After I thought about it for a minute, I decided they were right. It was better, for John, to have that time alone. So I waited in the VIP lounge with the Senior Medical Officer and the children.

A black car drew up at the door, and John got out. I could see that he was near the edge. I was on the edge of tears myself. 'I mustn't,' I thought, 'not if he's going to.' Guy was getting upset. If he saw both his parents in tears, he'd be bound to start crying too,

Toni would join in, and then where would we be – all weeping, collapsed in a wet little heap!

John just needed a few minutes to collect himself. He was painfully, impossibly thin.

26
Media Blitz

John Nichol: Throughout the whole process of release and repatriation, the Royal Air Force treated us absolutely magnificently. They asked us what we wanted to do, and then did it for us. What we wanted, not surprisingly, was the speediest possible reunion with our families and friends.

My parents had never left the shores of Great Britain before. The first time they ever did leave the country was to welcome home a son they thought had been killed. Not bad for your first trip abroad. The RAF detailed a VIP jet to pick them up in Newcastle, served them coffee on board from the VIP china, which thrilled my mother, whisked them over to RAF Laarbruch, put them up overnight in VIP accommodation, and provided a private room for our first reunion. We could not have asked for more, and we would certainly have expected less. For my parents, it was the trip of a lifetime.

My group of released POWs landed at Laarbruch on Sunday, 10 March, after the long flight from Cyprus, to the sight of crowds of well-wishers standing on the tarmac waving and cheering. As we took our first steps back onto home ground, the exploding flashes from the hordes of press photographers seemed to make the bright spring day even brighter. The Commander-in-Chief, RAF Germany, was there to meet us, along with his wife, a wonderful lady who seemed more overcome than the rest of us. It was a fantastic reception.

A car whisked me off to a private reunion with my mother and father, and Paul. I walked down the corridor to find them all standing in one of the Ops Rooms. I didn't really say anything. I couldn't. All four of us were just standing there holding each other; words were not necessary. After a while we sat down and chatted about little things like how the rest of the family were getting on. It soon became clear that everybody had had a worse time than I had, thanks to the relentless attention of the press and the wildly variable reports, both official and in the media.

I can forgive my captors for my own treatment, but I will never forgive them for the pain and torment that my family endured, all because the Iraqis refused to release the names of the people they held.

After our private reunion we adjourned to the Officers' Mess for a more public party.

It was undoubtedly the best day of my life!

It was Mothering Sunday.

When I returned home with them to the northeast of England, it was to what I can only describe as a hero's welcome. I didn't feel much like a hero, but they gave me the full treatment anyway. The local press had really picked up on the 'local lad shot down' story. It is hard to describe the intense quality of the local response, different in kind to the national attention, or to the more reserved acclaim John Peters told me he received down south. A warm people, the Geordies took me noisily to their hearts. It was great – the perfect antidote to the hatred and isolation of Iraq. My family has always lived in North Shields, and has all kinds of ties to the community. Across the road from our house is a large school. Its windows were colourful with Union Jacks, its walls bedecked with Welcome

Home posters, with Good Luck messages. The children there had adopted my cause for the duration of the war. This was true of several other schools in the area. I had a lot of thanking to do. I visited all the schools, met the children, or rather they mobbed me, yelling for autographs! I visited the local police force, which had done a superb job protecting my besieged parents around the clock. Finally, I called on our local British Telecom guys, who had been so helpful in stopping the press harassment.

Venturing out, the response was amazing, people stopped me in the street to congratulate and hug me. They were complete strangers for the most part, but they suddenly seemed like part of some giant extended family. I went out in the evening with my brothers and sister to some of the pubs we had frequented as teenagers. No sooner did we set foot across the threshold than the music would be turned off, someone would jump onto the stage and welcome us over the PA system . . . People would crowd round, competing to offer us free drinks. It was completely unexpected, and quite hard to believe. And it was wonderful.

The only thing was that every time there was a loud bang, or any kind of sudden noise, I jumped out of my skin. We had all noticed this, when we were on our way out, in Iraq and in Cyprus. We would be standing in a room, a door would slam, and there we were, all taking cover, terrified half to death. It was part of my post-traumatic stress, the result of the bombing, when the prison came down around our ears. There was a railway line about half-a-mile south of my parents' house. I lost count of the number of times I found myself sitting bolt upright, staring into the dark, sweating as a train went rumbling past. The noise was no longer comforting. It was just like the rumble of the incoming bombs.

During the war, everybody in the family was in touch every day. It drew them all closer together. It was something I noticed immediately when I got home.

I had received lots of letters from prisoners all over the world, Israel, India, Russia. Most of them were addressed very simply: The Navigator, North Shields, England. Or The Pilot, Newcastle. Flowers came every day, masses and masses of them.

John Peters: The next day, Helen showed me the scrapbooks, filled to bursting with the press cuttings she had collected over the course of the war and since. The extent of the coverage was staggering. In almost every case, there was a photograph of myself and John, *the* photograph, the one taken from Iraqi television. The impact of that shot! Along with the press reports, there was a sack of letters you could wade through, sent to me by well-wishers during the course of the war. There were literally hundreds of them. Helen had received between forty and fifty a day while the conflict lasted, and there had been hundreds more since my return home. Many of them were beautiful, some were funny, some religious in tone and some downright nutty! There were a few from other people who had been POWs and prisoners of conscience. I felt kinship with them, but unworthy compared with many, like the man who wrote about having spent eight years as a prisoner in the Soviet Union. I was determined to answer them all, and succeeded in the end.

With the letters was a small mountain of bracelets, mostly made of copper. These had my name and rank engraved on them with 'Iraq' and the date I went missing in action, so I would be remembered until I was released or confirmed dead. They also had little messages like 'Praying daily for your release'. Touching and charming, these bracelets were from Americans, from ordinary citizens who had started wearing them when news of my capture became public. People in the United States had begun adopting individual prisoners in this way during the Vietnam War. The idea was to send the bracelet to the prisoner when he (or she) got back home. John Nichol had a stack of letters waiting for him too; but where mine were nearly all from families, expressing wishes for my safe return, his were from women! Quite a few of them contained photographs. There were enticing physical descriptions of the senders, with suggestions that he might like to meet them: 'Hello, I'm blonde, five feet ten inches tall, and I live in . . .' Might? Try stopping him! It was going to be hell for him working his way through that lot . . .

Helen Peters: Some men are born great, some achieve greatness, and some have media attention thrust upon them. After John's capture, everyone on the station, from the checkout girls at the NAAFI Stores to the Station Commander's wife, was extremely kind to me. They showed me support in all kinds of ways. But because of the peculiar circumstances of his imprisonment and release, John came back about two weeks before the rest of the Squadron. Unfortunately, nobody on base was able to tell the other wives when their husbands would be coming back. Instead, there was a rumour circulating that XV Squadron might have to remain in the Gulf for a few months longer, as part of a post-war peacekeeping force!

It was impossible to hide the from incessant calls from interested journalists, and the camera-crews outside the gates. Some journalists were stooping to all kinds of low tricks, like approaching Laarbruch kids at the gates of the station school, which was off-base, and asking them questions like: 'Does your Daddy know any of the pilots who were shot down?'

John was having to visit the doctor daily for his knee and his back, and everyone was very helpful. On a base of about 6,000 people, 5,995 were just fantastic to us. But it was difficult to avoid bad feeling altogether. This whole business was a perfect test of character – it showed up the minuscule small-minded minority from the lovely, vast, generous majority.

We were able to pop away for a few days at this time, thanks to the Commander-in-Chief, Germany, who generously allowed us to use Service accommodation in Berlin. The RAF flew us out there with Rupert Clark and his wife Sue for four days of perfect bliss. It was like the war in reverse, suddenly being plunged back into civilisation. But in some ways, the best thing of all was that we were able to escape back into anonymity for a spell, have a rest, and sightsee in Berlin.

John Peters: Helen and I met up with John in London for *Wogan*. It is hard to describe how strange this all was: the nerves, the build-up. The last time we'd been on TV, we were answering questions with a pistol as prompter.

Terry Wogan, the genial host, proved in some ways a harder interrogator to outwit than the Iraqis. A great deal more charming, his questioning was a lot more difficult to handle. The BBC softened us up a bit first, paying for our overnight accommodation, and providing cars to the studio. We were very nervous, Helen, John and I, when they met us at Television Centre, though they did their best to calm us down, in hospitality, or 'hostility' as Wogan calls it, with a drink or two.

Another guest on the show, the American actor and singer David Soul, was in hospitality with us. John Nichol had his brother and sister-in-law with him, I had my brother and sister-in-law, Helen had her brother along ... David Soul looked around at all these people and remarked, 'Hey, you guys got more entourage with you than Sylvester Stallone!'

They escorted us downstairs. We watched from the wings as the warm-up man completed his routine. Then the studio manageress seated us in front of the audience. Wogan was wandering about among the cameramen at the back of the set, with a cup of coffee, chatting. They sat us down in the studio before transmission, to help us get used to the lights and the atmosphere. But the nerves came flooding back as the clock ticked down towards transmission time.

We had a set of fifteen questions, agreed between ourselves and the researcher, that Wogan had been briefed to ask us. The authorities had told us we were not to say anything about our time in the Gulf, from the moment our feet touched the ground after we were shot down in Iraq, till the moment they touched the ground in Cyprus after we were released from Iraq. There were, they said, various legal and security reasons for this. So Wogan was supposed to stick to his list of questions. He didn't.

At the start of the interview, he told the viewers, 'For diplomatic reasons, we've been asked not to talk about the circumstances of their capture, or their treatment in captivity.'

He began by asking a few basic questions: 'What is

it like to be home?' and so forth. But, like everybody else, he wanted to know what had happened to us in captivity, what had the Iraqis done to us?

He turned to Helen: 'It must have been horrific for you to see John's picture, of course, the pictures that were put up for propaganda purposes?'

'It was a relief, though,' she replied, 'because until then, I had no idea whether they were alive or not. So although it was obviously very upsetting and very frightening to see they being held by the Iraqis, it was also a great relief.'

'Yes, but they looked so terrible . . .' He paused. 'It looked as if they had been beaten up.'

We did not want to say, 'No, we weren't', because we did not want people to think we had gone down without a fight. On the other hand, we had been instructed to say nothing . . .

John Nichol jumped in to the rescue: 'He looks like that all the time.'

'Especially on Friday night,' I replied.

'Well, Saturday morning,' chipped in Helen.

'Were you instructed to say anything on Iraqi tele-vision?' Wogan went on, never one to give in easily.

'That's getting into an area that we haven't finished being debriefed from by our own people,' answered John quickly.

We were on live television. The RAF had not given us any public relations training, or advice on how to handle a professional like Terry Wogan. It would have come in useful. We were and are professional aviators, not media performers.

The only interesting thing about John Peters and John Nichol was what had happened to them during the seven weeks they were held in Iraq. Unfortunately, that was the one thing we could not discuss.

When we had been grilled by Wogan, his researchers and producer took us all out to dinner, about eighteen of us. It was a good night.

27

In Memoriam

John Nichol: Everyone asked us if our experiences in the Gulf had changed us in any way, and the answer, on the whole, was probably yes, although not in the way we, or other people, had quite expected. People thought that when we came home, our basic characters would be changed, that we might, for example, be 'broken'. But it was not like that, not as banal as that; it was more that we viewed life from a slightly different angle. Speaking for myself, I was more impatient, less ready to accept delay. At the same time, I was less argumentative than before. Now I will tend to let a point go rather than worry it to death, as I would have done in the past. The big thing is that I feel I haven't got time to waste. I live life to the full, even more fully than before. I no longer worry about money. I live my life as if it might end any day.

Sometimes, it lived itself for me. The first time I noticed it, I was driving on the A1, travelling to meet a girlfriend in London. I suddenly found myself back in Baghdad. I realised that these flashbacks had been happening for some time: I had regularly been reliving the fear without really acknowledging it. I found it very difficult to reconcile the fact that I was back in civilisation, leading a normal life, when a few weeks earlier I had been waiting for that step outside my cell door. Who was lying on that cell floor now, waiting for that footstep?

*

RAF FAIRFORD, GLOUCESTERSHIRE. *John Peters:* The main thing for me was that I had had seven weeks taken out of my life. That does not sound like a long time, and it isn't, when you consider that some of the US POWs in Vietnam spent seven years and more in the cage. But the point was that for those weeks I had absolutely no control over my life: they could give me food and blankets, or they could come in and kick me half to death. That is why I now wanted to get on with my life, to live it exactly the way I wanted. Other people had wasted enough of my time.

I can remember sitting in my cell, and thinking, 'I made a little money selling my house before I came out – that was a waste of time, wasn't it? Why on earth didn't we spend some of it?' Now, like John Nichol, I rarely hesitate when it comes to spending money. I am not sure if this is a good thing, or if it will last, but it is certainly a reaction to the time wasted in captivity.

One way in which the experience has changed me for the better, I hope, is by making me more attentive to my family. In prison, I became very strongly aware of how your family is a great source of strength. Sitting in solitary, one of my most bitter regrets was that I had failed to buy Guy a birthday present, before going out to the Gulf. With all the build-up to war, I got caught up in a big exercise out of RAF Leeming, and I was away for the actual birthday. That was fair enough. What was bad, though, was that I put absolutely no effort into buying his present, leaving the whole responsibility for it to Helen. It is easy, in the general run of things, to let these matters slide; there is always another birthday to celebrate . . . Well, sometimes there isn't. That was my lesson from the Gulf War, or one of them: I had to put in more time with my family. Sometimes there is no tomorrow.

Gradually, the combination tumblers of a 'normal' life began clicking gently back into place. It was fun becoming a daddy again. There remained, however, one big problem: the media. Anyone who has become the focus of intense media interest faces the same peculiar problem: choose the wrong stepping stone on your way to dry land, and you, your story, your credibility and perhaps even your career will be washed away in the flood of hyperbole.

But there was a good side to it. Suddenly, after the war, we were in a position to make a lot of cash for charity – the Gulf Memorial Fund. Together John and I did three airshows and were lucky enough to raise over £30,000. People were very generous. We were walking on air. For the first time, we really understood what it is to be free. Not only that, but everyone was treating us like heroes.

Sometimes, though, things happen that bring you back to earth, and cast your own experiences into shadow. At one of these airshows, RAF Fairford in Gloucestershire, the mother of a little boy with advanced leukaemia asked if he could meet us and look over the Tornado.

He was about six or seven. A baseball cap covered his head where the harsh chemotherapy had made him bald. Chatting quietly to his mother, she told us he was extremely ill. The first thing we did was gather up all the various prints and memorabilia we could lay our hands on, and give them all to him. His face shone with happiness, but he was still extremely shy. We walked him around the aircraft, both of us taking turns carrying him when he did not want to walk. Then we tried to help him up into the cockpit. He climbed the first two rungs of the ladder without help, but then shyness got to him and he started to cry.

None of us could coax him up the rest of the steps. We didn't want to lift him against his will, so we had to give up the whole idea. His mum crouched down, trying to console him. I looked at him standing there as his mother comforted him, a sad little figure weeping in his baseball cap. He made me think of Guy.

There we were, still in good health, and enjoying life; anything we might have been through, or that our families might have been through, paled alongside what that boy's mother, and the boy himself, had to live through. How did she cope with the knowledge that her child was very ill, and likely to die? How would she cope when he did die? We had been given the world's attention, accolades. What would this woman be offered on the loss of her child?

Even now, all some people see is the superficial glitter of the media attention. The 'glitter' has been fun. But for all the nice things that have happened to us, we would rather have flown twenty-one successful combat missions than get our guts kicked out in prison. Ours was a nasty, dirty, grubby little war.

CORNWALL. *John Nichol:* The whole Squadron travelled over to the UK in a VC-10 specially laid on by the RAF for Steve Hicks's funeral.

Steve's death hit me hard. On an official Squadron 'dining-in' night, his wife Lyn stood up and made a speech. It was a short speech, but it took real courage, and it was devastating. Here was the wife of a friend we had all lost, speaking bravely on behalf of her dead husband. Around the room, while Lyn was speaking, and afterwards, when she had sat down again, people were struggling to hold back the tears. It was as if all the pent-up emotions of the Squadron were being let out, a clearing of the decks. I remember standing with Lyn in the bar after dinner. We hung onto each other, sobbing quietly. Just that.

The funeral was held in the church near his family home. There we were, at the funeral of a friend, in the company of his wife, and what did the press do? They harassed the congregation, dishonouring the living who were assembled to honour the dead. Harrying both of us for an interview, the ladies and gentlemen of the media tried their best to make a nonsense of the whole occasion. While we could all understand they might want to cover the funeral of a Gulf War hero, we could not believe they were touting for our story at such a sensitive moment. This was plain disrespect for the dead. One or two of the senior officers present did their best to get rid of the intruders, and the service continued.

It was intensely moving, this memorial service for a dead friend. We were in beautiful old Cornwall. The mist was hanging on the wooded slopes around the church. There was complete quiet. The words of the service rang out in the still air.

Four Tornados executed a fly-past at the end of the ceremony, a mark of respect for the dead man. They were in 'finger four' formation, the four grey shadows approaching slowly through the mist. As they came overhead, the lead aircraft pulled up sharply, plugged in reheat, and roared away from the remaining three. It climbed vertically, heading straight for the stars, the bright flames of its engines flaring orange against the grey sky. This jet, disappearing suddenly from the middle of the 'missing man' formation, signified a departed comrade, the missing man. There was the long thunder of the engines, and then a complete hush. It was gut-wrenching. There was a stunned

silence. Then John Broadbent went up to the graveside, saluted, turned slowly, and deliberately walked
away. Individually, every other officer walked to the
graveside in his turn, paused, quietly saluted, and
walked out of the graveyard.

Some of the ties that had held us all together in the
war began to unravel. We discovered that the Squadron, which had fought so successfully in the Gulf, was
soon to be disbanded: Laarbruch was going to be
decimated. It was almost as if the fly-past at the
funeral had marked the passing of the Squadron, too.
Along with our own, 16 and 20 Tornado Attack Squadrons were due for the chop, and II (AC) Tornado
Fighter Reconnaissance Squadron was being moved
back to the UK. Impossibly quickly, in some cases
within days of their return, the people we had gone to
war with were being posted, leaving the Squadron for
ever.

Even as the Gulf crisis was developing, the crumbling of the Soviet threat had led to drastic cuts in the
British forces. XV would live on, just, as a reserve
Squadron – the Tornado Weapon Conversion Unit
(TWCU). Its boss, John Broadbent, who had been
decorated with the Distinguished Service Order for
outstanding leadership and bravery, was being replaced
by Wing Commander Andy White. Fortunately, the
distinguished Squadron number, XV, would survive.

It was depressing. The ending of the Cold War had
achieved what the Iraqis could never have hoped to
do.

John Peters: The pews of St Mungo's, Glasgow's gaunt
black stone cathedral, were packed with dignitaries:

the families of all those who had fallen in battle in the Gulf; Her Majesty The Queen and the Duke of Edinburgh; the Prime Minister and the British Cabinet; Neil Kinnock, then Leader of the Opposition Labour Party; Paddy Ashdown, himself an ex-serviceman, Leader of the Opposition Liberal Democrats; at least fifty Members of Parliament; a whole constellation of Generals (three-star and above only); forty-one ambassadors from around the globe; choristers, ushers, musicians and military personnel. Looking around at the distinguished guests, the royalty and the military brass, my nerves began to increase. You could hardly lift your eyes for fear of being blinded by all the medals and gold braid. Although I already knew it would be televised, the scale of the occasion hadn't dawned on me until then. I had a stinking cold and a sore throat; my voice had gone. It wouldn't have mattered – but I was supposed to be reading one of the lessons.

I felt unsure about my right to be there at all. John and I had been shot down on our first mission, mucked about in the desert for a bit, and then been captured. We sat out the rest of the war while our mates did the fighting.

The Memorial Service got under way with an address by the Minister of St Mungo's, Dr William Morris: *'We come to remember with pride our loved ones, who gave their lives in war . . .'*

Behind me a woman began quietly sobbing. Suddenly my nerves vanished. I realised I had every right to be there. I felt proud.

'Yes,' I thought, 'this one's for Steve, and for everyone else who died. It is for ordinary servicemen and their families.'

The dead. Forty-seven people on the British side

lost their lives during the war, twenty-four of them in action.

Did it matter to them who was at the service? The main thing was to remember them with honour.

'I to the hills will lift mine eyes, from whence doth come mine aid . . .'

The scale of the operation had been enormous. 45,000 UK Service personnel, together with 15,000 vehicles and 400,000 tonnes of freight, were moved 3,000 miles to the Gulf. The RAF alone flew over 4,000 combat sorties, dropping 3,000 tonnes of weapons: more than 100 JP-233 airfield denial weapons, some 6,000 bombs, over 100 anti-radar missiles and nearly 700 air-to-ground rockets. Even this was little compared to the American effort.

Saddam Hussein was still in power, still persecuting his own people, and much of the Republican Guard had escaped intact. You had to ask yourself the question, 'Was it all worth it?'

'They shall grow not old, as we that are left grow old:
Age shall not weary them, nor the years condemn.
At the going down of the sun and in the morning
We will remember them.'

We have learned there are some things you just cannot change, and that you have to accept. Our war was different. We took off once, we flew for a few hours on the first morning; the rest was survival. Our Squadron mates fought daily for seven weeks, yet we had the attention and the thanks, we had the praise and some of the rewards. People like Rob Woods and Chris Lunt, who had flown about twenty-one combat missions, got none of this.

Bravery lies in choice. Once we had been shot down

we had little choice – there was nothing brave about it. The brave ones were those who, knowing the risks they ran every time they flew in combat, nevertheless got on with the job. The Iraqi television pictures were a sharp reminder of what would happen to them if they were shot down. Going out to the aircraft, getting in it, and taking off for a bombing run through the 'tubes of molten metal' – that was the brave part.

I moved to the lectern, to read the Lesson of Thanksgiving, from Philippians, Chapter Four, verses 4–9:

> *'Finally, brethren, whatever is true, whatever is honourable, whatever is pure, whatever is lovely, whatever is gracious, if there is any excellence, if there is anything worthy of praise, think about these things. What you have learned and received and heard and seen in me, do; and the God of peace will be with you. Amen.'*

A Royal Marines bugle sounded the 'Last Post'. As its call faded away, the cathedral was filled with the skirl of the bagpipes, as a piper came in playing a lament for the dead.

Afterword

John Nichol is flying again, but in fighters, having recently finished a course at RAF Coningsby converting from the Tornado GR1 to the Tornado F3 Air Defence Variant.

John Peters is also flying once more, as part of 31 Tornado Strike/Attack Squadron based at RAF Brüggen in Germany.

Helen Peters has resumed her career in Marketing.

Toni Peters is an independently minded two-year-old with a very healthy appetite.

Guy Peters successfully completed his potty-training some time ago and is now a lively four-year-old.

Glossary of Acronyms

AAA	Anti-Aircraft Artillery (Triple-A)
ALARM	Air-Launched Anti-Radiation Missile
APU	Auxiliary Power Unit
ATC	Air Traffic Control
AWACS	Airborne Warning and Control System
BAI	Battlefield Air Interdiction
BFPO	British Forces Post Office
BMEWS	Ballistic Missile Early Warning System
CAP	Combat Air Patrol
CAS	Close Air Support
CAS	Chief of the Air Staff
CDS	Chief of the Defence Staff
C-in-C	Commander in Chief
COLPRO	Collective Protection
CPGS	Cassette Preparation Ground Station
CRPMD	Combined Radar and Projected Map Display
CSAR	Combat Search and Rescue
CSAS	Control/Command Stability Augmentation System
ECM	Electronic Counter Measures
ESM	Electronic Support Measures
EWO	Electronic Warfare Officer
FEBA	Forward Edge of the Battle Area
FLOT	Forward Line of Own Troops
4g	Four Times the Force of Gravity
GPMG	General Purpose Machine Gun
GLO	Ground Liaison Officer
HARM	High-speed Anti-Radiation Missile

HAS	Hardened Aircraft Shelter
HEAP	High-Explosive Armour Piercing (Ammunition)
HUD	Head-Up Display
IFF	Identification Friend or Foe
KKMC	King Khaled Military City (Saudi Arabia)
KTO	Kuwait Theatre of Operations
LMF	Lack of Moral Fibre
MASS	Master Arm and Safety Switch
MFBF	Multi-Function Bomb Fuse
MOS	Minimum Operating Strip
NBC	Nuclear Biological Chemical
OAS	Offensive Air Support
OCA	Offensive Counter Air
OCU	Operational Conversion Unit
OLF	Operational Low-Flying
PBF	Pilots'/Personnel Briefing Facility
PK	Probability of Kill
POL	Petrol Oil Lubricants
QWI	Qualified Weapons Instructor
RHWR	Radar Homing Warning Receiver
RPV	Remotely Piloted Vehicle
SAM	Surface-to-Air Missile
SEAD	Suppression of Enemy Air Defences
SQUINTO	Squadron Intelligence Officer
SSM	Surface-to-Surface Missile
TOT	Time On Target
TWCU	Tornado Weapons Conversion Unit
WOC	War Operations Centre
WSO	Weapons System Officer

Index